ELEMENTS OF RESEAI

Titus Hjelm

P

First published in Great Britain in 2024 by

Policy Press, an imprint of
Bristol University Press
University of Bristol
1–9 Old Park Hill
Bristol
BS2 8BB
UK
t: +44 (0)117 374 6645
e: bup-info@bristol.ac.uk

Details of international sales and distribution partners are available at
policy.bristoluniversitypress.co.uk

© Bristol University Press 2024

British Library Cataloguing in Publication Data
A catalogue record for this book is available from the British Library

ISBN 978-1-4473-6403-0 hardcover
ISBN 978-1-4473-6404-7 paperback
ISBN 978-1-4473-6405-4 ePub
ISBN 978-1-4473-6406-1 ePdf

The right of Titus Hjelm to be identified as author of this work has been asserted by him in accordance with the Copyright, Designs and Patents Act 1988.

All rights reserved: no part of this publication may be reproduced, stored in a retrieval system, or transmitted in any form or by any means, electronic, mechanical, photocopying, recording, or otherwise without the prior permission of Bristol University Press.

Every reasonable effort has been made to obtain permission to reproduce copyrighted material. If, however, anyone knows of an oversight, please contact the publisher.

The statements and opinions contained within this publication are solely those of the author and not of the University of Bristol or Bristol University Press. The University of Bristol and Bristol University Press disclaim responsibility for any injury to persons or property resulting from any material published in this publication.

Bristol University Press and Policy Press work to counter discrimination on grounds of gender, race, disability, age and sexuality.

Cover design: Robin Hawes
Front cover image: Irina Cheremisinova/iStockphoto.com
Bristol University Press and Policy Press use environmentally responsible print partners.
Printed and bound in Great Britain by CPI Group (UK) Ltd, Croydon, CR0 4YY

To

Alexandra Bergholm

Friend, Colleague, and Teacher Extraordinaire,
without whose support this book could not
have been written

Contents

List of figures and tables … viii
Preface and acknowledgements … ix

1	**Elements**	**1**
	Waldo and the history of witchcraft	2
	Catherine and coke in high places	3
	Alex and the archives	4
	Elements of research design	5
	Alignment and justification	9
	Steps and detours	11
	What is missing from the picture?	12
	Types of research interests	13
	Conclusion	15
2	**Question**	**17**
	Where do research questions come from?	17
	The principle of parsimony	20
	The funnel method	22
	Question types (and research puzzles)	25
	Dead end questions	28
	Conclusion	31
3	**Data**	**33**
	Numbers versus texts and images	34
	Naturally occurring versus researcher-generated	35
	First order versus second order	38
	Self versus others	41
	Articulated versus hidden positions	43
	How much is enough?	46
	Conclusion	49
4	**Method**	**51**
	Two bad attitudes and one good one	52
	How to choose a method?	54
	Quantitative versus qualitative	55
	The background assumptions of methods	56
	Methods of data collection	58
	Methods of data analysis	62
	Mixed methods	65
	Conclusion	68

5	**Literature**	**71**
	Orientation	73
	'Critical analysis and creative synthesis'	76
	Positioning	79
	Narrative versus systematic reviews	81
	Narrow versus broad reviews	84
	Literature or theory?	86
	Writing up and literature review checklist	87
	Conclusion	88
6	**Theory**	**89**
	Why theory?	90
	Research theory I: theory-testing	91
	Research theory II: theory generation	93
	Research theory III: application and development of concepts and models	95
	General theory	97
	Diagnoses of our time	98
	Fit-the-box theory versus creative theory use	101
	Conclusion	104
7	**Ethics**	**105**
	Beyond rules	106
	Ethical research questions	108
	Ethical literature review	109
	Ethical data and methods: informed consent	111
	Ethical data and methods: minimising harm and maximising benefits	114
	Ethical contribution	116
	Ethical writing	117
	The dark side of institutionalised research ethics	119
	Conclusion	121
8	**Contribution**	**123**
	Empirical claims	124
	Interpretative claims	125
	Theoretical claims	127
	Methodological claims	128
	Practical claims	129
	Overstretching claims	131
	Conclusion	134
9	**Writing**	**135**
	Writing strategy I: drafting (or, the 30:70 model)	136
	Writing strategy II: planning (or, the 70:30 model)	138

Contents

	Reading for writing	140
	Show, don't tell	144
	Revision, revision, revision	145
	Titles, abstracts and introductions	147
	Against procrastination	149
	Conclusion	151
10	**Proposal**	**153**
	What's in a proposal?	154
	The model proposal	156
	Introduction	156
	Aims and objectives	159
	Research materials and methods	161
	Work outline	163
	Project team and outputs	163
	Abstracts	165
	Conclusion	165
References		167
Index		181

List of figures and tables

Figure
1.1 The elements of research design　　6

Tables
5.1　Literature review checklist　　87
9.1　Reading for writing: the structure of 'One *Volk*, One Church? A Critique of the "Folk Church" Ideology in Finland'　　141
10.1　Research proposal questions and themes　　154
10.2　European Research Council template proposal structure　　155

Preface and acknowledgements

This is a selfish book. I have supervised countless BA, MA and PhD students in sociology, politics, cultural studies and religious studies at two universities (University College London and University of Helsinki) in the last 20 years. In both, students have taken some courses on methods and, possibly, theory. However, when the time comes to start thinking about the dissertation or thesis, almost everyone is confused about what a successful research project requires. In other words, they have little sense of research design. Thus, to avoid explaining the same thing repeatedly at supervision sessions, I wanted to write a guide that I can recommend students and early career scholars read when embarking on their research. Such books already exist, of course, but none of them quite did the job I wanted them to do. Hence this book.

In keeping with its origin – the table of contents is, basically, the outline of my MA seminar at the University of Helsinki – the tone of the book is unapologetically conversational. I have written it as I would discuss the topics in my seminars, in supervision sessions and with colleagues. It is not just a stylistic choice, however. I do not think a book on research design should present itself as a collection of hard and fast rules. Rather, my suggestions and prompts are meant to enable each budding (or more experienced) researcher to discover their own balance of elements. The book is personal in another sense as well: although I have endeavoured to cover a broad range of disciplines and themes in my examples, if you find yourself knowing more about the sociology of religion or about Finland than you ever wanted, I can only congratulate you and apologise in the same breath.

There are three ways that you can read this book: first, the chapters work as stand-alone guides to their respective topics. If you are struggling with a question regarding method, you do not need to read the chapter on data before that. However, I do recommend reading Chapter 1 first to get your bearings. Second, because all the elements of research design are connected, the traditional cover-to-cover approach probably works best, nevertheless. Finally, for best results, you should start putting together a research design portfolio while reading. You can take prompts from the chapters, note your reactions and make a record of how the ideas presented the book are relevant to your project. This way, at the end of the book you will have a collection of rough material which, when polished, can be turned into a research proposal.

A brief note on terms: throughout the book, I use the British terms for dissertations and theses. Thus, a 'dissertation' is the written work submitted at the end of BA or MA (or equivalent) level studies and a 'thesis' is what you submit to qualify for a PhD. There are probably few places in the text where this distinction matters, but it is worth mentioning just in case North American readers are wondering what I mean.

As with all intellectual endeavours, this book owes much to many people. It owes most to all the students I have supervised during my career as university teacher. There are too many to mention, but whatever wisdom there is in these pages, I owe it to the conversations with all of them. Students on the Study of Religion MA Seminar at the University of Helsinki deserve a special mention, because the structure of the book was 'tested' with them. Several colleagues read the manuscript, or parts of it, and kindly offered their insights. Thank you to Talvikki Ahonen, Alexandra Bergholm, Eric Gordy, Zeinab Karimi, Ilkka Koiranen, Richard Mole, Susanna Pagiotti and Allan Sikk. Only I am to blame for any silliness that may remain. Susan Palmer kindly sent me her article on research ethics. Maija Kühn made the 'holy trinity' figure come alive. I met Jim Spickard almost 20 years ago now, and I think I have thanked him in most of my publications since. Among other intellectual debts, Jim's book *Research Basics: Design to Data Analysis in Six Steps* is deeply wise and I have been much influenced by it, even if I take a somewhat different path in this book. A special thank you to Lloyd Langman, with whom I have had the pleasure to work with already a decade ago, and who kindly introduced me to the people at Bristol University Press and Policy Press. Working with Georgina Bolwell, Isobel Green, Bahar Muller, Paul Stevens, Freya Trand, Sophia Unger and everyone else at Bristol University Press has been a real pleasure. I am embarrassed to even think about the amount of time Alexandra Bergholm has spent advising me on esoteric issues having to do with teaching administration and day-to-day survival at the university. I hope to return the favour one day, but I'll start with dedicating this book to her. As always, it's the home crew – whom I wish I would remember to thank more often – that I owe the most. So, thank you, from the heart, Veronika, Lempi, Emil and Tahira.

1

Elements

Academic research is difficult. You cannot get away with interviewing two or three people, as journalists might. Neither can you get away with watching a couple of YouTube videos, like so many self-appointed experts on social media. There are principles, rules and traditions to follow in order to call research 'academic'. There is no shame in admitting that this is a tough path to follow, no matter what the stage of your career.

What makes academic research difficult? In my experience of both doing and supervising research, it is achieving the right combination of research elements, rather than ticking off any single element in itself, that presents the main challenge. That is, research questions sometimes take time to formulate, but eventually they click into place. Data collection may be frustrated by issues of access, but we swim in a sea of data, so a small tweak of perspective will enable us to look at other sources. Methods take a while to crack, but they are best learned by doing research. Theory and research literature require time to internalise, but as long as you have that, anyone can come to grips with both. However, what eludes many researchers, especially those at the novice stage, is how all these elements come together. How is my choice of data affected by my question? What then would be the appropriate method for data collection and analysis? Where does theory come in? How do I put it all together into a research report, dissertation, thesis or research article? In other words, how do I design my research?

The difference between beginning and experienced researchers is that the former often find this research design puzzle exasperating, while for the latter it is actually one of the attractions of the academic endeavour. The purpose of this book is to help you make the transition from exasperation to inspiration. In public discourse, 'scientific discovery' usually refers to papyrus manuscripts discovered in ancient tombs, or the discovery of a distant star. Few humanities and social science scholars can boast about 'discoveries' in this sense, but what they share with the researchers in the 'hard' sciences is that for both it is the interlocking of different research elements that leads to new knowledge. The chapters in this book discuss these elements and ways to make them 'click' in order to produce high quality research.

I have little to add to Schwartz-Shea and Yanow's (2012: 16) definition of research design, so I'll quote it here in full: ' "Research design" refers to the basic structure of a research project, the plan for carrying out an investigation focused on a research question that is central to the concerns of a particular epistemic community.' I like how the authors foreground the research question and how the research design is presented as a blueprint for conducting research. Instead of 'epistemic communities' I mostly refer to disciplines, although the former are broader than the latter. That said, I understand 'research design' somewhat differently from some other books on the topic. Many such books start with methods: how to do qualitative, quantitative, or mixed methods research. You will not find information about how to conduct multiple regression or qualitative content analysis in this book. What you will find are ideas and guidance about when using one of these methods would be appropriate – and when not. The problem with research literature (articles and books) is that few studies (with the exception of ethnographic research in anthropology and other disciplines) discuss how the combination of research elements came about (which is often through trial and error). The products of our academic endeavour – dissertations, theses or articles – hide most of the process that got us to the finish line. Therefore, throughout the book, I will illustrate with true and imagined stories how different choices in research design lead researchers to breakthroughs and dead ends. I will offer previous studies – including some of my own – as successful and not so successful examples. It will be impossible to convey all the tacit knowledge that accumulates with research experience, of course, but the aim is to provide a tool for avoiding major mistakes on the way to a finished study.

Now, let us begin with a couple of these imagined stories.

Waldo and the history of witchcraft

Waldo is a third-year history student freshly enrolled at a BA dissertation seminar. He has always been interested in the dark side of history: wars, the inquisition and witchcraft. He has read a couple of popular books on the latter topic and wants to pursue it in his own dissertation. There is excitement in the air at the first seminar meeting:

Supervisor:	So, Waldo! What did you have in mind for your dissertation?
Waldo:	I want to write about witchcraft.
Supervisor:	OK, what about witchcraft?
Waldo:	Well, the history of witchcraft.
Supervisor:	Yes, fine, history is why we're all here [awkward chuckles]. I meant something a bit more specific. What if you thought about your dissertation title? That often helps in condensing a broader topic. What could the title be?
Waldo:	'A history of witchcraft'?
Supervisor:	Erm, OK. But what is it about that history that interests you?

Waldo:	I'm interested in what happened.
Supervisor:	I think we need to move on. Please come see me during my office hours, Waldo. Now, Kristen, tell us about your ideas ...

What is wrong with this picture? Think about this for a minute and then read on.

Waldo's proposed dissertation does not have a research question. It has a topic, but no question it wants to answer, no puzzle it wants to solve. He might pull off a chronicle of events having to do with witchcraft (a very limited one at that, considering his word count limit), but it would not be research. (Another thing wrong with the picture is that a good supervisor would have already brought this up for the whole seminar to learn from.) Mind you, Waldo's idea would not pass even as a popular history book. Non-fiction books – at least good non-fiction books – targeted at popular readership are still driven by a question the author sets to answer. Hence, for example, Robin Briggs in his *Witches and Neighbors* (1998 [1996]) tells the reader that he wants to show how social context influenced European witchcraft beliefs – or lack of such beliefs – and, consequently, actions taken against suspected witches. He does not present it as an explicit question, but it is impossible to miss his aim. Without a question, there is no focus. A topic even as specific as witchcraft can be – and has been – approached from so many angles that no one study could possibly include them all. As Briggs (1998 [1996]: 10) puts it: 'A truly comprehensive study of European witchcraft would require not only several large volumes but also several lifetimes of study.' You only want to spend a fraction of one lifetime on a dissertation, thesis, article or academic book. That is why you need a good research question.

Catherine and coke in high places

Catherine is about to finish her MA in social anthropology. Inspired by her supervisor, who has written often-cited books about the family dynamics of ultra-rich people, Catherine wants to study drug use among billionaires. After one such billionaire made headlines smoking marijuana in a live web show, Catherine quickly checked and found that there is no research at all on the topic. Bingo! She feels this is a brilliant topic for a dissertation. It will make an original contribution and open doors to PhD study.

Catherine's first meeting with her supervisor is not exactly encouraging. He tells her that while he has had access to billionaires' homes, very few will want to talk about their drug use – assuming that they have used drugs in the first place! Catherine is adamant, though. She was taught not to give up before trying, so she proceeds with writing a proposal on the topic.

Her supervisor promises to ask around from his more amenable research participants, but warns Catherine not to get her hopes up. She has a card up her sleeve, though: James, who took the intro class with her in their first year, is a driver for a local billionaire. He will surely help her out. In addition, she sends several enquiries to the representatives of famous billionaires, telling them that she is interested in studying their 'recreational activities'. While she waits for replies, she reads relevant methodological and theoretical literature. Her supervisor recommends thinking about another topic, but she wants to wait another couple of weeks.

What is wrong with this picture? Again, think about this for a minute and then read on.

Catherine's dissertation could be truly ground-breaking, but it is extremely unlikely that she will ever have any data for it. She could perhaps find news reports of billionaires' drug habits, or perhaps read billionaires' memoirs for drug-related content. Alternatively, she might be able to track friends and employees of billionaires who would be willing to talk about the topic (anonymously). But these would all be different studies, most of them quite removed from the central concerns of her discipline, social anthropology. A study where the researcher gets to observe and interview billionaires about their drug habits would be truly sensational. It is also likely impossible to carry out.

I will admit the example is exaggerated and feels far-fetched. It *would* be a great dissertation, but even the most tenacious students usually have a more realistic sense of what is possible, especially within the limits of graduate study. However, similar cases are common. One MA student of mine wanted to study how immigration officials treat self-designated atheists seeking asylum because of religious persecution. First the officials did not respond for weeks, then said they only provide interview transcripts to PhD students or senior researchers. My student had to start from scratch in the middle of the MA seminar. It would be similarly difficult to imagine how an ethnic minority researcher could gain access to study a White supremacist gang – or to imagine how that would be safe. For some questions, the data is inaccessible. For other questions, there is no data at all (as I will discuss in the next section). If you find yourself in either situation, your research design needs tweaking.

Alex and the archives

Alex is a fourth-year theology BA student. They have spent a year in Germany learning the language and reading about an obscure German Protestant theologian. Alex's dissertation topic, discussed in advance with their supervisor, is the theologian's doctrine of sin. In addition to published works, a German university library has a box of the theologian's notes.

Alex plans to rummage through these in hopes of finding new leads on the formation of the theologian's thought.

Now, enter an awkward Zoom call with Alex and their second supervisor, a somewhat pesky sociologist of religion.

2nd supervisor:	Thanks, Alex, for sending me the first draft of the research proposal. I really enjoyed it, even if it is not my strongest area of expertise.
Alex:	Yes, err, thanks.
2nd supervisor:	I wanted to push you a bit more on some aspects, though. I know there are disciplinary differences, but even then, I think it will be beneficial for you to consider these issues.
Alex:	Right.
2nd supervisor:	You seem to have everything else in place, but can you tell me what you are going to do with your sources.
Alex:	Do? [Pause] Well, I'm going to go to the archives, there's a whole box of letters and notes, previously unexamined. And I'm reading the published works, of course!
2nd supervisor:	Yes, that's all fine. But what are you going to do with the materials after you have them?
Alex:	I will read the sources thoroughly. All of them.

What is wrong with this picture? One more time, think about this for a minute and then read on.

Alex's research lacks a method. They respond to the supervisor's question about sources by talking about the method of data gathering. What their supervisor has in mind, though, is method of data analysis. There is no doubt that Alex will read everything thoroughly. How they distil all the information in the documents into a cohesive interpretation of the obscure theologian's doctrine of sin requires more than reading, however. It requires a method of organising and interpreting the data. Students especially will need to follow their disciplinary and other traditions when assessing the role that method has in their work. Regardless of discipline and whether your written work requires a separate section on method, thinking about how to make the data answer the research question is a key element of research design.

Elements of research design

I have summarised my 'system' of research design in a figure that my students refer to as the 'holy trinity with halos' (see Figure 1.1). It is composed of six elements: question, data, method, literature, theory and ethics. In addition,

Figure 1.1: The elements of research design

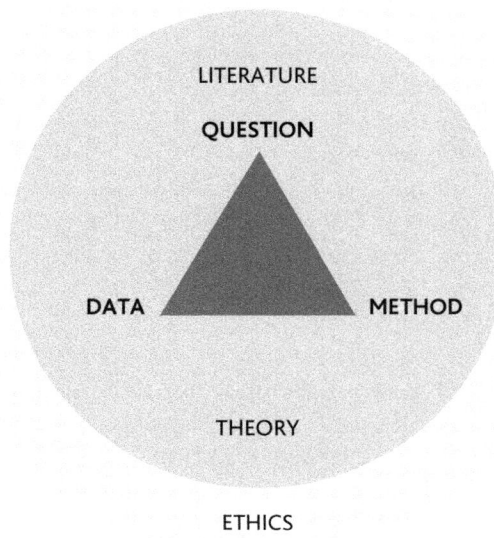

the final three chapters discuss how to think about the contribution your research makes, how to think about academic writing and how to put together a research proposal. I will briefly explain what I mean by each element in the following.

Question, data and methods comprise the 'hard core' in my scheme of research design. They are the indispensable elements. There can be interesting non-fiction writing, but there is no research without a focused problem that you want to solve, sources that enable you to answer your question, and a method of doing so. Understanding each of these elements and their interplay is the key to successful research. As the figure shows, these three are embedded in the field of previous academic literature, which is crucial to understanding where the gaps in your knowledge lie, how previous researchers have done their work and how your work fits into the field. Literature co-inhabits the field with theory, which is also a source of questions and the gateway to understanding the world in broader terms. Finally, the practice of research is embedded in the field of ethics, which ensures that the research we do is conducted in respectful and safe ways for researcher and researched alike.

Question. If you wondered whether Waldo in the earlier vignette was a realistic example, I can tell you that yes, he was. Waldo is only a slightly exaggerated version of myself in my European history BA seminar. I traipsed into the class thinking that I wanted to 'write about witchcraft'. I had a topic, but I had no problem I wanted to solve and, hence, no focus. Witchcraft in Finland? In France? China? What *about* witchcraft? There are few cases left in Europe where a narrative description of a witch trial (should one find historical sources for that) would be big news. I needed a puzzle to solve (and did not do so well, but that is another story). The question (Chapter 2) is the heart of any research project. It focuses your analysis and connects your work with earlier research. It is indispensable.

Data. Undergraduate dissertations are not necessarily expected to make an original contribution to research. This means that students can rely on secondary sources – that is, already published research on the topic – in their work. My/Waldo's dissertation could have been an analysis of earlier literature on witchcraft – although it still would have required a question; something that the previous literature was then harnessed to answer. At later academic stages and in other university systems, primary data is a requisite of properly scholarly research. This means conducting interviews, gathering newspaper clippings or analysing surveys to answer the research question. In disciplines such as philosophy, and some theoretical branches of the social sciences (and the natural sciences, for that matter), the concept of 'data' is, of course, different. In these cases, 'secondary' sources become 'primary'. Either way, data (Chapter 3) is a key component of research design.

Method. What most clearly differentiates academic research from journalism and general non-fiction is the way scholars conduct their work. Methodology is the broad conversation about how research in particular disciplines should be ideally conducted. Method, in the sense used here, is a narrower concept: it refers to the ways in which the data can be best collected and analysed to answer the research question. There are significant disciplinary differences between the humanities and social sciences – and within both! – as to the role method is given in research, but no one in any discipline would claim that they have no method (Chapter 4) at all.

Literature. Research does not exist in a vacuum. We build upon the work of earlier scholars, even when our mission is to repudiate them. More importantly, discussing particular research literature further focuses your work: it signals that you want to contribute to a particular conversation. In the current explosion of knowledge in all academic fields, it is important to recognise what your niche is. You cannot possibly know and take part in *all* the conversations, even within a relatively small subdiscipline like my own, sociology of religion. Knowing the relevant research literature (Chapter 5) is the key to making your research relevant to the field.

Theory. Here is where disciplines go their separate ways. Some disciplines, like history (Burke, 2005) have a fraught relationship with explicit theorising, whereas in some others it is part and parcel of the whole endeavour. The difference is usually expressed as a division between approaches seeking to produce generalisations about phenomena and approaches seeking to understand the meaning of unique events. Where your research falls will be influenced by disciplinary traditions, but not necessarily defined by them. Theory (Chapter 6) is also an important source for research questions and hypotheses. If you are using theory it is, however, very important to understand different types of theory and whether and how they fit into research designs.

Ethics. Some of the most fascinating studies of human behaviour – especially in psychology – have also been the most unethical. Stanley Milgram famously tricked his subjects into thinking that he was testing learning skills. One participant (the 'learner') was tied to a chair with electrodes and the other (the 'teacher') was given permission to administer electric shocks to the learner if they made a mistake. The intensity of the shock increased with each wrong answer. In fact, the learner was an actor and the teacher was the test subject. The experiment was about how far the teacher would go in obeying the experimenter's prompts to continue. Two-thirds of the test subjects went all the way to the possibly lethal 450 volts. Not only was the experiment based on deception, but also led to high stress for the participants. Later it was repeated by other psychologists, using six-year-old children as test subjects. Needless to say, there are potential harmful effects for adults and children alike (Baumrind, 1985). Nevertheless, I am old enough to remember a time without ethics committees and where there was little formal control over the ethics of research design. Professional associations may have had guidelines for research conduct, but these were never binding. In the last two decades or so, the situation has changed and most universities have an ethical vetting system in place. Now-universal ethics (Chapter 7) assessment is not just a box that needs to ticked. It affects all the other aspects of research design. That is why I have depicted it as the circle encompassing all the other elements.

If you understand the role that each of these elements plays in research, you are well on your way towards a less stressful research experience. In addition to these core elements, every study needs to consider its research contribution and the way that writing influences how your research is received. The former refers to the ways in which you explicate the meaning and significance of your research results. Results do not necessarily speak for themselves. Public crises like the COVID-19 pandemic, where scientific knowledge plays a leading role, have shown how people are great at drawing false conclusions from statistical figures. In addition to the elements discussed here, your research contribution (Chapter 8) connects you with the conversations you want to have in your discipline and beyond. Sadly, this point is often missing from research design training.

Finally, there are literally hundreds of writing guidebooks. My aim is not to compete with them. Instead, I want to discuss the ways in which your research design choices affect your writing choices and vice versa. Writing (Chapter 9) is also the aspect of academic practice where, for various reasons, perfectly fine research designs crumble. Bringing the research onto the page is about keeping focus on the research design and fulfilling the promises you have made. The way to do it, I argue, is to avoid thinking about writing as a painful birthing process and instead treat it as a routine. The research proposal (Chapter 10) is a document that is needed for many applications during an academic career, but writing one is also a good exercise in making sure that your research design holds together.

Alignment and justification

Recognising the different elements and their place in your particular study is the key to successful research design. Yet, it is not sufficient in itself. In addition to being present, the different elements need to be aligned and justified.

By alignment, I refer to the synchronicity between the different elements of research without which the design cannot work. I have borrowed the term from higher education pedagogy, where 'constructive alignment' (Biggs, 1996) has been used to discuss the relationship between learning objectives, teaching methods and assessment. The basic premise behind constructive alignment is simple: 'If students are to learn desired outcomes in a reasonably effective manner, then the teacher's fundamental task is to get students to engage in learning activities that are likely to result in their achieving those outcomes' (Shuell, 1986: 429, quoted in Biggs, 1996: 349). If you want to do research in a reasonably effective manner, then your fundamental task is to ensure that the elements of your research are related so that they are fit for purpose.

Most researchers have an intuitive sense of alignment – although few probably call it that – when planning their research. Certain statistical techniques only work with certain data, certain questions require interviews instead of surveys, and so on. Intuition, as important as it is for doing research, is a fickle guide for research design, however. That is why research design is so often a case of trial and error because alignment issues become explicit mostly when the elements are *mis*aligned.

In fact, most of the issues my students have relate to alignment. They know the elements – they have been to my seminar, after all – but fitting them into a working research design requires seeing the elements in relationship with each other. I have had several cases where students inspired by discourse analysis want to study, for example, how people construct gender identities in interviews. When they submit their first drafts, however, I typically see phrases like 'most of the informants thought …', 'three of the eight interviewees said that …', and so on. This kind of approach analyses the frequency of opinions in a (very small) sample, but it does not analyse how the interviewees discursively construct their identities. This would entail identifying how they talk about masculinity or femininity, for example. The question and (actual) method are out of sync. To go back to the visuals: the 'holy trinity' is an equilateral triangle when all the elements are in harmony. If your data is out of step with the question or your method is unable to process your data, one of the sides elongates or breaks off altogether and the harmony is lost.

Justification is corollary to alignment. Thinking about alignment helps you to fit the pieces of the research together. However, your readers will not know how that fitting process worked unless you tell them. Why are you using this particular data? Why does this method work best with your question and choice of data? The job of researchers is to crack mysteries, but there can be no mysteries in academic prose. You need to figure out the alignment and then explicitly justify your choices for the reader.

Justifying your choice of research elements is important because it works as a guide for your readers. They will not have to second-guess the rationale for the research design, and the analysis makes immediate sense when readers know what to expect. This is important to understand, since scientific rigour is assessed at every phase of an academic career. It is especially relevant for dissertation and thesis writers and those in the training stage of their researcher careers. As a supervisor, I may understand how your research design works, but without explicit justification, I cannot be sure whether *you* have understood! The same principle applies to professional researchers as well: in the role of academic journal editor, I have often been suspicious of the proposed combination of question, data and method in a submission. Yet, if the authors have taken their time to justify their choices, I am more inclined to send it forward for specialist review – even if I do not necessarily agree with all the choices. I am more inclined to reject the submission if it leaves me wondering whether the authors have understood the implications of their research design themselves.

In addition, I like to think that explicit justification feeds back to the alignment process. In my MA dissertation seminar, I normally discuss each of the elements in turn. At this point students have a more or less clear idea of their question, data, method, theory and secondary literature. However, by the time they need to pull the elements together into a coherent research proposal, many begin to have second thoughts. Even though they will have heard me repeat the point about alignment *ad nauseam*, it is often only when they write down their design – and seek to justify it – that they discover that some of the pieces in the puzzle might not click, after all. As disappointing as this is, it is much more preferable to realising that the design is off at the point when the data is collected and analysed. In this way as well, then, alignment and justification are intimately connected – and indispensable – features of any research design.

Steps and detours

James V. Spickard's *Research Basics* (2017) is my favourite book on research design (before writing this one, ahem). It is clear, comprehensive and compelling. I like almost everything about the book.

Except one thing.
The subtitle of the book is *Design to Data Analysis in Six Steps*. The overview of the book summarises the idea:

> This book offers a six-step system for designing social science research. You start by developing a good research question on the topic that you wish to investigate. You then choose a logical structure that will lead you to an answer. Together, the question and the logical structure identify the type of data you need to produce that answer. Once you know what data you need, you can pick the best data collection method for gathering it, the data collection site where you are apt to find it, and the best data analysis method to use. Do the six steps, and you've designed your research. (Spickard, 2017: ii)

Spickard is not the first (nor will he be the last) to portray the research process as steps or phases (see, for example, Blaikie, 2010). It makes sense in many ways: inexperienced researchers especially benefit from a sense of orderliness that such step models provide.

However, reality is almost always messier than that. In fact, I think presenting the research process as steps may be counterproductive if you are stuck in a step, thinking that you are doing something wrong there, when the problem is actually two steps back. You do not want to spend another year doing fieldwork just because your data does not work with your original research question. Rather, you tweak the question. All the precious time spent on learning about discourse analysis will do you no good if your interviews consist of 'yes' and 'no' answers mostly. Perhaps it would be more enlightening to count the number of 'yes' and 'no' answers and see what patterns emerge?

This is why I prefer to present research design as different elements rather than steps. The important thing is not whether you do a dozen detours, but that you cover all the elements on the way. Keeping the research elements aligned often requires going back to previous 'steps' and *that is perfectly normal*. If your research does not 'click', if it feels off in a way you cannot identify, thinking in terms of steps will not take you far. Thinking in terms of elements and alignment will.

In practical terms, it is of course sensible to envision the research process in terms of some sort of steps or phases. From the first idea to a written report, doing research takes time, and you will need waypoints and intermediate goals to split your project into manageable chunks. This is, however, different from thinking about the research process as a straight line from start to finish. Your waypoints will change depending on the rethinking and backtracking you need to do when assessing the alignment of the different research elements. In a strictly understood step model, you bury the previous steps once you proceed to the next ones. In the elements model the research process is alive until the last full stop in the written report. And that is as it should be.

What is missing from the picture?

If you have taken a research design course or browsed other research design books earlier, you will have noted that the 'holy trinity with halos' does not include some topics often associated with research design. I do not mention ontology, epistemology or 'research paradigms' such as positivism, interpretivism or critical theory. Why?

In my previous job, I came across a pattern in many politics and sociology BA and MA dissertations that I second marked, that is, texts by students I did not supervise myself. They would often have a very brief section inserted in the theory or method chapter titled 'ontology and epistemology'. That section would usually amount to a sort of declaration in a format such as 'I subscribe to an idealist ontology and proceed from a constructionist epistemology'. After some time I was able to trace the influence to Michael Crotty's *Foundations of Social Research* (2003), which was heavily used in one of the department's methods courses.

Crotty's book is brilliant, but I always squirmed when I read one of these declarations. They provided me with very little useful information. You can declare as much as you like, but how you *do* your research is what matters in the end. A declaration such as this certainly does not tell me whether *you* have understood what ontology and epistemology mean. In fact, more than once the actual research showed me that the students had not.

As a philosophy of social science buff (Hjelm, 2014) I think it crucial that researchers are able to position themselves in the broader context of social science and humanities research. Especially in the former, there are significant differences between epistemological approaches. However, the way I approach the issue is that in research design ontology and epistemology are the 'background hum' of your choice of theory and method. If you want to do discourse analysis of news reports about unemployment, your design by definition assumes a constructionist epistemology. If you want to do a statistical analysis of the impact of religiosity on the prevalence of premarital sex, then you are not likely to work within a constructionist epistemology.

In terms of research paradigms – established ways of doing research – I also like to think of them as products of your research design rather than the other way around. If you are interested in frequencies, correlations and causality, you probably work in some form of positivist or realist paradigm. (The former has acquired a bad name in some debates, but that does not change the fact that much of social research proceeds from a positivist position.) If you are interested in the meanings people produce in interviews, media or literature, then you work within the interpretative paradigm. Paradigmatic positions like this are rarely declared. Rather they become clear when the whole picture – question, data, method, whose theories and previous studies you cite – of the research becomes clear. Feminist, decolonial and queer approaches are some exceptions where the paradigmatic position is made explicit. However, even if it were not, it would be deducible from the combination of the elements of research design.

In sum, I am not implying that these topics missing from the choice of elements discussed in this book are unimportant. On the contrary. It is just that I do not think they are a fruitful starting point for research design. In the worst-case scenario, all these meta-questions may drag you to a black hole of philosophy of science. A colleague of mine started a PhD project on an empirical topic, but got so sidelined by epistemology that he despaired and never finished his degree. If your elements are all in place, aligned and justified, you will have had to consider your positions on these issues without being bogged down before even getting started.

Types of research interests

One more thing remains to be said before moving on to more detailed discussions about the individual elements. Although in this scheme, and throughout the book, I will repeat *ad nauseam* that balance between the different elements is key to successful research, people come to research with different agendas and motivations. I will briefly discuss the main types of interests I have come across in supervising students at different levels. The issue here is what drives the research interest and the pros and cons of different emphases. From this perspective, I find it useful to differentiate between data-driven, theory-driven, method-driven and, finally, question/problem-driven types of research interests.

Data-driven research interests. If I think back on my own career, the impetus for most of my empirical research has come from some interesting piece of data. I have analysed newspaper stories and parliamentary discussions that I have found fascinating. In dissertation seminars, students often have only a vague topic in mind, but often also mention that they would like to analyse social media posts, for example. Others, for example the student who wanted to study representations of religion in Terry Pratchett's *Discworld* novels, have a clear sense of their data, even if they do not yet know what it is that they want to do with it. The previous sentence also includes a clue to why a singularly data-driven research interest is insufficient: data never speaks for itself. We need recognised tools and theoretical frameworks to interpret the data. Most importantly, until we know what we want to ask our data, it will remain a chaotic mess; some would even say there is no 'data' before we know where to look. Anthropologists and ethnographers in other disciplines may tell you that we cannot always know in advance what is interesting in 'the field'. Hence, we need to submerge ourselves into the field and only after some sense of the data, start to work back towards the research question and theory. Only few researchers have this luxury, however, and no one goes into the field without any preconceived ideas of what they would like to find out. Data is a great (and very common) starting point for research, but it needs to be 'tamed' by the other elements.

Theory-driven research interests. Every year, there is at least one student in my seminar who 'wants to use Foucault' in their research (you can replace 'Foucault' with any relevant theorist in your discipline). Alternatively, these students are interested in 'identity theory', 'acculturation theory' or any other theory with a recognisable name. Now, of course, disciplines differ again. I would hazard a guess that few history dissertations are driven by a theoretical idea. In disciplines where theory is crucial, previous applications of theoretical ideas in empirical research often inspire imitation. As experienced researchers read more theory, they find combinations of theoretical ideas, which in turn may inspire empirical questions. This is as it should be. Theory is a major source of research questions and problem-definition. It is 'dangerous' only when it dominates the research design at the expense of the other elements. A person can spend an entire lifetime and never fully cover – or comprehend – the works of Karl Marx (I speak from experience here). Your knowledge of a theory will be incomplete by definition, because there are multiple interpretations and an ever-expanding commentary literature on most theories. Therefore, in individual research projects, both empirical and theoretical, the other elements force you to draw the theoretical line somewhere.

Method-driven research interests. Methods may sound like surprising sources of inspiration for doing research. Yet, every year I meet a student whose only idea in the beginning of the research journey is that they want to use a particular method. This can be expressed broadly, as in 'I want to do statistical analysis', or with a narrower approach in mind, as in 'I am interested in critical discourse analysis'. As a method buff, I am always delighted when this happens. If you do not have any sense of method, your research is in danger of becoming a descriptive jumble of anecdotes. However, no research design can survive on method alone. Methods are tools, but without the 'raw material' of research (questions, data) they are useless.

Question/problem-driven research interests. As I have already said and will repeat many times, there is no research without a research question or problem. Yet, few students start with a research question in their mind. This is understandable, because devising research questions is challenging. Few professional researchers wake up one morning with a clear research question in their minds either, but they are perhaps more attuned to seeing the research problems particular situations and phenomena suggest. As I will discuss in the next chapter, many of our everyday observations present problems, which may be turned into research questions: Why are racist tweets so similar regardless of the language they are written in? This could lead to a project that asks how racist discourse spreads internationally over social media. One could have the experience that male students in university-level classrooms take more space in discussions and speak over their female colleagues. This could be turned into a research question by asking, for example, whether this is true and to what extent. Further, another project could try to figure out *why* this is the case. Whether or not your interest in doing research is initially driven by a question you want to answer or a problem you want to solve, it should be by the time you have considered all the elements in your research design.

The typology here is based on concrete situations; what students say when I ask them about their research interests for the first time. The same applies for more advanced researchers. Everyone starts from a point of interest, whether a fascinating historical source, a new development in theory or a methodological innovation. These are all valid starting points. Yet, my contention is that all good research is question-driven or problem-driven. This does not mean you need to cast your favourite method or theory overboard, but it means you need to make sure that the 'holy trinity' is aligned. Therefore, it is useful to recognise what drives you research-wise and then accommodate and synchronise that with the other elements.

Conclusion

You may have many questions on your mind after this brief introduction. I would not have expected anything less. The point of this chapter has been to briefly summarise my vision of research design, which guides the structure of the rest of the book. Whenever you feel lost, the 'holy trinity with halos' figure should put you on the right path again. The heart of the figure is the relationship between research question, data and method. You will probably encounter previous research literature or relevant theory before thinking about these three elements, but these three decide the fate of your project. Further, the important thing to remember is that these elements need to be not only present in your research, but also aligned and justified. That is, they need to be in sync with each other and you need to tell your readers why a particular constellation works best for you.

Because my approach to research design is not a steps model, you can read the following chapters in any order you like. In addition to the topics in the 'holy trinity' figure, I have added chapters on research contribution (why your research matters), academic writing and drafting a research proposal, where all the elements come together. There will necessarily be some repetition, but you will get the best out of the book by reading it from start to finish. What I hope to have conveyed here – and in the following pages – is that research design is not a boring box you need to tick before moving on to actual research. The way I see it, there are two journeys of discovery working simultaneously in any research project: there is the discovery of new knowledge in the systematic analysis of real-world data (or theory and ideas). But there is also the discovery of how the different elements of research design 'click' in a way that guarantees that your analysis works. Research design is an indispensable half of the research journey. Now follow me.

2

Question

The research question is the single most important element in any research design. I do not hesitate to say this after 20 years of supervising students at all levels, and reviewing article manuscripts for scholarly journals. No matter what your fancy theory, unique data or rigorous methods are, without a question a research project is without direction. It may become a report that contains some interesting information, but it will not be academic research. In light of this, it is rather astounding that the research question continues to be possibly the most neglected aspect of researcher training. Research design books do talk about the importance of research questions, but many dissertation and thesis writers embark on their research journeys armed with only a methods course and perhaps some classes in the philosophy of (social) science. It is no wonder, then, that in many a first meeting with a supervisee my question, 'What is your research question?', has been met with a blank stare. Consequently, foregrounding the importance of the research question has been one of my main motivations to write this book.

The research question rests at the top of the 'holy trinity' triangle discussed in the previous chapter, because it guides all the other elements of research. Research should be guided by an interest in learning something new about the world. You may have previously undiscovered sources at your hands, but these are worthless unless you know what to ask them. You may have mastered intricate methods, but knowing how to analyse data is useless if you do not know what the purpose of such analysis is. As I will discuss in this chapter, data and theory can inspire research questions, but the best kind of research is always question-driven. Importantly, learning where research questions come from, how to draft good questions and how questions can go wrong is one of the best ways of learning about doing research, as it forces you consider your project as a whole. That is what we shall do in this chapter.

Where do research questions come from?

Before going into detail about what makes a good research question, it is useful to think about where questions come from. This is relevant because it affects the other elements in your research design (data, method, literature, theory) and helps thinking about your contribution to research (Chapter 8) at an early stage. I have divided these question sources into four types: lay theory; practical aims; gap in the literature; and formal theory.

Lay theory. As a fresh university lecturer, I tended to tell my dissertation seminar students that research questions are mostly derived from earlier research literature. I still think so, to some extent: many students say they are interested in a phenomenon they read about in an article or book on the reading list of another course. However, equally many are inspired by phenomena they have observed in their everyday lives.

I call this 'lay theory' (or 'implicit theory'), because whenever we observe a phenomenon, we start making connections between things and assigning causes. Repeated observations become sedimented into lay theories (Furnham, 2013). For example, if I observe politicians and voters of a particular political party repeatedly use racist language, I will be prone to think that racism is a major factor that attracts people to that party. A research question based on that lay theory could be something like 'How do racist attitudes affect voting preference?' I would, of course, have to check whether and how scholars have studied this question earlier. In this sense, lay theories can never be the *only* source of research questions, but equally, should be treated as important inspiration for research.

Practical aims. Sometimes research questions arise from an observed everyday situation that the researcher considers problematic. In these cases, the point of the research is to change the prevailing condition. The difference between lay theory and practical aims is thus that the former answers the question 'What is happening?', whereas the latter says 'This is happening. How can we change it?' For example, nursery/kindergarten-age boys report higher interest in science than girls do. Would a science literacy programme affect the gender discrepancy (Patrick et al, 2009)? Because it is easier to have impact on a local level – rather than, say, changing the practices of global trade – this kind of research is sometimes called community-based research. In community-based approaches, the questions arise from the needs of a particular community, not just the interests of the researcher. Such studies have been conducted on various topics, such as public health and education (for example, Strand et al, 2003; Minkler, 2005). Broader structural questions, such as racial discrimination and sexual violence, also inspire research aiming to change current conditions. The actual research can be either local (qualitative and mixed approaches) or on a national or international level (quantitative approaches).

Gap in the literature. At the end of the day, all research is about filling a gap in current knowledge. Nevertheless, it makes sense to talk about a gap in the *literature*, when that lack of earlier studies functions as an inspiration for new research. Often the process goes as follows: you read an interesting general work, which hooks you into the topic; you think about your research objectives; you read literature relevant to the objective; you identify the questions that have not been asked in the literature; you formulate the question in response to this gap. Experienced researchers can skip the literature review if they work on the topic of their specialisation. But experienced and novice researchers both go through a similar process when entering a new field of study.

When I speak of 'literature' here, I mean literature specific to your discipline or field of study. This is because while there should be no questions that cannot be asked, some questions are considered more relevant than others depending on your discipline and field. A very important aspect of fashionable interdisciplinarity is to introduce questions from another discipline to your own, and by doing so broadening the disciplinary vistas. However, dissertation and thesis writes will need to consult their supervisors about the relevance of their planned question in light of the disciplinary traditions. Since publishing in discipline-specific journals still tends to be the gold standard, more seasoned researchers also need to think about whether their question is considered relevant in the context of the disciplinary literature.

Another word of warning: looking for a 'gap' in the literature may lead to temptation. Originality is highly valued in academia and society more broadly, but claiming that *no one* has ever done the kind of research you want to do is a risky endeavour. It is true that an exactly same combination of research elements is highly unlikely. However, if someone has asked the same question using the same theoretical ideas, but different data, then you are not in uncharted waters. Or, the other way around, if you ask new questions from familiar data, the earlier research using that data is still relevant to you. Originality is, among other things, a rhetorical device, but should be used sparingly in research. Despite – or perhaps because of – the explosion in electronic search capability, there is little chance that anyone can trawl through all research even in emerging fields. When your combination of research elements is innovative, there is no need to hold back that information, but the occasions when our research is filling a complete vacuum are rare indeed.

Formal theory. What I call 'formal theory' refers to theoretical formulations, concepts and conceptual schemes, and typologies (see Chapter 6). Although sometimes overlapping with lay theories, they are more systematic and expressed in a logical manner. They are also distinct from gaps in research literature, which in my scheme refers to empirical studies (see Chapter 5). As noted several times in this book, there are important disciplinary differences regarding the role of formal theory. For psychologists theories provide the foundation for devising empirical tests. For example, Miner (2000) tested whether certain theoretical personality types would predict students' propensity for entrepreneurship after graduation. For cultural sociologists, a concept may spark a research idea, even if it is not 'tested' in the same way as psychologists understand theory. Even historians may be inspired by social theory, if only to refute its universalising claims. Importantly, even if your question is originally inspired by, say, practical aims, it may be tweaked and clarified in the process of reading relevant theory.

The principle of parsimony

The Merriam-Webster online dictionary defines 'parsimony' as 'economy in the use of means to an end' (Merriam-Webster, ndb). This is a more refined way of expressing my first rule of research design: *do less*! This applies to all aspects of research design: Do you need all those theories and concepts to understand your topic? Do you have to have two different methods for analysing your data? Does the research require you to gather interview data and press clippings, or could you do with just one source? Do you need to read *everything* that has been written about the topic?

The reason why I am taking up the principle of parsimony in a chapter on research questions is simple: *a good question implicates what data, methods, research literature and theories you need for your research design – and remains readable while doing all of the above.* Let us look at some examples.

The abstract of Kebede Kassa Tsegaye's article 'The Role of Regional Parliaments in Conflict Resolution: The Case of the Pan-African Parliament (2004–2011)' (Tsegaye, 2020) starts with the following questions: 'How do regional Parliaments contribute to conflict resolution? At what point in time do they intervene and with what impact?' (Tsegaye, 2020: 168). These are clear questions, which implicate the literature and theory the study contributes to (regional parliaments, conflict resolution). The reader does, however, need the article title to narrow the focus. The data pertains to the Pan-African Parliament specifically, and to a specific period. Both are important qualifications.

After introducing two vignettes from his case studies (Quebec and Catalonia) Marian Burchardt's (2020) book *Regulating Difference: Religious Diversity and Nationhood in the Secular West* kicks off with a string of questions:

> Why did Quebec's national representatives unanimously insist on the importance of a Catholic symbol, despite the often negative views of Catholicism that many Quebeckers hold? How and why, by contrast, did religious diversity turn into a dominant state discourse in Catalonia as reflected in the words of the former vice-president? How do both secularism and Catholicism (as the inherited majority religion) feature in nationalist discourses and imaginaries? And how is religion carved out as a salient aspect of citizenship through political discourses and practices in the first place? (Burchardt, 2020: 2)

The first two questions are about the specific case study vignettes and the latter two about the broader picture that the study wants to uncover. A couple of pages later, the author summarises his question in slightly different words: 'how ongoing nationalist mobilizations intent on defining the *demos* do or do not draw on religion as a cultural marker in the context of diversifying populations[?]' (Burchardt, 2020: 8). In both wordings, the research literature (religion, state, nations), the key theoretical concepts (nationalism, secularism, citizenship), the data (political discourse, analysis of key events/mobilisations) and even the method (some sort of text or discourse analysis?) are included in the question itself. Good research questions, then, aim to capture as much of the research design as possible, while showing that only necessary elements are included. That is why your first versions are bound to change through the research process, as the other elements become clearer.

You may have noticed that I often speak of a research question in the singular. This is not accidental. One of the best pieces of advice I ever got from a senior colleague was when religion professor Jeffrey Kaplan was visiting Helsinki in the early 2000s. I had just embarked on my own PhD study, but wanted to do a side project on a topic of Jeff's expertise. He listened patiently to my rant about all the trajectories I wanted to explore. After I had finished, he said this: "OK, that's all very interesting, but come back to me tomorrow with *one* research question. Just one. Then we'll talk." Sadly, that was the last time I saw him. I could not come up with a single question that would pull together all the disparate topics I had in mind. Embarrassed, I skipped the meeting and only emailed Jeff years after the incident. The lesson? There was no research project in the jumble of ideas I had. There were questions, for sure, but they were disconnected and disordered. I have ever since passed this wisdom down to my students as the *one question rule*.

It may be that it is impossible to condense your research into one question. Nevertheless, you should always try. If you find that there is no way of combining questions into one – one that is not a monster of subordinate clauses – you should ask yourself whether the principle of parsimony applies to your idea. An innocent looking 'and' in the middle of a very long question may actually hide the fact that to answer the different parts of your 'one question' may require completely different data and methods. Always ask: Is my project focused and coherent? The one question rule is a good exercise in practising parsimony and focus. You may end up with two or more questions, or a main question and sub-questions, but it is always good at least to attempt the one question rule.

Drafting good research questions is a challenging task. Coming up with one pithy yet informative question is a remarkable achievement. No one gets it right the first time. A phrase attributed to President Woodrow

Wilson (but sometimes also, likely mistakenly, to Abraham Lincoln) is relevant here. Asked about how long he required to prepare his speeches, the president replied 'It depends. If I am to speak ten minutes, I need a week for preparation; if fifteen minutes, three days; if half an hour, two days; if an hour, I am ready now' (Daniels, 1946: 624). The same goes for good research questions: it takes time to come up with a focused question that communicates all (or most) aspects of the research design.

The funnel method

How do you come up with that pithy yet informative question, then? Trying to summarise the process to my students years ago, I scrambled for a word and blurted out 'funnel'. That stuck and that is how the 'funnel method' was introduced to the *Elements of Research Design* system. I cannot claim originality for other than the term, however. Patrick White (2009: 33–35), for example, talks about the same principle by differentiating between topics, aims and objectives, and research questions proper. I will use his terms to demonstrate the funnel method.

Topics. Every academic year, when my MA seminar starts, we do a round where everyone says what they are interested in. Typically, these interests come in two forms. First, most students say something like 'religion and gender', 'LGBT migrants' or 'Giddens' theory of structuration'. Second, some identify with a particular discipline or field of study, like 'sociology of work', 'ethnicity' or 'cognitive science'. Both can be subsumed under the word 'topic'. They are the broad contexts in which the students would like to do their research, and as such perfectly fine. A broad topic will not, however, take you very far in terms of research design. The follow-up question is: What is it about religion and gender that interests you? Ethnicity can be studied from a myriad of viewpoints, which the topic itself says little about. This was the problem with Waldo, whom you met in the previous chapter. He had a topic (history of witchcraft), but no conception of which aspects of that broad topic he wanted to explore. In sum, everyone starts with a more or less vague topic, but it is just the first step towards a proper research question.

Aims and objectives. The next step down the funnel towards a focused research question is the formulation of an aim or an objective. British university administrators will tell you there is a difference between the two, but I treat the terms as interchangeable. Many studies in many fields actually park the car at formulating aims, without proceeding to research questions. So, for example, Eleanor Ross (2021: 849) states her aims thus: 'The aim of the research was to determine whether combining children's drawings and teacher interviews can help us to differentiate qualitatively between children with positive well-being and those with negative or compromised well-being.' The aims say little about the specific context of the study

(South Africa), but the formulation works, since Ross is conducting an exploratory type of research, which may provide methodological tools for social work everywhere.

Tsegaye's article (2020), which I mentioned earlier, placed the questions in the abstract. In the article itself, the purpose of the research is expressed as objectives:

> The overall purpose of the study is to understand the role of regional parliaments, using the experiences of the PAP [Pan-African Parliament] in conflict resolutions and the tools at their disposal. The specific objectives are:
>
> (i) To describe the overall short- and long-term mandates and functions of the PAP vis-à-vis conflict prevention, resolution and peace-building in Africa;
> (ii) To identify the mechanisms and types of intervention employed by PAP in conflict resolution, and
> (iii) To forward policy recommendations to further strengthen the role of the PAP for effective intervention in conflict resolution and transformation. (Tsegaye, 2020: 169)

Although rather wordy, the aims clarify the context and approach of the article exhaustively. Often, however, moving from topic to objective means formulating a still quite general statement, something like 'my objective is to examine the difference in religiosity between women and men'. This is an improvement from 'religion and gender', but says little about what exactly it is that you are going to study and how.

Research questions. At the tip of the funnel, then, are research questions proper. I often tell my students that once they have an objective, they should turn that into a sentence that ends in a question mark. Patrick White (2009: 43) once again summarises well why that is a worthy endeavour: 'reformulating your aims or objectives as research questions forces you to think more carefully about what you want to find out and can help you be more specific about what you want to achieve in your study'. Your question will narrow down the other elements of research, including the previous research literature you need to familiarise yourself with (for example, no one person can read all the relevant literature on 'social class', but you can get a solid sense of the literature on how women experience and perform their class position), the type of data, theory and even method. As Spickard (2017: 17) puts it with reference to data: 'A good research question tells you immediately what type of data you need.' While it is an encouraging thought that a good question does all these things, it is also the reason why drafting such a sentence with a question mark at the end is easier said than done.

Becky Kazansky's article, published in *Big Data & Society*, explores how people try to counter intensive data surveillance by the state and corporations in an ever-shifting context of data protection regulations. Her research question is 'how then, do affected groups and individuals determine how to counter the threats and harms of surveillance?' (Kazansky, 2021: 1). If we 'roll back' from the question (at the risk of putting words into an unsuspecting author's mouth), the objective could have been something like 'the aim of the research is to study how people react to intense data surveillance' and the topic simply 'data surveillance'. Here we see how the topic only designates a very broad field of study. The objective zooms in on the people experiencing surveillance, thus indicating that the data will be reports from research participants – in this case, interviews, participant observation and documents (Kazansky, 2021: 4). Finally, it narrows the broad aim 'how people react' to the question of how people end up with particular strategies for countering harmful data surveillance. The question is not, then, for example, *whether* people react to data surveillance, but how those who see data surveillance as threatening conduct their resistance. This narrows down the potential data and has methodological implications as well. For the 'whether' question, a representative survey would have been the most relevant approach, whereas for Kazansky a qualitative approach is more appropriate.

There are many types of qualifiers that further narrow down questions. Narrowing down the question to include, say, a particular timeframe, or only women, people of particular nationality or members of a political party, focuses the research even more. Sometimes the qualifier does not fit the question itself. For example, Tsegaye (2020), cited earlier, studies the Pan-African Parliament, but includes the date qualifier '2004–2011' in the title of the paper. Such qualifiers always serve the broader purpose of the research, of course. You should not randomly narrow down the period under study just because you want to read fewer documents. But it makes sense to narrow the dates if there is already research on another period, but not the one you are interested in, or the dates are historically meaningful.

Hypotheses. If your discipline is quantitatively focused, you may have been wondering what the point of all of this is. In what is usually referred to as the deductive model of social science, research questions seem to play little or no role. Quantitative studies of course also have an overarching problem they want to solve, but this is not necessary expressed as a tightly formulated research question. Instead, the tip of the funnel is often formulated as hypotheses. As discussed earlier, these are statements drawn from research literature and theory. They are formulated in order to demonstrate whether one or more factors (say, gender) influences another factor (say, alcohol consumption). Hypotheses are, in a way, inverted research questions, where the question is translated into a statement and then the accuracy of that statement is tested using statistical methods. Hypothesis formulation is a more formal process than coming up with good research questions, but the funnel analogy works equally well with hypotheses. Also, not all statistical studies use hypotheses. Sometimes, when the research is exploratory, charting the prevalence of particular beliefs or attitudes in a population without attempting to demonstrate correlations between variables, then research questions suffice perfectly well. This also works the other way around: unless limited to a clearly bounded population, it may be problematic to formulate hypotheses in studies that do not employ statistical tests. Because hypotheses often aim to uncover a social mechanism applicable to multiple contexts, it would be erroneous to claim that interviewing a handful of British women and men disproves or confirms the hypothesis that, *in general*, women are more religious than men, for example. Note that this does *not* mean that historical or qualitative research can never answer questions about causes (see Chapter 3). It does mean that these questions are rarely expressed in hypothesis form.

Question types (and research puzzles)

Now we know where the research question comes from and how it functions to narrow down and focus your research. What remains is the rather important part of formulating the actual question. For this, I have always found it useful to distinguish between three types of questions: what-questions (description); why-questions (explanation); and how-questions (process and change). Narrowing down the scope of the research is an important aspect of research questions. However, the form decides what the other elements of the 'holy trinity' will be.

What-questions. Much of academic research is about simply discovering what is out there in the world. We may read an interview in the newspaper telling us that a person with a 'foreign' name (whatever that means in each country) has a harder time landing a job than a person with a familiar-sounding name. This is a worrying phenomenon, but in order to have a scholarly opinion about it, we would need to study how frequently this happens. A team of Finnish social psychologists chose a large number of domestic companies and sent out two identical job applications to each, one using a Finnish name, and the other using a Russian name. The outcome of their experiment was that it was twice as difficult to be invited to a job interview if the applicant had a Russian-sounding name (Larja et al, 2012). An almost identical German experiment (with German and Turkish names) produced very similar results (Kaas and Manger, 2012). These field experiments answered a simple question: What happens when two equally qualified people with different names apply for jobs? The results describe the situation: the one with the 'familiar' name is more likely to get the interview. The study itself does not say *why* this would be the case, nor does it – or could it – say anything about how the recruiters end up with their choices. But before we can even ask these questions, we need to know what is happening. The baseline description can then function as a source for hypotheses regarding the causes, and questions about the processes of such discrimination.

In terms of form, descriptive questions include the obvious 'what', but also 'when', 'where' and 'who'. These all describe basic characteristics of a situation. Slightly deceptively, 'in what ways' can be both a descriptive question and a how-question. The point is that with one of these questions as your leading question, you are basically describing a situation or a phenomenon, but not burrowing deeper into questions of relationships, causes or processes.

Descriptive questions are important. For little-researched phenomena, they are crucial. In comparative research, for example, you need to get the basics right before you can delve into problems that are more detailed. Yet, there are situations where what-questions may not be the best choice. When a phenomenon has been widely studied already, there is a danger that you end up simply repeating what has been said before. Perhaps you use new data, but it is somewhat depressing to do a project, which requires a lot of time and effort, just to find that you knew the answer already. Sometimes it also feels that descriptive questions are simply an easy option: you gather the data, analyse it and say what is in there. However, unless you are working on a previously unexplored topic, that is not necessarily very exciting for you or your reader.

That is why I like to talk about research as puzzle- or mystery-solving. The question is the single most important thing that can make a pedestrian-sounding project fascinating. The topic may be thoroughly researched, you may work with much-used data and use the same methods as previous researchers, but if your question is posed so that you enter the well-trodden field from a new angle, that is when you have a new puzzle on your hands.

Now, coming up with research puzzles is not intrinsically valuable. If half of the energy that academics nowadays spend on desperate attempts at being 'innovative' was spent on quality basic research, academia would be a much happier place. So no, research puzzles are not a requirement for good research, but they tend to make it more exciting. That is why I often exhort my students to explore whether their topic and interests would be translatable into one of the other question types. This is because why- and how-questions by design imply a puzzle you want to solve.

Why-questions. Beyond description, scholars are interested in explanation, that is, why something happened or why some social arrangements or recurring social patterns are the way they are. In order to analyse the connections between phenomena (which one causes the other), you will of course have to have the baseline knowledge (the description) of the phenomena, so in that sense description is always a part of explanation.

Explanations can happen on many levels, from personal psychology to structural factors such as class position. There are also disciplinary differences: social scientists have a narrower view of how we can study why-questions than, say, historians. For many of the former, to talk about causes, we need statistical evidence and tests. Thus, for example, in trying to explain the ethnic discrimination discussed earlier, we could assess whether negative attitudes towards ethnic minorities result in more discrimination. A Swedish survey study (Carlsson and Eriksson, 2017) found 'clear evidence of a link between reported attitudes towards ethnic minorities and the extent of ethnic discrimination'. For the latter (historians and qualitatively inclined social scientists) causality may be inferred less formalistically. Thus, for example, Max Weber (2001 [1904–1905]) famously claimed that the 'Protestant ethic' was a key causal component in the formation of modern capitalism. He inferred this argument from the written documents left behind by Protestant theologians, philosophers and entrepreneurs. For thinking about research questions, the main point is not to confuse causes of unique events and causes of patterns of behaviour. Explaining the former does not necessarily help at all in explaining the latter. It is also important to differentiate between asking what people *think* are the causes of particular events or recurring social patterns, and talking about 'objective' causes independent of the actors involved. Here is where you need to consider the other sides of the triangle especially carefully to assess whether you are able to answer why-questions with the data and method you have.

How-questions. 'How' is a question about process and change. It encompasses description, because you need to know the characteristics of the phenomenon in question at point A in order to understand what it looks like at point B – but the focus is on the change. In 1930, Germany was a barely functioning democracy, but a democracy nevertheless. In 1949, there were two Germanies, one struggling with reinstituting democracy, the other ruled by a one-party elite. How did that come to pass? This is the basic question in historical research, most obviously. Historians also discuss causes and reasons, even if with somewhat different criteria than some social scientists, but change over time is their focus. Some social scientists also prefer 'how'-questions, but for different reasons. Those working with survey data often ask how two or more variables (say, gender and education) are related with each other, because showing more strict causal relationships requires different types of data (longitudinal or experimental). It is then the researcher's job to interpret what a strong correlation between variables means. Those identifying as 'constructionist' (or a variation of that term, see Hjelm, 2014), in turn, consider social reality as an outcome of social processes, where meanings and identities are constructed in human interaction. Thus, the process studied does not necessarily refer to long-term historical change, but rather to ways in which, for example, doctor–patient interaction affects the outcomes and quality of care (for example, Maynard and Heritage, 2005). How is the meaning of 'illness' constructed in the conversation between doctor and patient? How is the expert role of the doctor defined by the ways in which they do or do not afford the patient to interpret their own symptoms, and so on? Finally, how-questions can be asked not just to describe a process, but to think about how to actually change the state of things (Blaikie, 2010: 60). Walseth et al (2018) first identified from previous research that physical education (PE) classes in schools have a mixed track record in learning outcomes, especially when it comes inspiring students to physical activity. Their study asked how PE could be developed in order to meet the needs of all students, and resulted in several recommendations. This is again a slightly different way of understanding the 'how' question. There is, however, no reason, why all three approaches (change over time, social construction, activism) to process and change could not be combined in a how-type research question. In fact, many critical approaches (feminist, queer, critical race theory) do exactly that.

It is very likely that the form of your research question will change during the process of research. Unless you are replicating someone else's research design, or working on your research as part of a bigger project, where questions are predetermined, then the form the question takes will live until you have more or less decided on the other elements of your design. Nevertheless, formulating research questions is an important exercise in itself, because it forces you to think about all those other elements. As said before: a good research question tells you what the other elements of research are. Especially, practising research question formulation helps you keep from straying into dead ends.

Dead end questions

By now it should be clear that good research questions are always much-revised research questions. Some questions are, however, beyond salvaging. They are simply dead ends. As the question is the heart of your research design, dead end questions mean dead end research designs. I have three such examples in mind (although this may not be an exhaustive list): yes/no questions; questions beyond the purview of empirical research; and practically impossible questions.

Yes/no questions. If you look at social science and humanities research, the research question is rarely posed in a way that requires a 'yes' or 'no' answer. It is obvious that in, say, vaccine research you need to be able to say conclusively whether or not a vaccine will work against viruses. However, when we study humans, who always have the option to act against expectations, questions that require yes/no answers rarely work. This does not mean that yes/no type of questions are not asked. They are, all the time, especially in quantitative research. Resignato's (2000) article 'Violent Crime: A Function of Drug Use or Drug Enforcement?' is a case in point. He asks 'whether it is drug use that causes violent crime or drug prohibition and enforcement' (Resignato, 2000: 684). This is an either/or question, but taken apart it becomes a yes/no question: Does drug use cause violent crime? Does drug prohibition and enforcement cause violent crime? Now, look at Resignato's conclusions, typical to such studies asking similar question, and worth quoting at length:

> The belief that illegal drug use causes violent crime is widely held by the public in the United States and other countries. The results presented here, however, indicate that the relationship between the psychopharmacological/economic compulsion effects of illegal drug use and violent crime, *may* be weaker than assumed. Although many drug users may commit violent acts, it *may* not necessarily be the results of drug use itself. From these findings *it appears* that drug-related violent crime is more likely the result of systemic factors caused by drug prohibition and increased drug enforcement. Results from this paper and other recent research indicate that US drug policies *may* have more costly negative externalities than benefits. This result *may* be consistent across other countries with similar drug policies as the US. Alternatives to current drug policies, especially with respect to specific drugs, *could* reduce the overall external costs of illegal drug control. New drug policy strategies do *not necessarily* mean complete across the board legalisation. Instead rational fact-based policies ranging from legalisation and decriminalisation, to strict regulation and prohibition should be considered for all drugs. Violent crime *may* be only one of many negative results of increased enforcement and misguided policies. (Resignato, 2000: 688; emphases added)

Just to be clear: I picked Resignato randomly as an example here. His study is perfectly solid and his policy recommendations sensible. But it also shows how strict yes/no questions almost always produce much less strict answers. Note the number of so-called hedging modifiers, which I have italicised in the quote – especially the modals *may* and *could*. Add *it appears* and *not necessarily* (although here it is not used to discuss the results) and what you have is not a straightforward yes or no answer, but a 'more or less' or a 'kind of' answer.

In qualitative research, yes/no questions rarely work at all. If you ask 'Does exercise make people more happy?' and then proceed to interview ten people at your local gym, you have the world's shortest study in your hands. Because you are studying a sample that does not produce generalisable results, the best you can do is to write 'for some it does, for some it does not'. Even if everyone in that sample of ten answered in the affirmative, what would your discovery be? That the people who happened to be at your local gym agree with the statement will not take you far. There are few puzzles to solve in that question.

That is why it is often better to ask, for example, 'In what ways does exercise make people happy?' Now your result could be a condensation of different narratives of happiness and exercise. This would be new knowledge akin to Wienke and Jekauc's (2016) interview study, where they identified four 'factors' (perceived competence, perceived social interaction, novelty experience, perceived physical exertion) that triggered positive emotions in exercising adults.

Questions beyond the purview of empirical research. As a sociologist of religion, I am perhaps overly wary of certain kinds of questions, which may never appear on the radar of many other disciplines. These are the kinds of questions that presuppose an empirically unverifiable element. So, for example, an anthropologist would not ask a question like 'Did the forest spirit heal the injured tribal hunter?' because there is no data in the world that could answer that question. It would be perfectly valid to ask a question like 'Did the tribal hunters believe that the ritual honouring the forest spirit healed one of their injured members?' Although valid, that would be a yes/no question so a better one would be something like 'How does the performance of a healing ritual facilitate the transition of a patient from an agreed state of illness to a publicly recognized condition of health?' (Kapferer, 1979: 108). While the imputed source of healing is beyond our empirical reach, a clinical psychologist could also study the very real effects that the rituals of alternative medicine (as we call it in the West) have (Kaptchuk, 2013).

It should be noted that, again, there are disciplinary differences as to whether a question counts as 'beyond the purview of empirical research'. Take a question like 'Why was Dostoyevsky so concerned with guilt and punishment in his novels?' Most literature scholars would probably say that in order to answer a question like that, we would need to dig into the life history of the author, using diaries and reports of contemporaries. Looking at his novels would tell us *how* he addresses guilt and punishment, but would not take us far in answering *why* he did so. This, however, did not stop Sigmund Freud from claiming that Dostoyevsky's obsession with the themes was an outcome of his own guilt for wishing his father dead. For Freud, the proof is in *The Brothers Karamazov* (Mindess, 1967: 448). My point here is not to arbitrate between approaches, but to note that the 'purview of empirical research' is not just a matter of issues considered 'supernatural', but also a matter of theoretical traditions.

Last, but most commonly, *practically impossible questions* simply refer to valid questions, which, however, cannot be answered with the resources available to a researcher. 'Resources' here can mean several things. It can be a matter of access to data: ethnographic fieldwork, for example, was interrupted everywhere by the COVID-19 pandemic. Researchers had to either postpone their fieldwork or tweak their questions so that they could be answered using something other than observation data. It can be a matter of material resources and money: psychological experiments, for example, cost money to set up. An experimental design and question may need to be changed if material resources are not available. Most often, however, it is a matter of time, the most precious resource of all: many students start with a perfectly fine question, but one that would require half a lifetime of research to answer. Time as a resource is obviously most relevant to dissertation and thesis writers, whose research periods are limited.

It is always a disappointment to notice that your question might be leading to a dead end, for any of the reasons mentioned here. Luckily, the cure does not require a complete overhaul of the whole project. A small tweak of the question can put you back on the right track again. This, if nothing else, shows what a powerful difference the question makes in research design.

Conclusion

If, after all of this advice, you are still unsure what your research question is or should be, do not worry. That is quite as it should be. Unless you know the research literature, have read the theory and are familiar with the data, there is little chance that you could come up with a fully formulated research question at this point. Yet, the research question is the first element of research design I wanted to discuss in this book, because whatever you learn about the other elements, you should always reflect back on the question. Can you answer your question using that data or that method? Or, perhaps, in light of the limitations of data, for example, should you reconsider your question? Either way, the question is your guiding light during the research process. Most importantly, it is what makes your project more than a collection of random facts. Indeed, it is not only the answers you can provide, but also the questions you ask, which make your project academic research.

3

Data

Kellyanne Conway, former US President Donald Trump's political adviser, made her way into history books on 22 January 2017 in an interview for the NBC weekly show *Meet the Press*. Having been challenged about why White House Press Secretary Sean Spicer had made 'easily disproved claims' about the crowd size at Trump's inauguration, Conway responded by saying that Spicer had provided 'alternative facts' to his audience (Blake, 2017). The offhand remark, which she later amended, became an instant social media hit and, for many, a sinister sign of the administration's loose relationship with truth. Partly inspired by Conway, there was soon a spate of academic (Fuller, 2018; 2020; McIntyre, 2018) and popular (D'Ancona, 2017) books and magazine articles about 'post-truth', as the issue became to be known.

The question about 'alternative facts' touches upon central issues in epistemology and the sociology of knowledge, which is the topic of the books mentioned. For the purposes of this chapter, the interesting point is that Spicer and Conway wanted to push the narrative of Trump's inauguration as the biggest ever, while the available data – pictures from Barack Obama's inauguration in 2013 and statistics of Washington DC Metro users – did not support their claim. In other words, there was no evidence for it.

Unless you are doing research that is mainly philosophical or theoretical in nature, you will need to work with data. The point of empirical science – including the social sciences and humanities – is to back arguments with evidence. For this evidence, social scientists and humanities scholars need data from the human world. This data can be in the form of speech and text, observation of acts, public records, statistical information, or any combination of these and other types. Your research question will determine what kinds of data are best for you. After reading this chapter you will recognise different types of data and be able to justify why your data are the best possible for answering your research question. As you will remember, the point of the 'holy trinity' is that the different elements are aligned and justified. Now that you have at least a first version of your research question, it is time to start thinking about what data you could use as evidence.

This chapter takes the empirical research project as the baseline. That is, I assume that you are interested in gathering data about people going about their business, either now or in the past. However, if you are doing philosophical or theoretical work, or planning a review of literature on a topic or in a field, then the chapter will be partly useful. Some of what I say here is applicable if you just replace surveys, observation and so on with the texts you are studying. Some of it you can safely ignore.

This chapter approaches the role of data through a series of juxtapositions. I compare and contrast types of data from different angles: numbers versus texts and images; naturally occurring versus researcher-generated; first order (direct observation of actions and events) versus second order (telling about actions and events); data about self versus data about others; and articulated versus hidden positions. I will explain each in more detail in the sections that follow, but the point is that these contrasts serve to highlight three questions regarding data that you need to take into account when designing your research: What kind of data, why this type, and how much?

Numbers versus texts and images

I do not have data to back my claim(!), but I would hazard a guess that the first thing social researchers think about when thinking about data is whether it is 'quantitative' or 'qualitative' in nature. This is an unfortunate outcome of the tendency to equate research design with methods. While statistical data could be reasonably called 'quantitative', there is no reason why texts and images should be called exclusively 'qualitative'. Word counting has been used extensively for decades to track the relative weight newspapers give to different topics. For example, increased media attention (as measured by number of words) to obesity has been linked to pressure to find health policy solutions to the 'obesity epidemic' in the UK (Hilton et al, 2012). In the age of 'big data', it is actually imperative that we find ways of quantitatively assessing large text masses that cannot be analysed manually simply because of their sheer size (for example, Günther and Quandt, 2016). For clarity, then, I will use 'quantitative' and 'qualitative' when referring to the methods for analysing data. In terms of data, and to simplify somewhat, the main choice to make is between numerical data and texts/images.

Now, let me amend my claim that the first thing researchers think about when thinking about data is whether it is 'quantitative' or 'qualitative'. The actual issue, to hazard another guess, is that researchers make choices about data types *without* thinking much at all. In certain disciplines and fields, working at certain departments and under supervision of certain scholars, researchers are often expected by default to use one type of data or another. So, for example, American political science and sociology tend to favour quantitative methods. Hence their data comes in the form of survey and register data. Conversely, for anthropologists, the ethnographic method is the gold standard, where research data consists of observations of human interaction. Historians use historical records found in archives. And so on. We never do research in a social vacuum and academia has its own taken-for-granted ways of operating. As a student, you will probably have to abide by whatever your local conditions are. More enlightened supervisors will, of course, be open to a plurality of approaches, including the use of both numerical and textual/image data.

Ideally, from a research design perspective, the research question – not method – should determine what data are best suited for your research. Many social scientists would tell you that questions about frequencies, correlation and causality can only be answered using numbers. But a historian would immediately object: the point of historical research is not to just describe *what* happened over a period of time but to construct 'an ensemble of narratives that [add up] to a set of causal explanations' *why* it happened (Evans, 1997: 146). The data for explanatory research can consist of texts, images *and* numbers, but it does not require a particular method (for example, multivariate statistics). If explaining is your business, then you will need to figure out and follow your field's standards for causal explanation.

Philosophical debates regarding causal explanation are beyond the purview of this book, but what can be said with more confidence is that if you are asking a question about meanings, perceptions and experiences, then you will probably need textual data. Likewise – rather obviously – when you are analysing how texts and images construct a particular view of the world. However, note my use of 'best suited': it signals that, so far, most people have used one type of data to answer certain kinds of questions, but there is no reason why you should not come up with an original way to combine data types. As Becker (2017: 55) puts it, we should be 'ecumenical' about methods and focus on 'trying to create data that will serve as trustworthy evidence, capable of carrying the weight we put on it'.

Naturally occurring versus researcher-generated

One issue that is not necessarily often thought about much in advance, but which has a significant practical impact on your research process, is the choice between 'naturally occurring' and researcher-generated data (Silverman, 2007: 37–60). The former refers to data, which exists regardless of whether you are studying the topic. The latter refers to data, which would not exist if not for the researcher. Let me explain.

The reason the choice between naturally occurring and researcher-generated data is sometimes implicit in the research design is that the research question points to the data type so obviously. For example, when Boland and Katzive studied changes in abortion law around the world, they used 'the complete texts of new abortion legislation, most often obtained directly from government Web sites' (2008: 110). Needless to say, these legislative texts would have existed on those websites regardless of whether Boland and Katzive were studying them. Legislation happens independent of researcher interests and is thus, in our terminology, 'naturally occurring'.

South Africa is one of the countries where abortion legislation has become more liberal, following the trend Boland and Katzive identified. However, although mortality rates from previously illegal and unsafe abortions have plummeted, these unsafe abortions still occur because especially poor and rural women are unaware of the legal changes, which remove much of the stigma associated with abortion. To study this, Morroni et al (2006: np) 'investigated knowledge of the abortion legislation eight years after the introduction of legal abortion services in South Africa among women'. As the focus of the research is 'knowledge of the abortion legislation' the legislation itself is of little use here. Since there is no 'natural' circumstance where women would register their knowledge of abortion legislation, the researchers had to ask them. Using semi-structured interviews, the authors combined a dataset that could then be used to measure how well the legal context of abortion was known and, consequently, what policy implications the knowledge – or the lack of knowledge – had for public health. Clearly, in this case, the data was generated by the researchers. In statistical research, population registers and especially 'big data' collected by companies tracking our electronic lives, are an example of 'naturally occurring' data (data that would exist regardless of researchers), whereas surveys administered by researchers are an example of researcher-generated data.

There are data that do not fall neatly into either bracket. These include data generated by different state and other agencies. Records of police arrest rates, for example, exist regardless of your existence as a researcher. However, they are not primarily generated for research purposes, and they are generated by people with varying interests and agendas that may or may not be aligned with your interests. Therefore, it is paramount to be aware of how data gathered by agencies can be used in the first place. Despite appearances, they might not tell us much about the phenomena they purport to report. Some data, like court or parliamentary transcripts, are mostly unproblematic, although they miss much of the interactional element of such spaces. Some national and international surveys in turn usually include detailed descriptions of issues with data collection, which can be considered when interpreting results. Using this kind of secondary statistical data (data collected by others for research purposes) always requires diligence so that you understand the original purpose that the data was collected for in the first place. However, even reputable surveys (such as the American General Social Survey) may include systematic biases that are the outcome of survey interviewer actions (Becker, 2017: 142–143). Things get trickier when it comes to statistics about crime, death and so on (for a beautiful overview and discussion, see Becker, 2017). Sociologists noted already in the 1940s how crime statistics recorded crimes such as robbery and assault diligently, while what is referred to as white-collar crime (crime perpetrated by professionals in positions of relative power, for example, embezzlement, corruption) went unreported, or at the least, underreported. Our picture of crime in general is thus distorted by practices in defining what counts as 'crime'.

There are two solutions to this problem of data generated independent of the researcher but generated by others. First, you can try to triangulate official data with other types, which you may need to generate yourself. Becker (2017) discusses many path-breaking studies that have exposed the flawed nature of different types of official data so, regardless of your field, you will probably have guidance from earlier researchers that have grappled with similar questions. Second, you can flip your perspective (and research question) to focus on the process of data generation itself. Researchers have done fieldwork among police, for example, to analyse how an event ends up recorded as crime, how the attitudes of individual police officers produce a bias in the racial distribution of arrests, and so on (Becker, 2017: 122–128). If and when 'the statistics so created were *independent of the reality they were supposed to be evidence of*', then this kind of research 'helps us explain the fine grain of the "causes" of *the recording of police activity in the statistical records of police departments*', which, of course, is not evidence of the reality of crime 'out there' (Becker, 2017: 125, 128; emphases in the original).

Perhaps more than any of the other juxtapositions offered in this chapter, the choice between naturally occurring and researcher-generated data is a *practical* choice. Although the data type should always follow the research question first of all, there are three factors – access, skills and resources – that will influence your choice. First, not all naturally occurring data are available for researchers, nor do researchers always have access to interviews or observations that generate data for analysis. As I mentioned in Chapter 1, an MA student sat through half of my dissertation seminar with a firm intent to study how the Finnish Immigration Service assesses cases of self-declared atheists fleeing from Muslim-majority countries. She finished her proposal and read as much as she could in background literature – only to find that after waiting for a response for three months, the Immigration Service refused her request for asylum interview transcripts. Then she contemplated that she would interview asylum seekers about their asylum interview experiences, thus generating the data herself. Unfortunately, she had no contacts among the asylum seeker community, so gaining access to potential participants would have been a massive effort. Starting in March 2020, almost all research requiring participant observation in real-life situations stopped for about two years because of the COVID-19 pandemic. Research projects had to be redesigned on the go. A lot of interviews were changed to online interviews, while researchers patched up missing observation data with archival material or media reports, for example. Art historians had to be content with looking at reproductions rather than the real thing. The

COVID-19 pandemic showed what happens when many scholars lose access to their data.

Second, data gathering requires particular skills, depending on the data. Every year I have a student or two who want to do a survey or analyse big data. When I ask them if they know how to design and administer a survey (not even mentioning quantitative analysis methods at this point) or mine for data, it turns out they do not. While researcher training is of course all about learning data gathering and analysis skills, if you find yourself designing research that you do not have the skills to carry out, you need to reconsider. Some skills, such as participant observation and interviewing, are properly learned only by doing them, of course, but it is important to know what you are able to accomplish skills-wise with the time you have.

Which brings me to the third point: resources. In an ideal world, researchers would come up with a perfect design and then spend whatever time and money was required to finish the job. In the real world, however, you are constrained by exactly those two things. Whether it is the university's rules about submission deadlines or personal reasons (the business will hire you or the PhD programme will accept you if you graduate by a certain date), time is limited for all researchers. My student might have gained access to relevant participants for the asylum seeker project, but that could have taken many months – months that she did not have. Similarly, administering surveys is not just a matter of skills, but primarily about resources. To get a representative sample of even a relatively small population, you will very likely need the help of professional data organisations. An exception might be a survey administered to all members of a sports club, for example, when the study is about that club, and is not trying to generalise from the data.

As with numbers versus texts and images, some research traditions privilege naturally occurring over researcher-generated data – and vice versa. Which works best for you is defined primarily by the research question, but also the conventions of the discipline or field. If you have the access, skills and resources, a comprehensive project will try to combine both types of data to arrive at a fuller picture of the phenomenon under study.

First order versus second order

A slightly different distinction occurs in researcher-generated data. This has to do with the 'distance' that the researcher generating the data has from the studied phenomenon. To put it differently, the distinction is between the researcher as the reporter of events (first order) versus the researcher as the collector of other people's reports about phenomena (second order). Let us look at an example.

Workplace bullying is becoming an increasingly recognised problem around the world. Like school bullying, it leads to psychological stress and decreased functionality, and has adverse effects on the victim and the workplace community in general. Researchers have tried to analyse how and why workplace bullying happens and what could be done about it. Mille Mortensen spent five months in a Copenhagen hospital observing how workplace humour and teasing sometimes turns into bullying when the jokes serve a disciplining function (Mortensen and Baarts, 2018). People lower in the workplace hierarchy are 'put in their place' (my term) through shows of power. Mortensen experienced this first hand:

> He wraps his hands around my head to cover my ears. Because I'm sitting down and he's standing up, his genitals are right in front of my face. I can neither hear what he's saying, nor see the other surgeons' reactions. Everybody laughs when, a couple of minutes later, he takes his hands off my ears. (Mortensen and Baarts, 2018: 18)

Mortensen's description is an excerpt from her field journal, the main source for ethnographic analysis, used to record the experiences of a researcher immersed in the studied community. Also called 'participant observation' or just 'fieldwork' (sometimes interchangeably, sometimes meaning different things), the data of ethnographic research are the observations the researcher makes in the course of the study. The acts, behaviour and events that happen in real life are sources of data and the researcher is the instrument that records them.

Studying a difficult topic like workplace bullying is not always possible using participant observation, however. This is because people often behave better in the presence of an outsider and, by simply being there, the researcher makes the bullying invisible. In these cases, researchers resort to interviews, talking to people about bullying. Jaime Lester's research on community colleges, for example, has some chilling examples of stories of bullying:

> More than six years ago, we had a few deans who do not support what I was doing. One of them was really a racist. He said in a meeting, 'How bad can you get, you are a woman and a Mexican,' right in front of everyone. He said actually three things, 'how bad can you get: young, a woman, and a Mexican.' And another time, he told me, 'It's amazing what affirmative action can do for people'. (Lester, 2009: 450)

There are many similar studies, all of which use people's stories about their experiences of workplace bullying as data.

Now, what is the difference here? In the first example, the researcher observed and experienced the phenomenon of bullying herself. In the second example, the researcher listened to what people had to say about bullying. These are sometimes referred to as 'first- and second-order phenomena' (Spickard, 2017: 56–57). It is important for your research design to understand what kinds of questions the two types can answer and what challenges lie with each.

In a classic text, sociologists Howard Becker and Blanche Geer argued that 'participant observation makes it possible to check description against fact and, noting discrepancies, become aware of systematic distortions made by the person under study; such distortions are less likely to be discovered by interviewing alone' (Becker and Geer, 1957: 31). After 60 years, Becker (2017) is still suspicious of interviews and surveys, which record people's experiences of events – second-order phenomena – rather than the events themselves. Sometimes people simply do not know enough to help answer researchers' questions (Becker, 2017: 6–10). Sometimes people misremember, embellish and even lie when asked about their experiences. In the case of alleged 'satanic ritual abuse', researchers talked about 'recovered' or 'false' memories, where the experiences of shadowy cult proceedings – often said to have happened in childhood – were implanted by well-meaning mental health professionals interviewing their patients (for example, Ost et al, 2013). How do we reconcile this problem with second-order descriptions while wanting to understand a sensitive topic like workplace bullying without dismissing the participants' experiences as untrustworthy?

There are two immediate solutions: first, there is the idea of data triangulation (Layder, 1993: 121; Atkinson and Coffey, 2003: 420–422). That is, the veracity of the first type of data can be checked by using another type of data. So, for example, the stories people tell about workplace bullying can be checked against the workplace dynamics as observed by the researcher. This is what Becker and Geer (1957: 28) suggest when they say that '[p]articipant observation can thus provide us with a yardstick against which to measure the completeness of data gathered in other ways, a model which can serve to let us know what orders of information escape us when we use other methods'. For Becker and Geer, writing in the 1950s, 'facts' and 'distortions' were unproblematic concepts (Atkinson and Coffey, 2003: 419). Because of this epistemological view, discrepancies between different data can only be treated as a problem. Their solution was to privilege observation over interviews. But in some ways, we are back to square one again: How does one observe a phenomenon that becomes hidden by virtue of the researcher's presence?

The second solution takes a reflexive approach. By this, I mean that neither observation nor interviews are treated as unproblematic ways of accessing social reality. In reflexive ethnography, the observer is an active participant in the construction of observed realities. From this perspective, observational data is never 'pure' in the sense suggested by Becker and Geer, but filtered through the interpretive lenses of the observer. Likewise, in constructionist approaches interviews are treated as narratives and discourses, where the narrative construction of events and 'facts' becomes the object of analysis. Second-order data does not need to be complemented by first-order data – as in triangulation – because the focus shifts from accuracy and inaccuracy to the ways in which people make sense of their own experiences.

Research literature is full of creative ways to combine first- and second-order data. The two main solutions suggested here are controversial in their own ways and in some ways antithetical (for example, Atkinson and Coffey, 2003: 420–422). Method literature will help you dig deeper into the epistemological issues between the two. What is important in the context of data is to think about whether your data can answer your research question. If and when events and descriptions of events are different things, what information of events can you gain from first-order as opposed to second-order data? Your reasoning around these questions will determine whether you need to ask a different research question or whether you need to find different kind of data.

Self versus others

Another type of distinction could be considered a sub-case of second-order data discussed earlier. When you talk to people, or read historical records left behind by long-dead people, it is important to understand whether they are giving testimony about themselves or others (including something that they think 'everyone knows'). If you are studying the experiences of young people who have committed crimes and talk to the caretaker of a vandalised housing block, you will learn a lot – but about what? You can put together details of events using the caretaker's story, and you can very likely assess what the caretaker's opinion of the offending youth is. However, that story does not count as evidence towards answering a question about the experiences of young people involved in vandalism. Sometimes you may not have access to certain people, say, prisoners. You could talk to wardens, nurses or social workers to put together a quite accurate picture of life in prison. However, whenever your interviewees talk about their opinions, experiences or feelings – that is, the *meaning* of those daily events – the focus of your research switches from prisoners to the people working with prisoners. It is important to understand this difference so that you do not claim to know more than your data allows.

We are talking about 'the self' when you ask people about their opinions of issues relating to their lives, their life experiences and their feelings. I say 'ask', but the same applies equally to researchers using historical records. These can be quick answers on a survey form about the taste of a particular brand of yoghurt, long interviews about a person's religious journey, or the diary of a young mother in Victorian times. In short, these are data about the meaning people give to their own lives.

For example, while the media and politicians spend much energy on violent street gangs – sometimes to the point of moral panic – there is less research about how gang membership subjects young people to increased risk of victimisation. Using a state-wide survey of public high school students in South Carolina, Gover et al (2009) asked young people about their membership in gangs and their experiences of violence. They found that 'gang membership is significantly related to the risk of victimization for both males and females'. Analytically, the survey produced second-order data – which is the only kind available in a study such as this. It may be possible for a researcher to corroborate the reported experiences while observing one gang, but this would say nothing about the prevalence of victimisation among all self-identifying gang members. Importantly, the study was not about how prevalent South Carolina high school students think gang violence is, but how many had experienced violence while a member of a gang. The study's evidence came from people reporting about their own lives.

Now, what I call reports about 'others' – as opposed to reports about the self – can mean, literally, people talking about other people. This can be in the form of crude stereotypes, as for example when Finns talk about Latin American men and women in hyper-sexualised and sexist terms ('Women take care of their man and most have a principle that the man doesn't leave the house on an empty stomach and with filled balls') (Pakkasvirta, 2018: 102). However, I also include in 'others' so-called 'taken-for-granted knowledge' or 'common sense' – that is, what people think everyone knows. As with stereotypes, this may not be an accurate description of what is being described, but it says something about the people doing the describing; what they think people in a particular nation, community or subculture *should* know. Again, you need to be able to discern what kind of information your data yields.

Let me try to illustrate this with what is now known as the history of emotions. While it is easy to understand how historians reconstruct events from whatever documents people of the past have left behind, how can we study the feelings of people who have been centuries dead? Peter N. Stearns, a pioneer in the field, gives an example of studies on emotions in post-Reformation Europe, which 'have highlighted the pervasiveness of an atmosphere of melancholy—held to be an appropriate religious demeanor, given the snares of this world and the ravages of sin. Paintings frequently seized on melancholy, and diary entries characteristically portrayed dolefulness and grief' (Stearns, 2008: 17). The last sentence is interesting from a data perspective: diary entries are an example of data about the self, of course. But the reference to paintings is an example of 'common sense', or culturally shared beliefs. Early modern painters painted what they thought were typical expressions of emotion in their time. Or, more accurately, they painted what they thought *should* have been typical expressions of emotion in their time. Thus, the history of emotions is not so much about what people actually felt (although some forms of history writing claim to have access to that too), but rather about the 'feeling rules' in different times (Stearns, 2008: 22). That is, what people in the past considered appropriate displays of emotion. While this approach has its limitations (painters rarely painted peasants in their everyday settings, for example), it shows that data about 'others', or culturally shared knowledge and beliefs, can be used effectively as a source for analysis.

A subtype of 'data about others' is expert knowledge, which is not based on 'what everyone knows', but rather the opposite, on research or experience. Journalists, popular science authors and current affairs writers often use expert interviews as support for their arguments, sometimes juxtaposing two competing views. For academic research, expert knowledge can be a key data source for questions such as how well healthcare professionals understand the health needs of transgender people (Do and Van Nguyen, 2020). But unlike many journalists, you should not use expert knowledge to talk about another group of people that you could study directly. Access may of course be an obstacle, but as with the prisoner example, once the experts start talking about other people, the data you are producing is about the experts, not the people who are the object of the expert knowledge.

To talk about the difference between data about the self and data about others is not to privilege one over the other. Indeed, sometimes data about people's opinions, experiences and feelings is not available from first-hand witnesses. In the spirit of triangulation, discussed earlier, any data will do to complement gaps in knowledge. For example, the Vikings left a sparse written record of themselves, but we can learn something about them from Arabic sources (Hraundal, 2014). Despite the seeming distance between the two cultures, stories people tell about others are still useful data when used with care.

Articulated versus hidden positions

In the HBO hit series *Game of Thrones*, based on George R.R. Martin's *Song of Ice and Fire* books, Arya Stark, whose noble father has been just executed as a traitor, ends up as a serving girl for her archenemy Tywin Lannister. Under a false identity as a stonemason's daughter, Arya tries to gather information about the Lannister's plans, but the shrewd Lord Tywin sees through her façade. He tells her that 'lowborn girls say "milord", not "my lord". If you are going to pose as a commoner, you should do it properly' (*Game of Thrones*, S2E7). As much as she tries to pass as just another country girl, Arya, reared in a noble household, is oblivious to her manner of speaking, which eventually gives away her true identity. Like any good fiction, even a fantasy epic like *Game of Thrones* can teach us a lot about how society and culture work. Indeed, Arya's pretence is a good metaphor for this section: she articulates one type of social position (a 'commoner') but cannot avoid speaking in ways that reveal her hidden identity (an heir of a noble house). This distinction matters for data.

I call these articulated and hidden 'positions', with reference to different types of distinctions in society – whether gender, race, class, sexuality, ethnicity, religion, disability, and so on. Much of social research (but also historical and literary research) is interested in how people navigate, reproduce and challenge these categories. What makes them interesting topics to study is that some of these positions are clearly articulated, that is, people explicitly identify with a particular ethnic group, for example. At the same time, many people do not recognise – or they misrecognise – themselves as belonging in particular categories. They may not lie, like Arya Stark, but simply have not considered, or refuse to consider themselves as of a particular kind (cf Spickard, 2017: 64–65). Both are equally important aspects for researchers to study, but you need to know what kind of data can answer questions related to one or the other.

'Identity' is a useful shorthand for what I have here called articulated positions. It is one of those words that have trickled down into everyday usage and hence can be understood in a variety of ways, but Jenkins' definition is a good example of the academic approach:

> Identity is the human capacity – rooted in language – to know 'who's who' (and hence 'what's what'). This involves knowing who we are, knowing who others are, them knowing who we are, us knowing who they think we are, and so on: a multi-dimensional classification or mapping of the human world and our places in it, as individuals and as members of communities. (Jenkins, 2008: 5)

Just in case you are thinking that you did not sign up for a chapter on social theory, there are two relevant points here, data-wise. First, most scholars agree that identity is not something people possess, but rather that it is a process of identification. Second, following from this, it means – as Jenkins says – that identity is articulated ('rooted in language') by identifying with particular social positions. The people identifying as 'Peranakan' in Singapore, for example, navigate their identity between state-imposed categories (which classify them as 'Chinese') and actual hybrid identities (Rocha and Yeoh, 2023). The authors of the study, Zarine Rocha and

Brenda Yeoh, generated the data by interviewing 32 Peranakan people. They asked the participants about how they would classify themselves, but also about how they thought ethnic classification in Singaporean society worked in general.

Now, like Arya Stark, people also act in ways that they do not recognise, yet which are rooted in particular social positions. For example, we know from decades of large-scale survey and register research that people tend to marry within their class status. Middle-class people marry middle-class people, and so on. However, when it comes to love, Western culture is so suffused with the idea of romantic love centring on individuals that few people recognise this social pattern. This is different in India, for example, where both caste and class influence marriage choices quite explicitly. From a research data perspective, the issue here is that, should we want to examine the reasons behind this pattern, people's articulations of their experiences or general opinions on marriage and class would yield little useful information, because few would probably admit that they seek romantic partners based on the partner's position in the social class hierarchy. However, if we gathered ethnographic data of a group of people for an extended period, we could observe that middle-class people mostly meet other middle-class people in their daily lives – often without recognising or ever thinking about this fact. Getting romantically attached (economists and sociologists speak of 'marriage markets') to someone from a different social class would require a change in the social setting (see Kalmijn, 1998).

Hidden patterns are not data-specific as such, but a creative combination of data and method are usually required. Often, triangulation is involved. Few people have described the tangible effects of triangulation as well as sociologist of religion Mark Chaves:

> I do not have the literary skill to convey the drama of the evening in my office when I had in front of me all of these pieces of information – the counts from 18 dioceses, the percent Catholic in each diocese from the NSRI data, and the total population of each diocese from the 1990 U.S. census – and set about using my hand calculator to calculate a count-based church attendance rate for Catholics in these dioceses. Nor do I have the literary skill to convey the excitement I felt when, after a couple of hours, I pushed the ' = ' button on the calculator for the final time and saw the result: 28 percent weekly attendance rate, compared to a 50 percent Catholic attendance rate produced by conventional surveys at that time. Wow. I was staring at the same result – massive over-reporting – that Kirk [Hadaway] and Penny [Long Mahler] had found for Protestants in Ashtabula [county]. I have

never felt more like a scientist making a discovery than at that moment. (Chaves, 2013: 107)

Chaves' story is about counting church attendance, but it is a good example of how mixing data yields new discoveries.

Some methods foreground hidden patterns and positionings. Using particular words to describe the world is not a neutral endeavour, as different types of discourse analysis propose (Richardson, 2007). This is especially so when the described people and events are not familiar to us. That is why the language of the media is so often under a specific lens for bias. When reporting on the 1991 war against Iraq, the British press used very selective language – so much so that the British newspaper *The Guardian* (cited in Allan, 2010: 202) compiled a comparison of the different words the media used to describe the British and American troops on the one hand and the Iraqi side on the other. They found that the enemy ('they') engaged in 'destroying' and 'killing', whereas what 'we' did was 'suppressing', 'eliminating' and 'neutralising'. As people, 'they' were characterised as 'mad dogs', 'ruthless' and 'fanatical', whereas 'we' were depicted as 'heroes', 'professional' and 'brave'.

We can argue whether the perspective conveyed by the media is an unconscious decision ('hidden position') or a political choice. What is quite clear, data-wise, is that few journalists would admit to such bias, so asking them would help little in answering a research question about hidden biases (except that they would likely deny their existence – which is interesting in itself; see Chapter 4).

In some ways the contrast between articulated and hidden positions, as I call them here, is a matter of method. It is about what we *do* with the data rather than the data themselves. Looking for hidden patterns is a way to use the data in ways that are not necessarily obvious. Yet, you need to understand the distinction between articulated and hidden positions before you can start thinking about the best ways of finding data for the latter.

How much is enough?

Asking what kind of data fits your research question (alignment) and explicating why it is best for you (justification) while considering the practical limitations of your research are the logical first steps in thinking about the role of data in any research project. If my students are any measure, however, the question that arises soon after these – sometimes even before – is 'how much data do I need'. Frustratingly, the only sensible answer to that question – no matter whether you are doing a BA or MA dissertation, a PhD thesis, or a multi-year international research project – is 'it depends' (for example, Baker and Edwards, 2012).

It depends, first, on your approach. Although 'sampling' is not a perfect term, because it has connotations of representativeness and as such does not readily work with qualitative analysis, I will use it as a shorthand for thinking about 'how much data'. For the purposes of this chapter, it will suffice to say that if you plan to count things and work with statistical methods, then the question of sampling is somewhat simpler. Simpler, because there are tried and tested rules about how to reach acceptable levels of representativeness and mathematical formulae for checking for errors. Sampling principles and techniques are some of the first things quantitative researchers learn. I do not mean to imply that it is 'simple' to collect and analyse accurate data – on the contrary. My point is that if you run into a problem with your statistical project, there is a wealth of literature to guide you forward.

There is of course a wealth of literature about 'sampling' to guide researchers observing everyday life, doing interviews or reading archival documents too. But few of these guides purport to authoritatively claim that they are in possession of the philosopher's stone regarding sample sizes in qualitative research. It truly depends. It is important to remember, at all times, that the purpose of qualitative research is not generalisability, but description and conceptualisation (see Chapter 4). For many historians, the aim is to describe, understand and explain unique events in the past, so generalisability is not an issue by default (although historians may provide material for assessing social and cultural patterns over time; Burke, 2005).

There are, however, some principles you can follow regarding the amount of data when you work with something other than numbers. One of them is the idea of *saturation*, that is, that there is a point where new interviews or observations do not provide new information. There is a limited number of experiences young people can have at a religious summer festival, for example. Thus, even with 30,000 overall visitors, a saturated view of the youth experience can be achieved with 23 interviews (Nissilä, 2018). When these are complemented by *triangulation* using post-festival interviews and observation, a convincing picture of the youth experience emerges. A good rule of thumb, then, is to overestimate the initial number of interviews, or the time spent observing people. If your data reaches saturation point by the time you have done half of the planned interviews or in half the planned time, then it is up to you whether you want to stop there or play it safe, just in case. In the latter case, you will have more examples for your writing, but the data do not as such add to your evidence from the first half.

Another way of thinking about research that does not aim at generalisation is to treat it as *case study research*. This is a much-used term, but with mixed meanings. Often case study research is presented as a method of data collection and analysis – I see this especially in dissertations and dissertation proposals. However, a more accurate way of characterising case study research is, after Yin (1994: 13), that it is 'an empirical inquiry that investigates a contemporary phenomenon within its real-life context, especially when the boundaries between phenomenon and context are not clearly evident'. Thus defined, the case study is intimately tied to the research question and especially well-suited to examine the processual character of social life. (Problematically, Yin later replaced the better word 'inquiry' with 'method'; Yin, 2018). For example, O'Mahony and Garavan (2012) wanted to analyse how a quality management framework was implemented at an Information Technology Division of an Irish public university and what that implementation process could tell about quality management in the higher education setting more broadly. They argue that the process was successful and identify different factors enabling this success. They also argue that even though the example was limited to one division of one university, the research shows that incremental changes within one division, rather than organisation-wide overhaul, likely contributed to the success. This has both theoretical and practical implications beyond the single case. Most importantly for this chapter, however, the study used multiple types of data: documents, interviews and observation. These were all text-based data, but both Yin (2018) and other scholars writing about case study research (especially Woodside, 2017) agree that case studies can be conducted using whatever type of data, including numerical. It is the bounded, 'local' nature of the case that matters. The criterion for 'how much' should, then, be applied in the context of these local boundaries.

The second factor influencing qualitative data 'sampling' is access, which we have already discussed. If you have no access to suitable data, you will need to rethink your question. But what about limited access? If you can interview three people instead of the planned ten, do you still have a project? If it is a little-researched topic, you may be able to provide rich descriptions and conceptualisations, and thus generate new knowledge about the phenomenon, even with a small number of participants. Historians studying periods or topics with few surviving documents will use whatever they can get their hands on. As long as you acknowledge the limitations of the data – what you cannot ascertain and what you can ascertain with reservations – you still have a contribution to make. Dissertation and thesis writers will always need to check with their supervisor about acceptable standards.

Finally, there are resource issues, also discussed earlier. As mentioned, representative surveys are unrealistic for a single-researcher project with no extra funding, unless you are studying people in a bounded environment. Online questionnaires are attractive because they can potentially reach many respondents, but they are not an alternative for representative surveys, because the samples are not random and thus produce different kind of information. Also, if you have nine months to finish your dissertation, you may not have time to interview 20 people – and then transcribe and analyse the data. However, some students seem to have the idea that the appropriate number of interviewees depends on the word count of the report you are writing. So for example, five will be fine for a BA dissertation, but more than 15 would be needed for a PhD. This is nonsense. Whatever your justification for having the number of interviewees (or documents, videos, and so on), your word count is not it.

In sum, how much data is enough depends on your question, approach, access and resources. The trick is to always acknowledge and articulate the potential and the limitations of whatever data you are using. No amount of theorising and rhetoric will save you if your reader is not convinced that your data provides evidence for the argument you are making. Letting the reader know that *you* know what questions the data can answer and how well the data do it, is a crucial step towards better scholarship.

Conclusion

Data comes in many forms. The main questions on any researcher's mind when engaging in an empirical project are usually the ones I mentioned in the beginning: What kind of data do I need to answer my research question? Why is this particular type of data best for answering my research question? How much data do I need to answer my research question successfully? The identification of research design with a choice between quantitative and qualitative methods, which I have complained about already, is especially unfortunate since it reverses your priorities. You need to have a question and a solid sense of the data that you will use to answer that question before you can or should think about methods. Indeed, as Spickard (2017: 66) succinctly puts it: 'The type of data you want determines the data collection method.'

In this chapter, I have outlined some of the main ways of distinguishing between data types. If you go through each section with your research question in mind and think about where your data falls, you should have quite clear answers to the three questions presented. More than any other aspect of research design, however, access and practical considerations regarding data may require you to rethink your research question and your whole design. You can come up with the perfect research design, but sometimes the world interferes.

4

Method

My sociologist colleague at University College London had one adamant rule about student essays: whatever else you do, *never* quote a dictionary definition in your work! He thought it was intellectually lazy and led students astray when the sociological definition – there are academic discipline-specific dictionaries out there, too – might actually be quite different from the dictionary one.

So, that's exactly what I am going to do here (sorry Richard!). The Merriam-Webster (nda) online dictionary gives the following definition for 'method', closest to my purposes here: 'a systematic procedure, technique, or mode of inquiry employed by or proper to a particular discipline or art'.

As mentioned in Chapter 1, 'method' refers to the mutually recognised procedures for studying the phenomena we are interested in. *Methodology* is a broader concept; it is the conversation within and between disciplines regarding which individual methods are recognised and treated as legitimate ways of collecting and analysing data. Hence, anthropologists do not need to justify ethnography to each other, even if a political scientist employing survey research might find ethnography inexplicable – and vice versa. Although methodological discussion is crucial to any academic endeavour, the purpose of this chapter is to examine how different 'procedures, techniques, or modes of inquiry' – that is, methods – function as one element of research design.

I will add to this by offering my own definition: *methods are explicit frameworks of collecting and analysing data.* This definition suggests two things: first, methods are tools for collecting and making sense of the mass of data you need to answer your research question. Second, methods decrease the individual element (your background, ideological preferences) in interpretation, in the sense that methods make the analysis process more transparent – even if they do not guarantee 'objectivity'. Being explicit about your method enables your reader to understand why you have interpreted the data in particular ways, even if they disagree with the interpretation.

This chapter is, then, about these frameworks for collecting and analysing data. Importantly, when describing your method, you should always have something to say about *both* collection and analysis. I have read too many BA and MA dissertations that say that the method of the study is 'interviewing', for example. Fine, but what then? What do you *do* with the interviews once you have collected the data? Or vice versa, a description of method is incomplete if it says that data will be analysed using comparative multivariate analysis of variance and covariance, but no description of data collection is provided.

Because this book is aimed at people from a variety of disciplines and fields of research, a couple of caveats apply: first, as usual, some of the things said here are more or less useful depending on your discipline and field of study. However, as usual, it never hurts to think about method (or any of the other elements, for that matter) from an unfamiliar angle. Second, I will not feign to be able to present all relevant methods in a brief discussion such as this. Instead, I will examine different *types* of methods of data collection and analysis in order to illustrate what they can do for you. You will need to dig deeper into method guides for practical advice. Thankfully, there is an abundance to choose from. Finally, I have not structured this chapter along the common distinction between quantitative and qualitative methods. Although your hands may be tied, so to say, in terms of which approach your discipline prefers, there are good and bad reasons for adopting either. I will discuss some of the reasons in what follows, as well as reasons for and ways of adopting a mixed methods approach.

Two bad attitudes and one good one

Method textbooks will tell you how specific methods work. What they do not teach is different attitudes towards method. By 'attitude' I mean a general outlook regarding the role and significance of method among the different elements of research design. I have distilled these attitudes into three: method-driven, sceptical and balanced. I am sure more fine-grained typologies could be constructed, but these fit my purpose, which is to say that I find the first two unhelpful. As I discuss here, your attitude to method is shaped by more than your own interests, but whatever your discipline or field, I think it is in your interest to find a balanced attitude to method. Consider the vignettes that follow, think about where you fit best, and then ask yourself, 'why?'

You will have met the *method-driven* researcher already in Chapter 1. This person has a pet method that they have read about, perhaps practised on a method course, and which has somehow opened their eyes to how social or humanities research is done. In fact, I am speaking of myself in my student days, just before starting my MA research. I got my hands on a textbook about discourse analysis, the first of its kind in the Finnish language, and was immediately hooked. In a small country like Finland a publication of one method textbook may have a massive impact, which is exactly what happened back then. In addition, two recent dissertations in my discipline had used discourse analysis, so it was easy to take them as models to be emulated. When I started my MA seminar, I had a sense of my topic (but not the question) and some ideas about data, but most of all I wanted to do discourse analysis.

Method

You could insert whatever method in place of 'discourse analysis'. The point is that the method-driven person starts thinking about research design from the method corner of the triangle displayed in Figure 1.1 ('the holy trinity'). This means that the data needs to fit the method and, most worryingly, the question needs to be such that the method can actually help in analysing the right data in order to answer it. If you are dead set on using multivariate statistics, then you will have to rethink your plan to analyse what journalists mean when they talk about immigration. Why? Because your method is not aligned with your data and question. Of course, you can fit the other sides of the triangle to your method, but method alone will not provide you with a question (although it will point you to particular types of data).

Now, at the opposite end of the method attitude scale is the person who does not understand what all the method fuss is about. If you think this is an imaginary person, let me again reminisce a bit. A friend and fellow student of mine did his MA degree in a humanities discipline, where method clearly was not a big fuss. He then changed to a social science discipline for his PhD degree and was shocked about all the fuss. I could not locate his PhD thesis, so I do not have the exact quote, but I distinctly remember him fuming about the useless 'method fetishism' of his newly adopted discipline. Hence the moniker 'sceptical'.

There are of course disciplines and approaches that are not very invested in explicit methods. In some, 'interpretation' as a general concept is considered a 'method', which requires little elaboration. In others – old-fashioned and popular history writing comes to mind – method is not interesting, because the job of the scholar is to 'tell it like it was', the 'it' presumably accessible through the sources left behind. Either way, the problem with this attitude is that without some explicit framework, the reader of your research will have trouble recognising the parameters of your analysis. Has the data collection been systematic? Are sources analysed systematically, so that every interviewee, for example, gets the same treatment? Will a person coming from a different background be able to follow and accept your interpretations? Would their interpretation be anything like yours?

Both of these attitudes create problems, then. However, let me clarify what I am *not* suggesting before explaining what I am. I do not mean to say that every study needs to have a 'named' method, like 'discourse analysis', or 'qualitative comparative analysis'. In fact, using just a name to describe your method without explaining how you use it is as problematic as the two bad attitudes discussed. With the exception of some statistical techniques, methods in the social sciences and humanities do not usually have fixed meanings, which means that you will always need to be explicit about what *your* version of 'discourse analysis' (or whatever) looks like.

Although I suggested that it is a good exercise to think about whether someone else would end up with the same interpretations as you, I do not mean that simply having a method makes your research 'replicable'. Analysis of qualitative data is always about interpretation and cannot ever be strictly replicated. However, having colleagues analyse the same texts, for example, is a form of methodological triangulation. If your colleagues' analyses do not significantly deviate from yours, your interpretation gains support. And although quantitative research aspires to replicability, there has been much talk in recent years about a 'replication crisis', when new analyses using same methods have yielded very different results (see Chapter 8).

So, what is the 'balanced' attitude, then? To me, it means that method is seen as one of the three key elements of research design, organically adjusted to fit the research question and the data. To repeat: methods provide a systematic framework for your data collection and analysis. Methods enable you to make sense of your messy data and help the reader trace the logic of your argument. Being explicit about your methods means that your analysis is done according to the rules of inquiry shared in your discipline or field.

How to choose a method?

Although the point of this book is to demystify research design, I need to give fair warning about a too idealised picture of the process. Ideally, the choice of method would be a matter of aligning the sides of the triangle so that your data can answer your question, and your method enables you to analyse that data in a systematic way. In practice, however, there are at least three reasons that have nothing to do with the 'holy trinity' that will affect your choice of method: disciplinary tradition, time and resource limitations, and personal preferences.

I have already discussed the role of disciplinary traditions in the chapter on data. I will just reiterate here that in some cases the choice of method is out of your hands, unless you want to spend extra time and energy in convincing your field that your unconventional method choice is legitimate. This may be especially daunting for degree students. Even broad-minded supervisors may be reluctant to approve unconventional method choices, not because of some unwritten rules, but rather because they are trying to protect their students. Uncontroversial method choices mean passed degrees and funded research proposals. However, if you feel that your choice of method is justified in light of the alignment of the elements of research design, then you have every right to make the case to your supervisor and/or your peers.

I also discussed time and resource limitations in the data chapter and have little to add here. Representative surveys require funding usually beyond the means of degree students. Ethnography, in turn, requires immersion in the lives of your participants to the degree that may not be possible within the timeframe of the project – again, particularly in the case of BA and MA dissertation researchers. The problem is not only one of data collection methods. Doing comprehensive discursive analysis on a large amount of text may be prohibitive in terms of time, even if the textual data is readily available. Qualitative method software does not similarly yield 'results' as statistical programmes do. Even if you are able to mine and organise the data with a software package, the programme will not tell you what the different types of discourse *mean* in the context of their usage. The only way to figure that out is to read the texts, no matter how many there are.

The third point is slightly different. In general, I do not think it is helpful to categorise researchers according to their preferred methods ('I am a quantitative scholar', 'I am an ethnographer'). Personally, I have found it enriching to do all kinds of research, text-based, ethnographic and quasi-experimental. That said, there might be something to the point Blaikie (2010: 207) makes when he comments that 'I have long suspected that each group [quantitative and qualitative] of methods attracts different kind of personalities, with level of comfort in being close to people an important factor'. This may not be a conscious choice – how many of us really know what our 'personality' is? – but social research methods involve varying degrees of 'intrusion' into the lives of participants and hence a different distance between the researcher and the researched. Some could never contemplate inserting themselves for an extended period of time in a community whose language they barely know. Conversely, some would find reading mouldy papers in an archive for two years immensely boring. I certainly found ethnography much more demanding than analysing newspaper texts. Even plain interviewing was less stressful, because there is a structure to the research event, whereas in ethnography everything was potential data. Keeping an eye on all the potential data in addition to navigating everyday human relationships is no mean feat. I like to think of myself as sociable, but I was exhausted after every day in the field. You may not have thought about 'personality' as an issue when thinking about methods, but it may be, especially if you are thinking about a qualitative approach involving living, breathing participants who sometimes have bad days like everyone else.

Quantitative versus qualitative

Now that you have figured out the external constraints, you may focus on assessing what methods would best fit your question and data. Here you have a choice to make, and one bad reason to make that choice is to think that some methods are better than others by default. Both quantitative and qualitative scholars have contributed to the 'method wars' by claiming superiority. Luckily, the worst excesses of the debate are behind us and with the exception of some disciplines, qualitative research has found a legitimate place in the methodological pantheon of social science. Similarly, traditionally exclusively qualitative humanities research has expanded into quantitative territory with the advent of digital humanities and some specialisations, such as economic history. Although research design and method textbooks sometimes perpetuate a hierarchical view of quantitative versus qualitative, this is not how I view the issue, nor how you should view it.

How should you view the issue, then? If you have paid attention so far, you will already know my view: *methods are only as good as their fit with the data and the research question*. Neither quantitative nor qualitative methods are 'better' simply by virtue of their premises. 'Better' is what better aligns with the other sides of the research design triangle. Research questions point towards a preference for data based on either numbers or texts/visual/audio data (including descriptions of observations). These data in turn point towards methods devised for analysing that kind of data. In many cases, the questions point to a combination of data and, thus, 'mixed' methods. The boundary between the two can also be innovatively blurred beyond the use of particular methods. In her book *Birth Control Battles*, sociologist Melissa Wilde (2020) uses qualitative data (church-affiliated periodicals), but the design and logic of her study imitates a model familiar from quantitative research. She talks about 'falsifying' alternative explanations, offers justifications for her 'sample' of studied churches and their periodicals, and discusses comparability (Wilde, 2020: 5–24). In a meeting with my students, I asked Wilde whether she thought my assessment of her design made sense. She said 'yes', and added that her main aim throughout the study was to be 'relentlessly explanatory', no matter what her data. The important point here, then, is the overall approach, which for Wilde is 'explanatory'. That is, she looks for causal connections instead of a looser understanding of the phenomenon. In that, she is not too worried about conventional boundary marking between methods. And that is how it should be: the distinction between qualitative and quantitative methods sits deep, but the point is to make methods work for you – not the other way around.

The background assumptions of methods

In the beginning of this book, I argued that starting to think about empirical research from the perspective of philosophical concepts like ontology and epistemology is disheartening. It may bog you down, when nothing in the research process requires you to begin with the most abstract aspect of research. Your research interest and, ultimately, your research question determines your ontological and epistemological position. That, in turn, determines what kind of data are most useful for answering the research question. Logically, looking at our familiar triangle of elements, the next thing to be fitted in the picture is method.

Methods come with different background assumptions, however. The most common assumption, which is sometimes referred to as the 'objectivist' approach (Crotty, 2003: 8–9), is that data (in whatever form) more or less accurately reflect the world. When historian Adrian Gregory (2008) uses personal diaries as data to analyse the British public's reaction to the outbreak of the First World War, he treats them as accounts of actual feelings experienced at the time. Like any critical scholar, he acknowledges the problems of using such material, but from an epistemological perspective the diaries provide access to a world that we cannot experience ourselves anymore.

Some methods, however, come with different kinds of background assumptions. These include especially text-analysis methods such as discourse analysis, narrative analysis and rhetoric. These methods treat text and talk not as unproblematic reflections of the world, but active constructions of it. In other words, they start from the premise that our access to the world is mediated by the meanings that people give it. The epistemology ('how can we know?') of these methods is, hence, different from the standard 'objectivist' account. That is why they are sometimes referred to as 'constructionist' methods (Hjelm, 2014). People's constructions of the world are by definition partial in both senses of the word: they are incomplete and they are subjective. People can at best describe a small slice of the word they inhabit and what the slice looks like is influenced by their preferences, ideology, and so on. For these reasons, the focus of these methods shifts from trying to present a more or less accurate description of the world to trying to figure out what people accomplish (and hope to accomplish) by constructing a particular version of the world.

Going back to the First World War, Martin (2015) takes a different approach to war diaries. Unlike Gregory, she analyses the diaries as tools that frontline soldiers used to 'authenticate the newly militarised, masculine self'. She is not even interested in whether the events described happened as the diaries portray, but rather how the diary became a way to construct a new identity very different from the civilian one: 'the combatant diarist, in a sense, *writes* his newly militarised self into being' (Martin, 2015: 1260; emphasis in the original). Martin traces this construction of a new identity by analysing the narratives, word choices and rhetoric used in the diaries.

My point with this excursion is *not* to claim that one epistemological stance is 'better' than the other. Neither should you think that once you have chosen an epistemological stance, you are stuck with it. Different studies require different approaches. The point, then, is simply to help you recognise which methods align with your question and data (and which do not). It is partly a question of quantitative versus qualitative, because methods that produce numerical data are better for some questions than other questions – and vice versa. However, that dominant distinction does not fully cover the issue here, because interviews and observations can be used in an 'objectivist' way, as unproblematic accounts of the world. The point is more about what you then do with the data. Data does not speak for itself; methods make data speak. It is your job to recognise whether the background assumptions of your methods make data speak different languages.

Methods of data collection

Data collection needs methods for the same reason methods are needed in the first place: transparency. Your reader needs to know how comprehensive your 'sample' is (although that word makes less sense for qualitative analysis) in order to appraise how broad the claims you can make based on your data can be. Are you missing crucial data? Are the gaps in the data outcomes of resource restrictions or selection bias on your part? In this section, I briefly list some main types of data collection methods (in alphabetical order), specifically with an eye on what kind of questions and data match the method best. The list is not exhaustive and, as said before, for further information, you need to consult specific method guides.

Action research. Action research refers to an approach that aims to change the situation it analyses. In it, 'research can become a systematic intervention, going beyond describing, analysing and theorizing social practices to working in partnership with participants to reconstruct and transform those practices' (Somekh, 2006: 1). Researchers are often practitioners themselves, which is why the action method is popular in education, nursing and social work. For example, teachers may collect observation data in order to analyse classroom dynamics while teaching in order to uncover patterns of interaction between students, and then change classroom arrangements in order to improve a situation. A variant of this is participatory action research, where the students would not be treated as passive participants, but as data collectors and analysts. This aims to further empower both researcher and participants (McIntyre, 2008). Note that action research is not a method of data collection as such. It uses other data methods, but it is distinct from these because the research has a practical aim of changing the researched situation. Clearly, action research method is made for research questions that include an emancipatory element. The data fit depends on the actual method used, but since action research is done in practice settings, observation and interview data are common types.

Archival research. I use 'archival research' to refer to all data collection that takes place in designated repositories where old and new documents are kept – 'archive' being the most common term for such places. Archives are the home of historians and folklorists, especially, but social scientists studying contemporary organisations, for example, need archives as much as historians do (Ventresca and Mohr, 2017). The type of data found in archives varies wildly, so digging up archival documents may be related to questions about the average salary of employees in a company, or to questions about the love lives of 18th-century nobility, and everything in between. One of the key skills is finding the relevant sources among a potential abundance of documents.

Ethnography. Frustrated by the various and vague uses that the term 'ethnography' nowadays has, Howard Becker (2017: 44) semi-seriously suggests 'that its use be forbidden'. Perhaps we do not have to be that drastic, but it is true that the word alone does not tell us much about anything. Often used interchangeably with 'fieldwork' or 'field research', sometimes the term encompasses both observation and interviews, sometimes just the former. An anthropologist colleague of mine is very adamant that interviews are *not* ethnography. I think many would agree. Here I refer to ethnography especially as a method for generating observation data. That data can tell you about what people do, what they know and believe, and how what they know and believe affects what they do. It can also show you how people's actions are influenced by their social position (gender, race, and so on), even when they do not recognise this influence themselves (see Gobo, 2008).

Experiments. In the popular imagination, experiments are associated with medical and psychological research. You choose a sample group with a medical condition, give one group with symptoms a drug and another group with symptoms a placebo. Then you test them again at the end of the medication period to see whether the drug has had an effect. The same logic has been applied beyond the laboratory as well, however. For example, research on literacy has employed experimental (or quasi-experimental) methods to assess the success of literacy programmes (for example, Kim et al, 2010). If the aim of the study is to assess causal effects, then experiments are the go-to method (Green, 2022). Experiments in real-life situations cannot of course replicate the sanitised conditions of the laboratory, where external factors have been minimised, but experimental social scientists have devised controls for these. Social experiments often transform qualitative data (for example, written tests) into numbers in order to measure the impact of an intervention and use statistical methods to analyse the data.

Focus groups. Interviewing one person enables asking about private issues and may provide 'in-depth' information about a person. Sometimes, however, it is more important to find out how people talk about a topic within a group, to see how the interactive situation affects their opinions. Focus groups are group interviews originally employed in marketing research, but since then used widely in social research as well. A single study usually employs multiple focus groups. The composition of the group may serve different purposes (people from similar versus different backgrounds, for example), but Nisbett and DeWalt's (2016) study of what young people think about celebrity influence in politics, for example, only specifies that the participants were recruited at a university and provides a breakdown of their ethnic distribution. They do not specify how the ethnic groups were spread across the eight focus groups, however. Sometimes my students think that doing focus groups means that they are increasing the number of interviewed people, and thus increasing the validity of the interview data. But the point of focus groups is not generalisation. That is why the groups are rarely chosen through random sampling. The point is, rather, that the interaction between participants potentially illustrates how people justify their opinions and expressed values when confronted by people in the group who may disagree (Barbour, 2007). The disadvantage of focus groups is that the researcher has less control over the situation than in one-on-one interviews. Some participants may dominate, or the discussion may disintegrate into a shouting match. Focus groups are good for exploratory research about a topic which involves opinions and shared knowledge, but less so for talking about feelings or personal experiences. Focus group data may be analysed as text or transformed into numbers.

Material, visual and audio methods. The social sciences especially tend to think of data in two main forms: numerical and textual. However, researchers in art history and archaeology, for example, are working with material objects. Analysing sculpture, whether exhibited in the Louvre or dug up from under a hill in Jordan, requires specific methods, whether they refer to the style of sculpting or the carbon dating of the artefact. Sometimes the objects themselves are not available anymore, but pictures of them remain. For example, if you wanted to study early 19th-century Parisian architecture, there are few buildings left to visit in the city centre from that period, but you could glean information from drawings, plans, even contemporary literature that describes building style. Digitalisation has changed the research world dramatically when masses of visual and audio materials have been made accessible at the click of a button. Musicologists have known for a long time what composer Johannes Brahms' Hungarian Dance No. 1 looks like in notation. Previously, if you were interested in knowing how Brahms wanted it to sound you would have to rely on conjuncture from the broader oeuvre of his work. Now, you can go on YouTube and listen to Brahms play on a digitised wax cylinder recording from 1889. It is important to remember, as always, that there is a difference between studying the object itself and its representations. Visual methods help in decoding the representations of gender roles in film, for example, but need to be used with more caution when drawing conclusions about gender roles in the societies the films depict.

Interviews. Sociologist David Silverman (2007: 43) argues – with a note of annoyance – that we live in an Interview Society. Television is full of interviews, marketing companies call us to ask about our favourite brand of shampoo, and we want to use interviews as a method of research data collection. There are many good reasons to use interviewing. For example, interviews are the only way to find out about an event, which you could not witness yourself and of which no other records exist. One of the attractions of interviews is that they are a relatively easy way to gather information about people's knowledge, opinions, identity and accounts of their behaviour. The problem lies in thinking that interviews are by default the best – even the only – way of generating data. Perhaps because of this 'interview society', this is a common notion among my students. In my experience, interview data is also often misused in two ways. It is either used in a quantitative way, where the frequency of particular types of talk is considered somehow important ('most of my participants thought …'). Alternatively, interviews are used to 'illustrate' points that the researcher wants to make, but which are based on impressionistic rather than systematic analysis of the interview data. Interviewing is a key skill in the method repertoire of social scientists and humanities scholars, but it means more than just talking to people, and requires methods of analysis to complement the data collection.

Solicited writing. Better known as the 'diary method' (Bartlett and Milligan, 2021), what I call 'solicited writing' encompasses diaries but also memory-work writing. Diaries can refer to the everyday use of the word, that is, unstructured notes on what the person thinks was important in a day. The time-diary method is something else. Here, participants are asked to note down what they are doing at regular intervals and for how long (Robinson, 2002). Time-diaries are a way of triangulating and correcting survey data, because they avoid the so-called compliance effect. When people are asked in a survey how often they cook at home, they may be prone to overestimating their home-cooking, because it is commonly thought of as healthier than eating out or serving frozen food. A time-diary may avoid that because they are collected for no single purpose, so people have no incentive to inflate the amount of home-cooking they do.

The memory-writing method is again somewhat different. In memory-writing, the participants are asked to reminisce about a particular topic in their own past. In some countries, institutions collect this kind of memory-writing. The Finnish Literature Society, for example, maintains a network of respondents who are regularly asked to write about different topics. Recently they have solicited writing with questions such as 'What do you remember about the 1990s?', 'What do you think of different generations?' and 'How have you reacted to the events in Ukraine?'. The hundreds, sometimes thousands, of texts are then available for public use and are used frequently by folklorists, especially. In all of these examples, the participants are collecting the data for the researcher. Diaries and memory-writing function in lieu of interviews and time-diaries as an alternative to observation. Note that the data that is generated is thus better suited for slightly different purposes. Regular diaries and memory-writing are best used to analyse people's experiences and their constructions of the past. Time-use diaries in turn tell us about people's actual behaviour – even if they include the possibility of people 'doctoring' their daily routines.

Surveys. Survey research is ubiquitous in today's world; you have probably answered a marketing survey even before you were thinking about university studies. All survey research aims to describe a population and analyse patterns of influence (for example, how level of education affects salaries). Surveys generalise from a sample, unlike censuses, which cover the whole population. The difference between surveys and register data is that the latter are not collected primarily for research purposes and are updated regularly. Surveys can be snapshots of one point in time or administered at different points, enabling study of social change. They are a powerful tool for social analysis but also quite prohibitive for students for practical reasons. Probability sampling, which is required for generalisations from a sample, is difficult to administer. In practice, it is often relegated to specialised data collection companies (such as Gallup), which charge for their services. Non-probability sampling, such as a survey posted online, where anyone available and interested may respond (also called a 'convenience sample'), yields interesting information, but becomes problematic if used for generalising about a phenomenon. Surveys are also different depending on whether they are self-administered (like an online survey) or collected by interviewers with a structured interview schedule. Survey data comes mainly in numerical form, although questionnaires may include open-ended questions.

Methods of data analysis

Once you have collected the data, methods of data analysis enter the picture. As I mentioned earlier, 'interviewing' would not pass for *the* method in a study using interviews, because what you have after the data collection is a potentially extensive mess of talk. Analysis methods provide you with those (more or less) transparent frameworks for making sense of the mess. There are, however, literally hundreds of different 'named' methods in the social sciences and humanities, each with disciplinary variations. What follows is a drastic synthesis and reduction of this variety.

Content analysis. This term should actually appear in scare quotes, because like some other 'named' methods (discourse analysis, for example), 'content analysis' has come to mean so many things that it should not be used on its own, without explicating what you mean by the term. Earlier, 'content analysis' used to refer to word counting and analysis of text with statistical methods. Drisko and Maschi (2016) call this 'basic' content analysis. In addition, their three main types include 'interpretive' and 'qualitative' content analysis. The former does not rely on quantitative checks for validity and reliability but retains the idea that content analysis is replicable. The latter, in turn, is interested in categorising the meanings of texts as they appear in particular contexts. In that sense, it comes closer to what I call discursive methods (see pp 64).

The aim of content analysis in all its forms is to reduce and categorise data. The function of content analysis is, therefore, largely descriptive. For example, Howse et al (2022) analysed Australian newspapers' coverage of an alcohol policy debate. They first screened the data found through a database search and then quantified the frequencies of stories that were either supportive, neutral or opposed to the alcohol policies. They also identified actors represented in the news and analysed the frequency of who gets to talk in national media. Their study would fall in the 'basic' content analysis category. Qualitative analysis software may be helpful in dealing with large amounts of data, but it will not interpret the data for you. Even the simple slotting of newspaper articles into 'oppose' or 'support' in Howse et al's case already requires interpretation. Similarly, creating typologies out of text data involves creative thinking so far unavailable in analysis programmes. Things are changing rapidly, though, as algorithms become more powerful.

One more thing about content analysis: content analysis is more than coding, but coding in some form is involved in all types of content analysis. 'Coding' has become a general term, sometimes also used to give qualitative analysis an aura of objectivity. Coding is not, however, a mechanical process, but involves choices that do not simply arise from the 'raw' data. Further, content analysis, when used as a method in a study embedded in a theoretical framework, does more than just organise the data. It interprets it in light of previous theoretical ideas or generates new theoretical thinking based on the reduction of data (see pp 90–91).

Descriptive statistics. Mine is a very simplified schema, but once you have collected your quantitative data, you have basically two options with the analysis: description and explanation. The first, discussed here, refers to statistical analysis of distributions, frequencies and trends. A study of adolescent pregnancy rates across 21 countries (Sedgh et al, 2015), for example, found that although adolescent pregnancies were decreasing, the overall level remained high in some countries. Adolescent abortions also varied, but live births were more common in countries where adolescent pregnancies were more common. Here the authors describe what the statistics say, and point to some trends, but explicitly admit that 'we did not examine the factors that explain the differences across countries or trends over time' (Sedgh et al, 2015: 228). Nevertheless, as the article shows, the descriptive statistics provide an important starting point for discussion about contraception, sex education and the impact of socioeconomic inequality. Quantitative studies often include a descriptive element, before proceeding to explanation, but they are equally often important in themselves.

Discursive methods. 'Discursive methods' is an overarching term of my own making, which encompasses discourse analysis, narrative analysis, (new) rhetoric and conversation analysis, for example. Not everyone doing these types of analyses would even agree that they should be grouped together as 'discursive methods'. I use the term to refer to methods that operate within a constructionist epistemology, as discussed earlier. That is, that these methods treat texts as drawing from the social world, but at the same time contributing to new understandings of that social world. The difference between this and content analysis, even the qualitative kind, is that discursive methods are not content to just describe what is being said. They take the analysis a crucial step forward by focusing on what is being *done* when something is said (Hjelm, 2014). What is accomplished when British media calls the actions of Iraqi soldiers 'killing' and 'destroying', but the actions of British/American soldiers are called 'suppressing', 'eliminating' and 'neutralising' (see p 46)? The question already suggests that discursive methods require also contextual analysis, because the function of discourse is only apparent in particular contexts. In fact, discursive methods may use some form of (computer-assisted) content analysis to make sense of the mass of data first, but their particular focus then requires a second step, where the meaning and social function of the constructions is analysed.

Explanatory statistics. The statistics most people are familiar with are almost exclusively of the descriptive kind. News media show us the changing fortunes of political parties, the average number of cars in a household, and the rising temperatures on the planet. Most statistical research aims to do more, however. Specifically – and this, some scholars argue, is what distinguishes quantitative from qualitative methods – explanatory statistics aims at mapping relationships between variables in order to demonstrate significant correlations and causal connections between some of them. Let us take eviction – expelling tenants from properties by legal means – as an example. Descriptive statistical analysis could tell us the total number of evictions in a country, where evictions happen most frequently, and whether evictions have increased or decreased over time. In the United States, for example, the number of filed evictions has decreased in recent years (Messamore, 2023). Now, that is interesting, but it sheds little light on *why* this decrease might be happening. Messamore (2023) analyses how community organising – anti-poverty and tenants' movements – affects eviction rates in larger American cities. Using elaborate statistical techniques, he shows that 'plausibly causal estimates of the role of community organizations show that an addition of ten community nonprofits per 100,000 city residents is associated with ten percent reduction in eviction filing rates'. Since statistical operations only allow an estimate of causality, the language is often cautious, but provides important new knowledge on a little-considered topic. One of the reasons the different types of explanatory statistics are popular for answering why-questions is that they offer a transparent procedure and logic for thinking about causality not readily available for other methods of analysis.

Grounded Theory. Of all the equivocal terms used in this section, 'Grounded Theory' is perhaps most misunderstood and misused. It is some ways more a method than theory (at least in the traditional sense), but its aim is theory generation, so the term really refers to a process of systematic data analysis, which produces theorisations. Different types of practitioners, such as social workers (Oktay, 2012) and educators (Hutchinson, 1986), have been keen to apply Grounded Theory principles in their research. Indeed, Barney Glaser and Anselm Strauss (2017 [1967]), the progenitors of Grounded Theory, suggested themselves that the approach provides tools for practitioners to theorise their real-world experiences. Grounded Theory has also been popular among ethnographers, who observe communities from the 'inside'. Not all ethnography employs a Grounded Theory approach, however, so the two are not synonymous (Layder, 1993: 44). Grounded Theory is even less synonymous with 'qualitative methods' as a whole – even if some people seem to think that is the case (Suddaby, 2006: 633).

Grounded Theory is interested in patterns of experience or, to put a slightly different spin on the issue, how lived reality and interpretations of that lived reality structure people's interactions. This is studied by close observation and detailed coding of these interactions. Through these codes, it is argued, patterns emerge, which suggest theorisations, which in turn feed back to data sampling and analysis and so on. This is referred to as 'theoretical sampling'. For example, Yan (2008) found that 'cultural competence' in social work was a much more complicated issue than previously assumed, when she looked at cultural tensions from minority social workers' perspective. Through her fieldwork, she suggested a new theorisation of cultural competence. In Chapter 6, I discuss why 'grounded theory' is often used in problematic ways, but for the purposes of this chapter suffice it to say that it provides a procedure for exploring little-studied phenomena and, when used with skill, a way to reassess even familiar phenomena.

Mixed methods

I sometimes have students approach me for supervision with a proposal to interview, say, ten people and then do a survey – or the other way around. I usually present them with a standard battery of questions about their statistical skills, how they are planning to collect a representative sample survey, and how (on earth!) are they going to accomplish both interviews and a survey in the very limited time that they have. These are all practical questions. Once again, even an otherwise well aligned and justified research design falters if it is practically unfeasible. However, the more important question is *why* they would want to have both a qualitative and a quantitative element in their research. I suspect that in many cases, the eagerness to mix qualitative and quantitative methods stems from a fear that the former are not 'scientific' enough – specifically, that it is impossible to generalise from qualitative data. Mixed methods can enrich a research design, but there should always be a good reason for using such an approach. In this section, I explore three types of mixed method approaches and reasons for using them. These are the exploratory, explanatory and triangulation approaches.

The *exploratory* approach is used when you want to study a phenomenon quantitatively (in order to examine its prevalence or how it affects and is affected by other factors), but there are no standardised statistical operationalisations for the phenomenon. (Note that this not the only way the term 'exploratory research' is used; see Swedberg, 2020.) In other words, you cannot measure the phenomenon without knowing which things measure it. In this case, you need to first figure out qualitatively what the phenomenon means for people. Or, to put it differently, the qualitative part of your research provides the quantitative part with hypotheses. For some quantitative scholars this is the only legitimate use for qualitative research. Interviews or observations provide ideas for operationalisation and hypotheses. Then the 'real' research can proceed. For example, in a study of Turkish and Yugoslav immigrants' political attitudes in Germany, Doerschler (2004) first interviewed 25 immigrant-background students. From these interviews, he formulated hypotheses regarding the relationship between education experiences and the development of immigrants' political attitudes, which he then tested using panel data from an established German household survey.

In the *explanatory* type of research (even more so than already discussed, 'explanatory' is used in other senses as well), the order of analysis is reversed. That is, you would first collect and analyse survey or register data and then complement that with qualitative data in order to illustrate or 'deepen' the insight from the quantitative analysis. For example, the 'Sexual attitudes and lifestyles of London's Eastern Europeans (SALLEE)' project described its methodological design as follows:

> The project consisted of a quantitative arm and a qualitative arm: a cross-sectional survey of CEE [Central and East European] migrants, augmented with semi-structured in-depth interviews with a purposively selected sample of CEE migrants. The principal aim of the cross-sectional survey was to provide generalisable data on sexual and reproductive health, risk behaviours and health

service use of CEE migrants in London. The qualitative research was designed to complement the quantitative survey by further exploring these issues and identifying additional important elements. (Evans et al, 2009)

As you can see from the language of the description, the qualitative element was in place to 'augment' and 'complement' the quantitative, primary, element. In this type of approach, the qualitative element may provide ideas for further research, but the quantitative study would be based on already existing measures and questions. The SALLEE project researchers, for example, used the British National Survey of Sexual Attitudes and Lifestyles as a basis for their questionnaire.

Finally, we speak of *triangulation* when researchers use a different method to corroborate results attained using another method. Triangulation can refer to data, method or theory. I already discussed data triangulation in the previous chapter. So, for example, you could interview people and ask them to write a diary – two different data types – but then analyse both with a narrative method. Alternatively, you could have these two types of data, analyse the interviews using a narrative method, and then do a quantitative frequency analysis of instances of particular words in the diaries. In the former case, you would have data triangulation, but not method triangulation. In the latter, you have both. Note that unlike in the previous two types of mixed methods research, the emphasis with triangulation is on corroboration. It is not to construct variables (exploration) or to identify issues that a survey may have missed (explanation), but to argue that the research results are valid because multiple data types and methods support them.

Mixed methods raise three further issues. First, the different methods can be used sequentially or concurrently. The exploratory design is by definition sequential, because the variables for the quantitative part are drawn from the qualitative analysis. For the other designs, the timing of the different methods depends on the research interests. Is it, for example, important to know the results of a survey before devising an interview schedule? Or is it enough to ask clarifying questions to complement possibly ambiguous survey questions regardless of what the survey results are? The latter might be even accomplished as open-ended questions in the questionnaire itself.

Second, mixed methods require extra consideration when the previously discussed background assumptions of different methods diverge. When Mark Chaves (see Chapter 3; Chaves, 2013) counted church attendance numbers from different sources, he was doing classic triangulation. The numbers were different, but checking them against each other, he could come to an estimate of what was the most likely accurate number. This, in turn, told him that people were inflating their self-reported church attendance. That is an interesting finding, which was enabled by a uniform method and approach: no matter how the numbers differed, all the data were treated as more or less accurate reports of reality. The point was just to ascertain which data source was most accurate (or, in this case, least accurate).

However, if your aim is to study what attending church means to people, the methods most useful for you would probably start with the assumption that the narratives of your participants will provide you with important information, whether or not they are accurate descriptions of reality – as a constructionist epistemology would suggest. How people narrate their lives says a lot about their values and identities even when they misremember or lie. You might first ask participants about their churchgoing habits, and then observe and count church attendees and catch a 'frequent' churchgoer missing church every single Sunday, but that does not mean that you need to throw away the interview material as worthless. It does mean that the two methods cannot be used to 'triangulate' in the traditional sense. It also means that the discrepancy is not a blip to be corrected with some other method, but rather a source of new research questions: Why do people claim they are frequent churchgoers when they are not?

Finally, it is important to note that in practice few mixed method research designs are slotted neatly into one of these categories. Many who do explanatory research think of using two or more methods as 'triangulation', for example. It all depends on how you see the design unfolding – as exploratory, explanatory or the triangulation type. As sequential or concurrent, and mixing methods with different epistemological and ontological premises. Most significantly, it matters how you spell this out. Not everyone spells out these things in a research proposal, but if you do not, make sure that you are not claiming triangulation with incompatible elements. Similarly, you need to be sure that you do not claim equal value for methods if the design actually shows that you are prioritising one method over another.

Conclusion

There is a popular meme doing the rounds in academic social media. It is a photograph of a footnote that says: 'This was once revealed to me in a dream.' The joke is that we scholars wish we could use the same line instead of meticulous tracking of our sources. The same applies to method: if someone asks you *how* you can know that your research results are valid, you cannot refer to a dream. Methods are the shared rules for collecting and analysing data. They make the 'how' of scholarship transparent. I suggested earlier that methods are 'explicit frameworks of interpretation'. They enable your audience to trace the logic of your argument – even when their interpretation might differ. This is a crucial element of research and, as such, of research design. Methods should serve your research question and the data suggested by the research question, but different disciplinary traditions and practical issues may limit your choice of method. Importantly, 'method' refers to both methods of data collection and methods of data analysis. Individual methods can be combined in creative ways – and this is not just a matter of quantitative versus qualitative – as long as the background assumptions of the chosen methods are compatible.

5

Literature

Popular history of science is mostly 'great man' history. You probably know Da Vinci's drawings, Galileo's experiments, Einstein's E=mc², and so on. You might have heard of Marie Skłodowska-Curie and some other women scientists, who have been, until recently, virtually invisible. Stories of scientific discovery sometimes make for gripping reading, especially when the private lives of the scientist are at stake, as in the case of Skłodowska-Curie getting cancer from her experiments. The problem with these popular narratives of scientific discovery is that they create a misleading impression of scientific practice. Science – including social science and the humanities – is not a solitary endeavour, but a social endeavour *par excellence*.

Scientific ideas progress through an assessment of peers before becoming received knowledge. Scientists, not as individuals, but as a community, decide which ideas best help understand the world. For example, for more than a century the phenomenon of combustion was explained with reference to a substance called 'phlogiston'. Burning gave off phlogiston, so it was believed, which saturated common air, at which point the burning ceased. In the 1770s, French chemist Antoine Lavoisier concluded after experimenting that instead of producing 'phlogiston', combustion requires a gas he had isolated in experiments. He called the gas oxygen. Lavoisier's evidence required abandoning the old theory, but the scientific community of the time was so wedded to the established ways of understanding combustion through phlogiston that it that it took time before the modern theory of combustion became universally accepted. Philosopher Thomas Kuhn called these established ways of understanding scientific questions 'paradigms' (Kuhn, 1996 [1962]). Kuhn referred to the natural sciences, whereas in the social sciences and humanities the matter of established ways of understanding the human world is somewhat different. Nevertheless, the point remains the same: scientific ideas only become accepted through assessment by peers.

How is this all relevant for a book on research design?

It is relevant because I want you to start thinking about your research as part of a *conversation* (for example, Huff, 1999: 3–5). The literature review is, literally, your review and critical assessment of the previous research relevant to your topic. All of the key elements in your research design – question, data, method – depend on what other researchers have discovered earlier and how they did it. That is why, in Figure 1.1, I have depicted the 'holy trinity' as floating within a field of literature. Without knowledge of the conversation in your field, you may be reinventing the wheel. In order to think about your contribution (Chapter 8), especially if you are making any claims to novelty, you need to know what the previous conversation is. I think it is important to understand the role the 'holy trinity' plays first, but to put that understanding really into practice, you have to have a clear sense of where you stand.

I want to underline already at this point what the literature review is *not*: it is not a summary of everything you have read for your research. The point is not to show that you have read studies on your topic – that is expected anyway – but rather that you have read the *relevant* studies and, most importantly, that you are able to synthesise what is important about those studies for your research question. Also, although I have discussed research questions in terms of a 'gap' in literature, the point of the literature review is not to gloat over what other people have not done, but to think about where your research fits in the conversation and enter into dialogue with studies relevant to your interests.

Indeed, I like to think of the literature review as part of the argument of your work. It is where you position yourself in relation to earlier research. There are countless ways of approaching a topic; the literature review is where you show what is yours. The term 'literature review' often conjures images of a compulsory chore, but I hope after reading this chapter, you will think of it as a way to show where you stand in terms of your research topic. That is indispensable to good research.

Again, as with some of the other elements, disciplines differ in what they think of as a 'literature review'. This chapter is built upon the assumption that you are working on an empirical project, where you need to assess the previous literature in order to sync and justify your question–data–method triangle. Philosophical and theoretical dissertations, theses and research papers are, in a way, literature reviews themselves, lacking a designated 'literature review' section. Also, in many degree programmes (BA, taught Masters) the dissertation is not an empirical project, but rather an extended literature review in itself. If that is what you are doing, this chapter will still be helpful, but I recommend checking discipline-specific guidebooks and advice on how to structure your work.

The chapter starts with a discussion of what I think of as the three functions of literature reviews: orientation (identifying the conversations in the field), analysis (integrating and criticising previous research), and positioning (identifying your place in the conversations). These focus on the reading and 'thinking about' part of literature reviews. The following sections then examine the planning and writing stages of literature reviews, by looking at different types of literature reviews and providing a checklist for a successful literature review process.

Orientation

The first function of a literature review is to orient you in the field. Simply, you need to know what is known and what is not known about your topic. If your interest in the topic does not arise from practical concerns or personal familiarity (see Chapter 2), the orientation phase is also where you start figuring out a feasible research question. It may be useful to think of orientation as the mapping of the research landscape. Mapping does not mean, however, simply describing what is out there. You are already making choices about what to include. Without this kind of sorting, 'the map of the research landscape would be as large as the research landscape itself' (Randolph, 2009: 3), and would be of little use.

How to discover and discern what the key conversations on a topic are, then? Today, when so much information is available at the click of a virtual button, it is understandably overwhelming when your keyword search returns 24,000 hits. In light of this abundance, the most common question I get when students are engaging in literature reviews for the first time is 'How do I know which studies are relevant for me?'. In the narrative review format (see pp 82–83), typical in dissertations and theses, there are no clear-cut inclusion rules, so it is easy to feel rudderless. In a later section, I will discuss how to present a condensed review of much-researched topics, but here I will offer some tips on locating and identifying those key conversations.

Keyword searches are indispensable in today's research environment, but often uninformative and overwhelming by themselves. Citation numbers give you some sense of relevance, but there are other and probably more instructive ways of identifying the key conversations. I am thinking of five sources in particular:

1. *Review articles.* Academic journals regularly publish articles, which are, as the title says, literature reviews of topics and approaches in different disciplines and fields. The problem is that review articles tend to focus more on concepts and theories, less on the state of the art in empirical research on a particular topic. But often review articles would be the first place to identify the conversations and the most relevant and recent literature.
2. *Handbooks.* Many academic publishers publish large handbooks even on rather narrow topics. Chapters in these handbooks are mini-review articles in themselves and often present a particular point of view on a topic. They are good resources for finding out what the current conversations are.
3. *Book introductions.* Although scholarly books avoid the dissertation/thesis structure with a designated 'literature review' chapter, the introductions

to many studies often survey the field in order to position the book in the conversation. Here you can find the key arguments and references.
4. *Dissertations and theses.* Of course, earlier dissertations and theses on the topic are valuable sources as well, both in terms of their actual research and the literature they use. The problem may be that the authors have an incomplete view of the conversation, so you should check it against any other possible sources.
5. *Expert opinion.* If it really happens that neither keyword searches nor any of the previous four sources yield anything useful, you can always turn to experts in the field. Some are busy and will not respond, but most, I would say, are usually happy to oblige requests also from students other than their own. They may not be able to give you references to your topic exactly, but they may be able to point you to similar literature in adjacent fields and topics.

Remember that bibliographies enable you to assess what the author deems relevant literature, to reach back, so to say, from the current text. In order to assess how research in a topic has evolved after the publication, you can 'reach forward' by examining who has cited them in turn. For example, Priyamvada Gopal's chapter 'Renegade Prophets and Native Acolytes: Liberalism and Imperialism Today' in *The Oxford Handbook of Postcolonial Studies* (Gopal, 2013), cites David Harvey's book *The New Imperialism* (Harvey, 2003) several times, so in order to understand the entanglement of liberalism and imperialism more deeply, that is probably a good source to check. Going forward, Peter Blair (2016) cites Gopal's chapter in his encyclopaedia entry on 'liberalism'. This will probably also be a good source on the topic. You can repeat the procedure for Blair's text in turn, and so on. Review articles and handbook chapters will always miss some studies, but generally speaking, you can remain confident that such review texts offer a reliable picture of the key conversations, arguments and approaches.

What about the opposite problem, then? What if the topic is very specific and the only thing written about it is a Bachelor's dissertation in a university repository? Do not worry: it is unlikely that you will really be in a situation where you have precious few previous studies to cite. Yes, it may be so that few or no scholars have looked at *exactly* the same thing as you are looking at. This does not mean, however, that no one anywhere has studied a similar topic. Especially, this does not mean that you can shrug off the literature review by claiming no one has studied the topic ever. This is almost never the case and enables your readers to 'catch' you in an easily falsifiable claim. Instead, look for research in another national context, older publications, another discipline or field, or an adjacent topic.

It is likely that there are many blank spots in knowledge about phenomena in particular national contexts. Teaching in a Finnish university, this is often the case. We don't know many things about Finnish society and culture, simply because there are relatively few scholars to study these things. A student of mine wanting to study Scientology in Finland would, indeed, have little domestic research to build upon. However, what about Swedish scholarship? Sweden is close enough to be relevant for Finnish research on any topic. In fact, a study of Scientology in Brazil would still be very useful for analysing the research design, even if comparing the results would require taking into account social and cultural differences between the two countries. In this case, that Brazilian study should be included in the broad review. Language limitations can obviously be an issue, but most abstracts are published in English and machine translation is nowadays smart enough to easily get a sense of what the main arguments of a study are in any language.

When we look for research literature, the basic advice is to look for the latest, the 'state of the art', on a topic. However, it may be that your topic has fallen out of fashion for whatever reason. As long as you are able to justify why this topic remains relevant, it is perfectly fine to rely on older literature. In fact, having few contemporary studies gives you a good rationale for updating knowledge on a topic. You will need to be careful when discussing the results and methodologies of earlier research, however, as contexts change and methods advance. For example, Émile Durkheim's *Suicide* (1979 [1897]) has been long considered a classic of sociological suicide scholarship both in terms of the results and the statistical methods he employs, but more recent research has argued that Durkheim's antiquated methods require a completely new approach to the issue (Stark and Bainbridge, 1996: 31–51).

Today's electronic resources enable searching across disciplinary boundaries, but you might be tempted to think that only research in your own discipline or field is worth investigating for the literature review. It is true that students of German literature learn best about how a topic has been approached in their field from other German literature researchers, but leaving out all the rest would be a mistake. It will almost certainly enrich your analysis if you examine how, say, sociologists, religion scholars or gender studies researchers have read the German novels you want to study. Sometimes it is required to move beyond the usual ways of doing things to discover new questions about your topic.

Finally, if casting your net beyond national and disciplinary boundaries still does not yield relevant studies to review, try looking into adjacent topics. Let us say that you want to conduct a sociological study of the experiences of 'Flakka' users. Flakka is a relatively new street drug, so it is unlikely that there is much research on users anywhere or in any discipline (see Palamar et al, 2019). However, knowing that Flakka is also known as 'poor man's cocaine', you could read studies on users of similar street drugs, like crack cocaine and crystal meth. Research on powder cocaine may be useful as well, but because the socioeconomic profiles of users are quite different, you would have to read it more critically. Even if the topic of a study is somewhat removed from your immediate concerns, you can always learn from the research design.

'Critical analysis and creative synthesis'

After reading as widely as possible on your topic, you should have a solid idea what research exists on your topic. Why not get the literature review out of the way, then? Let us imagine I was studying the employability of international students. My literature review (or part of it, at least) could look like this:

> In their study of international students in Australian universities, Gribble et al (2015) show that increased employability is a major reason for studying and working abroad. This is confirmed in the research by Soares and Mosquera (2020). Often international recruitment is seen by universities as a source of revenue (de Wit, 2020) or, as Humfrey (2011: 650) argues 'HE is now viewed as both a commodity and a service'. Römgens et al (2020) argue that so far employability has been understood in a narrow, 'Western' sense. Yorke (2004) argues that employability has become increasingly important for government policies regarding higher education. Marginson (2012) states that 'international students are affected by two different national regulatory regimes, in the nations of citizenship and of education. But they are fully covered by neither'.

What is wrong with this example? Think about it for a second and then read on.

The problem with the example is that it is not a 'review' in any sense of the word. It is a glorified list of studies on the topic. My reader would learn some things about employability and international students but would have little idea what I want to study and how this research is relevant to what I want to do. Granted, this is not as bad as some first drafts of literature reviews that I have seen. They are not even glorified lists, but simply lists. I might as well look at the references section of those kind of 'reviews' and learn as much from the titles of the cited articles. That is because the previous example and such list-like 'reviews' are lacking any sense of analysis and synthesis.

The previous example was my bastardisation of Omolake Fakunle's (2021) fascinating study of international students' perception of 'employability development opportunities during their study abroad'. Fakunle's actual text shows how the literature review is done right:

> Considering that employability is cited by international students as the main motivation for studying abroad (Gribble et al., 2015; Soares & Mosquera, 2020), it is surprising that there is a paucity of research into international students' perceptions on developing their employability. Two main reasons account for this deficit: (1) as has been widely acknowledged, national and institutional strategies and policies on international student recruitment are driven by economic rationales (de Wit, 2020; Humfrey, 2011); and (2) employability is a priority for national policy-making within country contexts (Purcell & Elias, 2004; Römgens et al., 2020; Shah et al., 2004; Teichler, 1999; Yorke, 2004) which excludes international students. This phenomenon reasserts international students' 'outsider status' in a nation-bound world (Marginson, 2012). The outcome is international students' exclusion in employability plans and policy yet to be addressed. This gap is critical considering growing international students' numbers up to 5 million globally according to OECD, 2018 figures. (Fakunle, 2021: 576)

Every citation in Fakunle's actual text serves the purpose of argument. She synthesises various studies to condense the reasons why her topic has been so far little examined. In addition to showing where she stands in the conversation and how she is filling a gap in the literature – the academic relevance – she also answers the 'so what' question (Chapter 8) by showing why this topic matters beyond the academic realm. This is all in sharp contrast to my poor version, where the citations, at best, served the purpose of showing I had read some relevant works.

In answer to the opening question, you should *not* 'get the literature review out of the way' after you have read what feels like a sufficient number of previous studies. Knowing what is out there enables you to identify the conversations in the field. That is step one. Step two is to make sense of the cacophony. In order to do that, the literature review needs to be 'a *critical analysis and creative synthesis* of the literature included in the review', which is accomplished by 'identifying themes, patterns, relationships, and gaps in understanding' (Elsbach and van Knippenberg, 2020: 8; emphasis added).

With practice, researchers begin to detect these themes, patterns, relationships and gaps without thinking actively about what exactly they are looking for. However, if this is your first time reading a larger body of literature, it may not be clear how to engage in 'critical analysis and creative synthesis'. The following checklist should get you started on the analysis part (cf Knopf, 2006):

1. *Argument.* What is the question the study wants to answer? What is the answer? Why is the question important? Why is the answer important?

By the standards we have established in this book, every academic study should answer these questions. However, often there are several questions scattered over an academic text, sometimes leading to different goals. Sometimes there is an answer, but it is not an answer to the question posed. An argument is the main point of the study, supported by evidence and filling a gap in empirical or theoretical knowledge in a logical manner.
2. *Evidence*. What evidence is used to support the argument? Does the evidence lead convincingly from the question to the conclusions? Although many types research do not operate with numbers, mathematical formulas offer a useful metaphor for them all: you may get the answer right, but if you cannot show how you ended up with the answer, you are not demonstrating an understanding of the formula. In empirical research this means showing the evidence and, specifically, that the evidence supports your conclusion.
3. *Meta-positioning*. What are the background assumptions of the work? In sociology, for example, the classic divide is between scholars who prioritise social structures and those who prioritise individual actors. Often these priorities are not spelled out (hence 'background' – or meta – assumptions). This is not necessarily a problem, but you need to be able to recognise the different assumptions, otherwise you may end up comparing apples and oranges, in a way.
4. *Positioning*. Where does the study sit in the conversation? Where do the authors see themselves vis-à-vis other research on the topic? In addition to the explicit positioning, your synthesis may reveal new patterns in the literature. Perhaps antagonistic approaches are not so far removed, when looked at from a new angle – and vice versa.
5. *Clarity*. How well do the authors articulate their argument? Is it possible their place in the conversation has been misunderstood because of ambiguous formulations? Unclear writing is, I would say, the main source of red pen in dissertation and thesis margins and negative journal article reviews. Often seemingly major problems can be fixed by paying attention to whether the argument or idea is expressed clearly. In your review, the point is not to get stuck with someone's typos, but to assess whether the argument could be interpreted in different, even opposing, ways because of unclear formulation. If so, you may judge the previous points differently.

I once made the mistake of providing my students with this checklist without talking about the synthesis part, and what I got in return were lists of publications, which were taken apart point by point. This is, in a way, critical analysis, but not in a sense useful for a literature review. The main point of being critical is not to find weak spots in individual studies, but to understand how different studies form patterns according to the argument, evidence, background assumptions or positioning they present. You read the literature critically, yes, but what ends up in the written part should be a synthesis of all that, not criticism of individual studies. Your analytical and synthesising literature review is creative to the extent that you are able to see – and make your reader see – the relevant literature in a new light.

This may mean uncovering new patterns in one field, or creatively combining previously unconnected conversations. What emerges from these dialogues is creative simply for the fact that the topics or approaches are presented as relevant to each other for the first time. For dissertations and theses, I have – once again – recommended a funnel approach. You start with the larger issue and narrow it down towards your own topic, all the while assessing and synthesising the literature. For example, my former University College London PhD student Charlotte Doesburg wrote her thesis on the adaptation of Finnish folk poetry in contemporary heavy metal music. In the study, she asked how the adaptations reflected issues of national identity. The outline of her thesis's literature review section looked like this:

3.1. National Identity
3.2. Finnish National Identity
3.3. Popular Culture
3.4. Finnish Popular Culture
3.5. The Global Metal Scene
3.6. Finnish Metal

Charlotte (now Dr Doesburg) took the three main topics of her thesis (Doesburg, 2022) – national identity, popular culture and metal music – and analysed the current research literature in each and then narrowed each of them down to focus on the Finnish research. (She discussed folk poetry both in the theory and data sections.) While there has been research on national identity and popular culture, even national identity and metal music, through this one type of funnelling, she was able to narrow down the literature to the point where she could demonstrate that her research was making a contribution to the field. In other words, the orientation, analysis and synthesis enabled her to position herself in the conversation.

Positioning

Now that you have mapped the literature that is out there and discovered patterns and trends in it, it is time to take the third step. That is, your intimate knowledge of the existing research should enable you to answer the key question at the end of any literature review: Why and how does your research matter for the conversation? This is what I call positioning. Positioning is important both in the beginning of a research project and at the very end.

As already discussed in Chapter 2, previous research literature is one of the sources of your research question. After reading the literature you identify gaps in it. Your project then aims to fill these gaps. Even if your research question arises from a personal experience or a practical incentive (changing an existing state of things), you still need to know what others have said about your topic in order to figure out how to do the research. This is how you position yourself before having results of your own. But the gaps can come in several forms: empirical, conceptual-theoretical and methodological.

Most commonly, a 'gap' in the literature refers to lack of empirical knowledge about a phenomenon. If we go back to Fakunle's article that I cited earlier, she clearly identifies the gap in the literature: 'there is a paucity of research into international students' perceptions on developing their employability' (Fakunle, 2021: 576). She shows what we don't know about the phenomenon of international students and employability and positions her research squarely in that gap. Obviously, you cannot make a statement like this without knowing what is out there.

A conceptual or theoretical gap exists when a phenomenon has been studied empirically, perhaps even extensively, but has not been interpreted in the light of a concept or a theory. This is often the case with – but not limited to – the variety of critical approaches to the human sciences like theories of gender, race and class. Often these approaches show how even a familiar phenomenon becomes 'strange' when looked at from a critical perspective and by so doing unmask how many aspects of our societies and cultures are built on gendered, racialised and classist stereotypes. The study mentioned earlier on job applications with 'foreign' sounding names is a case in point.

Another way of identifying and filling a conceptual-theoretical gap is to bring concepts and theories from another discipline into dialogue with your own. This is what I did with my own *Religion and Social Problems* (Hjelm, 2011). The point was to examine the ways in which sociological thinking about religion and sociological thinking about social problems might intersect. It was not the first time anyone had thought about this nexus, but it was a fresh attempt to systematise these connections and in so doing filled a gap in the research literature.

Conceptual-theoretical positioning is not only about filling gaps, but also about recognising the agreements and disagreements about the 'big picture' in your research field and finding your place in the picture. International Relations, for example, has been long characterised by a split between 'realists' and 'constructivists', who disagree on some of the fundamental aspects of what politics is about (Guzzini, 2013). There have since been many attempts to reconcile these two approaches, but they have become 'paradigms' in the sense that I discussed in the introduction to this chapter, which means that identifying with one or the other, or some sort of middle way, is required almost by default. Not all disciplines are as explicit about their major fault lines, though, so you may need advice from supervisors or colleagues about this 'big picture' positioning.

Finally, it may be the case that your topic has been extensively researched and you are content with the conceptual-theoretical approaches to it. Yet, you can still produce original research even with the same data and same theoretical framework if you can show that a new methodological approach will produce new insights into the topic. This is the case, for example, with various discursive, narrative and rhetorical approaches to qualitative data. Instead of stopping at *what* is being said in government texts, the media, or in interviews, these approaches zoom in on *how* things are said, and how the ways language is used may influence our understanding of the issue. For example, Catherine Bouko and her collaborators say this quite explicitly in their study of the social media language of Islamist radicals: 'Understanding *how* extremist Salafists communicate, and not only *what*, is key to gaining insights into the ways they construct their social order and use psychological forces to radicalize potential sympathizers on social media' (Bouko et al, 2022: 252). Methodological innovation is also a standard way of looking at familiar statistical data in a new light. Whether qualitative or quantitative, the point is to show what the previous research misses because of methodological choices.

What about the role of the literature review at the other end of the research project? Positioning in the beginning enables you to discern the relevance of your research question to the broader field. Positioning at the end of your research enables you to assess the significance of your answer to that question. To put it a bit differently, it is the 'basis for your critical evaluation of your own findings in the discussion chapter' (Greetham, 2009: 242–243). Here we are moving into the territory of your research contribution (Chapter 8), but it is important to remember that without a sense of how your findings relate to what was known about the topic earlier, it will be difficult to argue for the significance of your research. When looking for gaps in the beginning of your process, you squeeze yourself into existing patterns in the literature. If your research yields interesting results, no matter how small, your findings may require a reshuffling of these same patterns. Next time others are positioning themselves within the literature, they will have to position themselves vis-à-vis your contribution to the conversation.

Narrative versus systematic reviews

There is no commonly shared understanding of what a literature review consists of. In fact, 'literature review' is best understood as a generic term for the analysis of existing research on your topic. There are multiple ways of doing the review. Disciplines, methodology and research questions all affect the type of review that you should engage in. There are elaborate ways of distinguishing between different types of literature review (see Grant and Booth, 2009: 94–95), but for the purposes of this book, two types – narrative reviews and systematic reviews – are the most important. In the next section, I will discuss, on a slightly different level, the difference between narrow reviews of mature topics and broad reviews of emerging topics.

The *narrative review* is what I think of as the standard type you see in dissertations, theses and research articles. In my opinion, it is called a 'narrative' review for two reasons, one 'positive', one 'negative'. On the positive side, it highlights the fact that the literature review is part of the larger narrative of your dissertation, thesis or article. It narrates what relevant things previous research has said about your topic and how your study fits that picture. The review is also presented in narrative form, as opposed to, for example, meta-analyses (see pp 83), which combine statistical data to summarise and evaluate knowledge. This is all rather uncontroversial.

On the negative side, narrative reviews are criticised for not being comprehensive and for their lack of transparency about the selection and evaluation criteria used for reviewing the literature. How can you justify that the discussed literature is enough, if the reader does not know how you have chosen the studies you have? The next question, then, is how did you choose these particular studies and not others that could be equally relevant? If the review goes beyond description – a good thing – it is not necessarily clear why you think some studies are worth emulating, while others are relegated to the indifference pile.

This criticism is not unfounded. I rarely see even a short description of how the reviewed literature was chosen in dissertations or theses, or why some authors/studies were preferred over others. Partly this is convention, partly an outcome of the status of the literature review as a chore part rather than a core part of research. The issue of transparency is a valid concern, but comprehensiveness (which seems to bother students more) can be problematic as well. You need keyword searches for comprehensive reviews, but keywords are not entirely 'objective' either. They often reflect implicit assumptions about research fields. Keyword searches also ignore much interesting research, while including a lot of repetitive noise. A narrative review can, if done well, be a much more nuanced affair than critics suggest.

A narrative review should, then, include research that is immediately relevant to your research question. I would say that one of the reasons people avoid transparency – in addition to not thinking about it in the first place – is that it would show how much of the literature is *not* discussed in any single review. If you lead with the research question in mind, this becomes less of a problem. Yes, there might be hundreds of research papers relevant even to your narrow question, but it is possible to come up with a 'revealing but manageable sample' of these papers (Alvesson and Sandberg, 2020). At this point, it is important to remember that a review of key works should fulfil the functions that we discussed earlier: orienting, positioning and analysis. It will probably mean that you will need to read more than ends up in the actual review, simply to get your bearings. What you end up writing is a different thing, and there it is better to aim for relevance than accumulating everything you can find.

A *systematic review*, in turn, is a type of review that seeks 'to draw together all known knowledge on a topic area' (Grant and Booth, 2009: 102). The point of systematic reviews is not simply broad coverage or exhaustiveness, however. One way of distinguishing systematic from narrative reviews would be to say that where narrative reviews are part of a larger research design, systematic reviews have their own research design. A systematic review includes an exposition of the principles of data gathering – 'data' in this instance being the previous research – the method of analysis, and a discussion of the validity of the results of the review. A systematic review that combines statistical data in order to provide a composite picture of quantitative research on a topic is called *meta-analysis*. Other types may combine analysis of quantitative and qualitative research, but always with the methodology of the review spelled out. For example, Adamczyk et al (2017) assess the link between religion and crime in 92 articles (quantitative and qualitative) published between 2004 and 2014. They first review previous reviews of the religion–crime connection in order to justify the time range and then outline in detail how they ended up with the 92 articles finally selected. Their analysis of the selected studies focuses on data sources, methods, theories and the types of journals where research on the topic is published. This produces a comprehensive picture of the field that, importantly, also points out the shortcomings in data, method and theory, in order to improve research in the area.

As research in the social sciences and humanities has exploded, it has become impossible for any one scholar to keep up with current research, even in smaller subfields. Systematic reviews are thus an important way to provide up to date overviews of the state of the field. As such, they require not only particular skills (Cooper, 2017), but also time. Published systematic reviews may take months for a team of researchers. In other words, systematic reviews are research projects in themselves.

Although called 'the most frequent kind of literature review in the social sciences' (Cooper, 2017: np), it is probably clear by now that this is not what is meant by a literature review in the context of BA or

MA dissertations. Some PhD theses, especially quantitative ones, might utilise a systematic approach, but otherwise a full-blown systematic review is probably beyond the scope of research reports written as part of university studies. That is why Grant and Booth (2009: 102) talk about 'systematised reviews', which 'attempt to include one or more elements of the systematic review process while stopping short of claiming that the resultant output is a systematic review'. Even if a systematic review, as depicted here and in the literature, is beyond your particular project, it is a good idea to take heed of the principles guiding systematic reviews, especially the transparency about the criteria for selecting studies, and apply them as much as possible to a traditional narrative review, making it more 'systematised' in the process.

Narrow versus broad reviews

Now, jumping on to a slightly different level, there is another distinction that is useful for thinking about literature reviews. On the one hand, you may be looking at a field that is well scoured and the issue is how to make sense of the mass of research on the topic. On the other hand, you may have been so successful in your funnelling of the research question that you have ended up with a little-researched topic and few previous studies to cite. Elsbach and van Knippenberg (2020: 7) call the former 'relatively narrow reviews of mature topics in need of reconceptualization' and the latter 'relatively broad reviews of emerging topics in need of synthesis'.

For the first type, *narrow reviews* of mature topics, I would like you to focus on the word 'narrow'. A consistent perception among my students, everywhere I have taught, and a claim I sometimes see in research manuals as well, is that a literature review has to be *comprehensive*. We can argue about semantics – I sometimes see a distinction between comprehensive and exhaustive – but comprehensive does not mean that you need to include everything written on the topic. With 'mature topics' this would be impossible anyway, with decades of research to absorb.

Elsbach and van Knippenberg (2020: 7) talk about 'reconceptualisation' as the function of narrow reviews, but they are talking about published review articles that are meant to say something original about the field of research. For an empirical research dissertation, thesis or article, the scope of the literature review is defined by the literature's relevance to your research question. For example, if you are a sociologist studying suicide, you will probably mention Émile Durkheim's book by the same name (Durkheim, 1979 [1897]) in your review. As mentioned earlier, it is a classic in the field, after all. However, unless your research question is directly linked to assessing Durkheim's contribution, you should not spend too much time on his work. There is a hundred years of scholarship after Durkheim, which is much more relevant to you. Mentioning *Suicide* – the book – is a way to flag the research tradition you are conversing with, but analysing recent research is much more relevant for estimating where you stand in relation to the field. Note that 'relevance' is something that only you can judge. The worst kind of 'literature review' is the kind that trusts search engines to define relevance. I have come across literature reviews where the text is literally a summary of the first ten hits of the keywords on Google Scholar. Do not do this. Just don't.

Broad reviews of emerging topics, the second type, are actually the same *length* as narrow reviews. 'Broad' here refers to the coverage of your review. In little-researched, emerging topics, it is possible to review all of the relevant literature. Put differently, the 'boundary conditions' (what to include and exclude; Elsbach and van Knippenberg, 2020: 6) are broad, but what you do with this corpus is the same as with narrow reviews. The point is to say something analytical about the state of the art in the field, to integrate insights from the reviewed studies in order to be able to assess what the conversation is – which questions are asked and which are not. To give an example from my own research, 'religious literacy' – the idea that if we know more about religion and different religious traditions, we are better able to live together in a religiously diverse society – is a topic of public discourse that has exploded in recent years in North America and Europe. Looking at academic literature on religious literacy shows that existing research tends to be conceptual (this is how we can understand the concept) and normative (this is what we should do in order to promote religious literacy). However, there is a dearth of empirical studies evaluating the claims made in the conceptual and normative literature. Since it is a new field, it was possible to come to this conclusion by reviewing more or less all published research from the last two decades. The analysis clearly shows a gap – an empirical one – in the field. Just keep in mind, as already mentioned, that literature relevant for you does not stop at national or disciplinary boundaries.

In sum, thinking about the type of literature review helps you focus your energies on doing what is best for your dissertation, thesis or other text. It also helps you think about what more you need to know about doing good literature reviews. It is a waste of time to spend days learning about systematic reviews if your work does not really require one, or to try to include everything if your topic is already well studied. There are also other types of literature reviews (Grant and Booth, 2009: 94–95), and learning about them may help you think about your task ahead. The point to remember is that the literature review, whichever type, always serves your research question.

Literature or theory?

I run into a recurrent problem in my seminars: many students do not know how to tell literature reviews and theory apart. In practice, this often means that they start writing a literature review, but what emerges is a discussion of the different theories used in their field. Does this go into the literature review or the theory section? This may not be a relevant question in many fields or disciplines, but teaching in a multidisciplinary environment has taught me that it is common enough to deserve a brief discussion here.

An easy answer would be to say that empirical research goes into the literature review and theory in the theory section. However, if and when the point of literature reviews is to provide insight into *all* elements of research, then surely concepts and theory are part of it? Indeed, Elsbach and van Knippenberg (2020: 9) argue explicitly that the best types of review (they talk about 'integrative' reviews, specifically) lead to conceptual and theoretical development. In principle, then, literature reviews are 'holistic' simply because of the idea presented earlier: the gap sought in the literature is not just a dearth of empirical research on a topic but can also be a question of applying particular methods or conceptual frameworks in analysing empirical cases. In the article format, this is not necessarily a problem. A typical quantitative article, for example, will usually start with an exposition of an empirical idea and then discuss the empirical studies that have previously tested the idea, before outlining why the current design is required to complement existing knowledge.

Things get trickier with dissertations and theses with their designated sections, including literature review and 'theoretical framework', or something similar. In these cases, splitting the discussion becomes a practical question. What goes where is always for you (and your supervisor, when applicable) to decide, but I have suggested the following rule of thumb for my students: the theory section should include only discussion of theories relevant to your empirical analysis.

This means that in the literature review you can discuss theories *relevant to the field*: a broad review of a little examined topic can and should include discussion about the conceptual and theoretical frameworks so far used to understand the phenomenon. Similarly, it is important for a narrow review of a familiar topic in need of reconceptualisation to review the concepts and theories that you wish to replace with your own. A study of anti-immigrant prejudice, for example, could review the 'contact hypothesis' (contact decreases negative attitudes) and the research testing the thesis in the literature review section, simply because it is such a prevalent approach in the field. If the study then decided to use a 'symbolic prejudice' framework for the empirical analysis (for example, Muslims are perceived a threat because their religious attire deviates from secular and/or Christian imaginings of Europeanness), then that would be properly discussed in the theory section. In that section you discuss theories that are *relevant to your empirical analysis* in this particular study.

As said, this is just one suggestion, which caters specifically for structured dissertations and theses. If distinguishing literature and theory feels like a problem, explore different options and compare your solutions with those of others, if possible. The point, as always, is to demonstrate that you understand the difference in the context of your research and that however you solve the problem, you are able to provide a justification for your solution.

Writing up and literature review checklist

By the time you have completed the orientation, analysis and synthesis, and positioning parts of a literature review, you may or may not have written much in terms of a logical narrative. If you have done all the previous steps with care, you should have a sense of what should be included the written literature review. If your review is genuinely analytical and synthetic, you should not end up with a list of random stuff that has been published on the topic, but a balanced picture of the 'state of the art' in your field of study, and a sense of how your research contributes to that field. Please see Table 5.1 for a checklist before starting the writing process.

Table 5.1: Literature review checklist

Action	Function/phase
Choose topic	Orientation
Decide type of review: narrative versus systematic/narrow versus broad	
Explicate method of literature collection and criteria for inclusion	
Search databases for keywords	
Locate key literature (review articles, handbooks, and so on)	
Analyse: key arguments, evidence, positioning	Analysis and synthesis
Synthesise: patterns in the literature (agreements, disagreements); combining different literatures	
Identify gaps (empirical, theoretical, methodological)	Positioning
Position: your place in the conversation; your research question	
Outline review: funnel approach	
Write review	

Conclusion

Perhaps surprisingly, the literature review is the element of research with which my students often struggle most. They understand the idea that you need to know the field in order to know what more needs to be known, that is, what I call 'finding the gap'. But trouble often starts with distinguishing literature and theory and with making the review analytical. Fair enough, in the context of a BA or an MA dissertation, everything said in this chapter may feel a bit overwhelming: Are you really supposed to break new ground, within word count limitations, by synthesising the relevant literature – *in addition* to doing the empirical analysis? Time and space constraints will obviously limit what you can do, but that does not mean you should not strive to make the literature review an integral part of your research. You should not think that a literature review needs to be done, because someone told you so. Instead, think of the literature review providing you with a better question, a better sense of what data and method is needed to answer the question, a better understanding of how theory is used in your field, and a better sense of your contribution to the field. Then you will see that a good literature review is part of your argument, part of your analysis, and an unmissable part of any good research design.

6

Theory

More than any of the other chapters in this book, this one's utility depends on your discipline and approach. As I have already noted, historians rarely stress about theory, while for most social scientists it is an inseparable part of research. That said, no discipline is monolithic. There is theoretically savvy history as well as historically deep political science. This has always been the case: Adam Smith, Karl Marx and Max Weber – just to name a few of the foundational names – are best known as theorists, but much of their oeuvre consists of historical treatises (Burke, 2005: 7, 10). Whether your research follows or deviates from disciplinary traditions in terms of theory use is for you to figure out. *If* theory is relevant for you, then this chapter will help you to think about how to use it in research.

Put differently, the point of this chapter is to understand theory as part of *research practice*. This is different from 'general' theorising, by which I mean the construction of theories that do not necessarily build on empirical cases. So-called 'theorists' theory' is built on conversation with earlier theories. In contrast, theory as research practice, the way I understand it here, focuses on the role of theory in empirical research. As I discuss in this chapter (under 'general theory'), the two are not entirely disconnected, however. Hence, the best way to approach theory as part of research practice is, I think, to differentiate between uses of theory, each with different implications for research design. In what follows, I will discuss five such uses: theory-testing; theory generation; application and development of concepts and models; general theorising; and diagnoses of our time. Discussing these types also helps to think about what 'theory' means in the first place. That is why I do not give a definition of theory here in the beginning. Theory is what you make it in a particular piece of research.

Most importantly, I want to convey that you do not need to consider yourself a 'theorist' in order to 'do theory'. Too often students approach the 'theoretical framework' (or similar) part of their dissertation or thesis with trepidation. Sometimes this leads to shallow name-dropping, sometimes to rigid claims that a theory has been 'disproven', even if the research does not quite warrant the claim. In both cases, the function of theory has been misunderstood. Understanding how theory can be made to work with your research question, data and method is the key to making the 'theoretical framework' more than just a box to tick.

A reminder, though: as with method, everything you say about using theory in your research is a *promise*. I have seen too many dissertations and theses, which demonstrate admirable theoretical literacy and skill, but then fall flat because none of that eloquence is actually applied in the analysis of data or in the discussion about the significance of the research. You may love Bourdieu's theory of distinction, but if your research only uses Bourdieu as a token to fill the theory section and never goes back to his ideas in the rest of the work, that is a promise betrayed. You have been warned.

Why theory?

Even if you have a good sense of the role theory plays in your discipline or research tradition, all the functions of theory may not be entirely clear. The problem is that theory books focus on the substance of theories, but rarely discuss how theory can be used in empirical research. In my view – and there may be other views – the main uses of theory correspond with different stages of the research project. Before gathering and analysing your data, theory helps in figuring out what to ask from the data. In other words, theory is a source of research questions. During the research, theory enables you to organise your observations. In other words, theory gives you analytical lenses. After analysing the data, theory connects you to a broader conversation. In other words, your case study becomes significant beyond the analysis of a national or group context, as it engages theoretical issues that transcend case study boundaries. I have already discussed theory as a source of questions (Chapter 2) and how theory organises data (Chapter 3). In Chapter 8, I will discuss theory as part of the contribution your research makes. However, it is useful to briefly summarise the ideas here.

Theory and the research question. While many research questions arise from mundane observations or practical concerns, theory is also an important source of questions. Researchers often make theoretical claims based on an analysis of a particular national context. An important way of checking the validity of those claims is to test the theoretical claims in another context. In a less strict sense of 'theory', theoretical concepts can inspire research questions. For example, 'democratic consolidation' has been used to describe previously authoritarian regimes, which have managed to avoid regressing after a democratic transition (Schedler, 1998). As such, it provides a kind of lens, which focuses attention to particular issues, such as popular legitimation, the diffusion of democratic values and party building. The concept can then be applied to a particular case study, as Chandler (2000) did when he asked how democratisation had been conceptualised in the case of post-war Bosnia.

Theory and data analysis. Riffing on philosopher Immanuel Kant's slightly different formulation, it could be said that 'theory without data is empty and data without theory is blind'. In less ableist language, this means that theory functions as a tool with which the chaotic jumble of data is organised. It organises data in the gathering phase by, say, influencing what questions you ask in interviews. It further organises data in the analysis phase by sifting through disparate text or numbers. For example, if you were studying radicalisation – a much-debated theoretical concept (Kundnani, 2012) – you could not ask the interviewees 'How were you radicalised?', because that is a value-laden question in itself. Therefore, in the analysis phase you would need to pay close attention to all snippets of information that would be relevant from the perspective of radicalisation theories – life experiences, disappointments, social networks, and access to radical ideas and groups – while sifting through a lot of other, less relevant information. The exception to this kind of use of theory is Grounded Theory. As I discuss in the following, in Grounded Theory approaches you do not use an existing theory to organise data, but rather develop theory from the data.

Theory and the research contribution. If the point of theoretical contributions had to be summed up in one sentence, it would be 'to join a broader conversation'. Your empirical case may fill a gap in knowledge, but in the best-case scenario, your research may also have something relevant to say about the key tools – theories and concepts – used in your field. In fact, if you have applied a theory or theoretical concept to your question-formulation and your data analysis, your reader will expect that you will have something to say about whether your research has any implications for the future use of said theory or concept. Thinking about how your research contributes to theory means joining a conversation beyond the limits of your particular topic, data and context. Therefore, I always encourage it, whenever it fits the work. Going back to 'democratic consolidation', the concept not only inspired Chandler's (2000) overall question regarding democratisation in Bosnia, but he also remarks how the concept is highly problematic since there was no agreement in the literature – or among international institutions – about which 'hoops … new democracies [had] to jump through to prove themselves' (Chandler, 2000: 16; see also Schedler, 1998: 92). Indeed, Chandler argues that the concept has become a tool for justifying Western intervention in countries deemed insufficiently democratic. That is a powerful addition to the theoretical conversation.

Research theory I: theory-testing

The classic model of social science, often referred to as the 'positivistic paradigm' or the deductive model of scientific research, is to take a theory, formulate hypotheses from the theory (see Chapter 2), operationalise the key variables, and then test the hypotheses with quantitative data. Much of the dissatisfaction in the social sciences in the 1960s was directed against this kind of mechanical model of analysis. The impact of this critique has varied considerably, with sociology expanding into more qualitative horizons, political science perhaps less so, and economics practically not at all (but see Starr, 2014). It is therefore fair to say that when theory appears in social science research, it most often appears in its theory-testing form.

In theory-testing research, theory is built into the research design, as the name implies. A study that tests a theory (by constructing hypotheses and testing them statistically) confirms, refutes or modifies the theory in question. For example, Lin and Miller (2020) tested how gender affects risk of delinquency in a nationally representative sample of American adolescents. They draw their hypotheses from social control and routine activities theories, the former which suggests that close bonds with parents suppress delinquency and the latter that youth are more susceptible to 'risky' behaviour the less parental controls they have. The aim of the study is clearly expressed: 'This study addresses the literature voids by examining the strength of these protective factors *simultaneously* and testing how these factors work differently for boys and girls on aggressive and non-aggressive delinquency' (Lin and Miller, 2020: np; emphasis in the original). Using sophisticated multivariate statistics, they demonstrate how the suppressive effects of parental bonds and control are different depending on one's gender. Although the main thrust and aim of the study is empirical, their findings call for a rethinking of the traditional theories.

It should be noted, however, that theory-testing is not inherent to quantitative approaches. Many quantitative studies are descriptive or provide sort of ad hoc explanations for patterns in the data. But because theories are supposed to be generalisable, their testing logically requires data that allows generalisation. But does this work the other way around? Can we test theories using qualitative data?

The intuitive answer – and the answer that quantitative researchers tend to give – is no. This is why I continue to be surprised by dissertation and thesis proposals that replicate the deductive model of theory-testing, but use qualitative data. An ethnographic study of ten yoga enthusiasts is hardly proof of the failure of secularisation theory – just to use a type of argument that pops up frequently in my own field of research. The theory does not claim that religion is inevitably bound to decline everywhere and at all times, only in particular circumstances. More importantly, even multiple cases of religious vitality do not challenge the broader statistical trends (see Bruce, 2017). They might challenge the ways in which we conceptualise religion in the first place, but that is a different conversation. Using qualitative data for a deductive, theory-testing research design leads to problematic questions regarding generalisability, most of all.

Not all qualitative researchers are willing to forsake theory-testing, however. Some scholars (for example, Bitektine, 2008; Yin, 2018) suggest that theory can be tested deductively in a limited case study research. Here the point is not generalisability, but assessment of the explanatory power of theories regarding social and group processes. In this type of design, theories provide a pattern of expected outcomes, which are then matched with the pattern of observations. Then the process is repeated at a different point in time to check for the validity of the original analysis. Through a process of falsification, researchers can also weigh between multiple competing theories (Bitektine, 2008: 162). The point to remember, then, is that the problem is not theory-testing research using qualitative data as such, but bad research designs where theory and qualitative data are combined inappropriately. Here we are straying into method territory, but the discussion demonstrates that if theory matters for your research in the first place, then it is inseparable from the other elements.

Research theory II: theory generation

Later I will discuss 'general theorising', which is of course (regardless of discipline), 'theory generation'. What I have in mind in this section is more the kind of theory-building that happens as a side product of empirical research. In this sense, 'theory generation' encompasses a broader spectrum than formal theories and includes models and concepts (see the next section). So, for example, historians, who usually focus on events rather structures, have nevertheless made some lasting conceptual contributions, such as E.P. Thompson's 'moral economy' and Eric Hobsbawm's 'invention of tradition'. Both continue to inspire historical and social scientific research (Burke, 2005: 1). In my own assessment of the new interest European governments are showing towards religious communities as potential welfare providers, I coined the 'paradoxes of expediency thesis'. It says that '*[p]ublic authorities' increased tendency to treat religion as expedient interpellates religious communities to formulate legitimation strategies. These lead, by definition, to authenticity struggles which, in turn, can lead to schism, polarisation and radicalism*' (Hjelm, 2015: 10; emphasis in the original). This is a 'testable' thesis – although not primarily quantitatively – that grew out of reading secondary literature. For example, a Norwegian study showed that when a Christian umbrella organisation wanted to update their gender policies under pressure from the government, which funds much of the member organisations' work, the issue led to serious disagreement, especially among the conservative members (Østebø et al, 2013). The novelty of my 'thesis' was that no one had proposed the process as a more general pattern for religion and state relations. The theoretical formulation grew out of empirical observation (even if based on secondary data, in my case).

Understood this way, theory generation is especially relevant as an element that broadens the scholarly contribution of your empirical research. Theory is generated, so to say, at the back end of the research process. However, there is a distinct tradition of social science, which *begins* from a theory generation perspective. This approach is called *Grounded*

Theory. I have detailed the methodological process of Grounded Theory in Chapter 3, but here I want to discuss how it is sometimes used as a 'theoretical framework', especially in dissertations and theses. I focus on the problematic uses, even abuses, of the term, not because I do not think that approach has no merit, but because the critical assessment hopefully throws light on some practices you should avoid when thinking about theory as part of research. I have three points in mind in particular: first, Grounded Theory as an excuse for not reading the literature; second, ticking the 'theoretical framework' box by calling descriptive research Grounded Theory; and, third, misunderstanding coding as a positivistic technique for qualitative research.

My own first brush with 'Grounded Theory' came as a journal editor. A paper submitted to the journal analysed a well-known topic, but the authors said that they would refrain from discussing earlier literature on the topic, because they wanted to start from a 'clean slate', without theoretical preconceptions, and then work towards their own theory. Not an expert on Grounded Theory, I found this a very problematic approach, thinking, like one early reviewer of Glaser and Strauss' foundational book *The Discovery of Grounded Theory* (2017 [1967]) put it, that 'presuppositionless inquiry is self-deception or pretense' (Wagner, 1968: 555). As many scholars employing Grounded Theory (for example, Suddaby, 2006: 635) have argued, however, this was never the authors' intention. Rather, it seems that Grounded Theory is used – possibly especially by dissertation and thesis writers – as an excuse to avoid delving into the literature (Suddaby, 2006: 634).

Dovetailing with this, the fixation with having a 'theoretical framework' in social science dissertations and theses sometimes leads to questionable practices. Even if the research itself is basic exploratory qualitative research, the theoretical framework part is ticked off with calling the research Grounded Theory. Ethnography and Grounded Theory both fit well with exploratory research, where little is known about a phenomenon, but calling ethnography Grounded Theory does not yet make it theoretical.

Finally, theory generation in the Grounded Theory sense is often misunderstood as the mechanical application of coding to data, from which then automatically some theories emerge. There is sometimes a tendency to use 'coding' to make research look more 'scientific', like quantitative theory-testing research, but Grounded Theory as method and an approach to theory generation is thoroughly interpretative. Qualitative software programmes will not generate your theory for you. Also, as Layder (1993: 45) argues, Grounded Theory is a process, so that unlike in other types of theorising, the end result is not 'a theory' with axiomatic, testable propositions, but rather that 'theory should be viewed as a constant and flexible accompaniment to the incremental collection of data and the unfolding nature of the research'.

My point here has not been to pick on Grounded Theory, much less to discourage researchers from applying it. Rather, it has been a gentle plea to not abuse the term and find out what the developers of Grounded Theory actually said (Suddaby, 2006).

Research theory III: application and development of concepts and models

Application and development of concepts is a special case of theory as part of research practice. Concepts, models or typologies may not be as comprehensive as theories, but they are crucial in distilling something of the complex social and cultural realities we study. Often the dissertations and theses that I supervise revolve around one or several key concepts, rather than one identifiable theory. Concept application and development can take several forms. Next, I discuss three such forms: assessing and clarifying concepts; developing new concepts; and applying models.

First, research can aim at clarifying an existing concept in light of empirical results, or assess its usefulness in a particular field. George Ritzer is an American sociologist who coined the concept 'McDonaldisation' in the early 1980s (Ritzer, 1983) and whose book by the same name became a hit in the early 1990s (Ritzer, 1992). Building on Max Weber's concept of 'rationalisation', Ritzer argued that the paradigmatic example of rationalisation in the contemporary United States was not bureaucracy, as Weber had suggested, but the fast food restaurant. The time-saving and profit-maximising techniques developed at McDonald's restaurants were, according to Ritzer, increasingly applied to various spheres of society. 'McDonaldisation' struck a nerve and there have been numerous studies applying the concept in equally numerous fields. Franklin (2005), for example, analysed local newspapers in the UK using the derivative concept 'McJournalism' to describe the outcome of centralised news production. He argued that the features of McDonaldisation (efficiency, calculability, predictability, and so on) characterised well the structural changes in local news production, thus demonstrating the usefulness of Ritzer's concept through a case study.

Second, research can develop entirely new concepts. These can be genuinely new words, or concepts transposed from one discipline to another and gaining new meaning in the process. David Herbert (2011), for example, showed how earlier accounts of secularisation took little notice of developments in the media (technological advances, liberalisation of media markets) and how these developments challenged the assumption on the declining presence of religion in the public sphere. He called this process religious 'publicisation'. This was partly a case of linguistic transposition, as 'publicisation' is a common term in French, but not so in English.

Used in the context of theories of religious change, Herbert used it in an innovative way.

Third, models can be considered a sub-category of concept application. However, the word 'model' has different meanings depending on discipline. For natural scientists and economists, 'modelling' signifies what I have here called theory-testing. In other social sciences and the humanities models are rather understood as heuristic lenses, which help us *think* about empirical phenomena, even if not explain it as such. For example, in the field of social problems research, Hilgartner and Bosk (1988) developed a 'public arenas model' for studying how some issues, such as the youth delinquency mentioned earlier, become objects of intense social concern. They propose several different factors that either amplify or dampen the success of issues in developing into full-scale social problems. As the name implies, this is not a testable theory, but provides a perspective – a model – for examining how some issues (such as youth delinquency), but not others (such as youth poverty), become widely (even if sometimes incorrectly) recognised social problems.

Models can also take the form of 'process charts', where the development of a phenomenon is conceived as particular steps. Again, in social problems research, Herbert Blumer's (1971) classic article outlined a five-stage process where a state of things becomes recognised as a social problem and how society reacts to that recognition:

1. the emergence of a social problem;
2. the legitimation of the problem;
3. the mobilisation of action with regard to the problem;
4. the formation of an official plan of action; and
5. the transformation of the official plan in its empirical implementation.

The details of the individual stages need not concern us here. What is relevant is that Blumer's model has inspired a lot of further research and theorisation on social problems. Again, it does not exactly explain *why* people begin to perceive a particular issue as a social problem, but it does help us understand what it takes to draw people's attention to the problem and to consolidate efforts to eradicate it.

Classifications, taxonomies and typologies can also function as 'models' in the broad sense. They can help us understand common social and cultural features across cultural and historical boundaries. Comparative politics makes better sense if we can find a way to classify the huge variety of national political parties. Hence, party typologies have become a staple of political science literature. Historically, for example, political parties can be classified as legislative-electoral parties (loose networks created to gain legislative power for individuals), electoral mass parties (semi-professional parties bent on winning elections) and organisational mass parties (permanent organisations with a strong ideological base) (Sartori, 2005). Importantly, no single party that we can observe empirically needs to fit the description exactly, or it can be several types at once. But the typology helps in understanding comparative party development and organisation. Max Weber used the term 'ideal type' for theorising about types of phenomena that do not exist in pure form anywhere, but which empirical examples approximate to various degree (Kalberg, 1994: 81–91).

Concepts and models are perhaps especially important in qualitative analysis, in cases where theory-testing is challenging, or when studying topics for which no comprehensive theories exist. A key concept or classification can serve all three functions of theory (inspiration for research questions, analytical lens, and an aspect of the research contribution) in research practice. However, with loose rules of application come potential pitfalls as well, which I discuss under the theme of theoretical creativity.

General theory

I have already mentioned what could be called, for lack of a better term, 'general theory' (see, for example, Layder, 1993: 6–7). This is theory that discusses the fundamental concepts of social science, such as social structure, culture or the individual. It usually draws from insights in research theory, but not necessarily. So there are endless books on general Marxist theories of society, for example, which do not necessarily check the theories against updated empirical facts and research theories, but rather discuss the logical construction of the Marxist system or weigh it against competing general theories. Often in the social sciences there is a rather notable gap between empirical 'toiling' and theoretical 'dreaming', where the latter is reduced to the study of the theoretical classics in any given field (sociology, political science, and so on), or to abstract conversation between theories, removed from everyday realities.

This is an unfortunate and unnecessary divide. To add to the confusion, many theories that in this chapter's terms would be 'research theories' are called 'general theories' (for example, Gottfredson and Hirschi's *A General Theory of Crime*, 1990). The point to remember is that research theory is always built upon a particular understanding of more fundamental concepts. Theorisations of 'ethnicity' are built upon an understanding of 'social identity', which in turn is built upon an approach to 'culture'. Hence, a theory of ethnicity will have a general theory of culture built into it (this is not to meant exhaust ethnicity as a cultural category only, but to demonstrate one possible way of looking at different levels of theoretical concepts; see Parker et al, 2015: 10–11). From this perspective, general theories and theories relevant for empirical research should not be seen as opposites, but rather as positioned on a continuum.

General theories can also connect with empirical studies in more direct ways. Layder suggests two ways to apply insights from general theories to research:

> [G]eneral theory can be employed both as an initial part of the research design (loosely conceived, of course) as well as a post-research strategy. Both forms have the effect of stimulating innovative forms of theory either by using ideas or concepts as initial 'sounding boards', or as a retrospective means of establishing an explanatory pattern on the data. (Layder, 1993: 65)

So, for example, questions of micro (individual action) and macro (structure) levels of society are central to sociological general theory. The debate about the relationship between these levels can inspire questions regarding the (unobservable) social structures enabling or constraining the (observable) actions of people. For example, men engage in more 'imprudent airline passenger behaviour', such as passing gas or swearing at people who repeatedly bump one's seatback, than women do (Meldrum, 2016). If we do not want to stop at that observation, we could ponder about how gender as a socially structuring category affects such situations. The general theory of structure versus action is abstract, but it can sensitise research to pay attention to the micro–macro connection or use it to interpret the results of empirical analysis.

Often these 'basic' or 'fundamental' concepts and theorisations, that is, general theories, are implicit in the further 'derived' or 'subsidiary' theorisations and conceptualisations. Put differently, they are the 'frame of reference' for research theories (Noro, 2000: 322). Layder (1993: 15) suggests that where these kind of frames of reference or background assumptions are implicit, 'they should be made explicit and the relevant connections detailed'. The key word here is 'relevant', because in practice, in the writing scholars produce in various forms, there is rarely room to dig deep into the more general theoretical aspects of a research project. In fact, this makes for tedious reading. However, in some cases explicating the basic conceptualisation is called for, and in *all* cases, it is important for the researcher to acknowledge the more fundamental general theory assumptions, even if they are not explicated in the written reports – or, rather, when they have to be deduced from the operative research theory.

Diagnoses of our time

The fifth and final type of theory that I want to discuss is a special case. It is such in the sense that it is recognised as an actual genre of writing only in sociology (as far as I know), and even there only by a minority. This is what is referred to as the 'diagnosis of our time' (from the German *Zeitdiagnose*). These diagnoses of our time purport to answer questions such as 'Who are we?' and 'What is our time like?'. Essayistic rather than presented as strictly logical arguments, they are broad-sweeping visions about what defines the times we live in. It is their embeddedness in disciplinary thinking that makes them *sociological* visions.

Opinion differs on whether all sociology includes, or should include, diagnostic elements such as these, or whether the genre is reserved for popularisers and journalistic accounts. The fact is that many 'big name' sociologists have written treatises that are best characterised as diagnoses of our time, starting from the classics. Hence, Max Weber (2001 [1904–1905]) wrote about 'the iron cage of rationality', which characterised modernity as he saw it. Similarly Émile Durkheim (1979 [1897]) used 'anomie' to describe a typical condition of modernity. More recently, Ulrich Beck (1992) has talked about 'risk society' and Zygmunt Bauman (2000) about 'liquid modernity', both trying to catch something about the character of the times within a master concept. As sociologists, they all have been specifically concerned to understand the emergence of modernity (or postmodernity) and its characteristics.

Why is a discussion of such a specific type of theorisation relevant for a non-discipline-specific book on research design? Because, as sociologist Klaus Lichtblau puts it:

> [T]he literary genre of the 'diagiosis of the times' is certainly no privilege of sociology as such; instead, it possesses a long tradition of its own in intellectual history. That history is expressed both in the various philosophical and culture-critical attempts to read the 'character of the times', and in the literary, aesthetic and journalistic reflections on the conceptually amorphous and often whimsical 'spirit of the times'. (Lichtblau, 1995: 25)

This is important, because sometimes research ideas and questions are inspired by popular cultural criticism or concepts circulating in public discourse. One such example is 'Finlandisation', a Cold War term used to signal a 'conviction that the Finns, after World War II, trimmed their system and policy to suit Soviet needs, even by anticipation. The picture was one of creeping Sovietization: Finland today, the rest of Europe tomorrow' (Hjelm and Maude, 2021: 105). Although 'Finlandisation' was mostly used polemically to discredit left-wing politicians around Europe, it also made an impact in scholarly policy discussion. Its usefulness as a heuristic concept, even less a 'theory', has been rightly questioned, however (Mouritzen, 1988).

The diagnosis of our times genre is most obvious with the kinds of books and articles that purport to distil the character or spirit of times, as Lichtblau put it, quite explicitly. Hence, we have historian Eric Hobsbawm's famous quadrilogy *Age of Revolution*, *Age of Capital*, *Age of Empire* and *Age of Extremes* (Hobsbawm, 1962; 1975; 1987; 1994, respectively). They may be the best-known examples of the use of such periodisation in historical writing, but the diagnosis of our times is a regular genre for books dealing with the contemporary world as well. Take, for example, Shoshana Zuboff's recent (2019) *Age of Surveillance Capitalism*, or Michelle Alexander's (2010) *The New Jim Crow: Mass Incarceration in the Age of Colorblindness*, just to note two at random. Both are research-based, but also do not shy from saying what is wrong with their respective 'ages'. Diagnoses of our times are often critical in the sense that they suggest how to change the times we are living in. They are always guided by a vision – whether acknowledged or not.

How do these kinds of diagnoses of our times work as 'theory' in the sense of theory as part of academic research practice? Looking at citation data, Zuboff's and Alexander's characterisations of the age (surveillance capitalism, colourblindness) have been referred to by many other researchers. For the purposes of this chapter, I have not done a comprehensive analysis of how their diagnoses have been used in subsequent research, but the impression from a limited sample is that often an 'age of' type of diagnosis may be a loose contextualisation, useful for setting the scene for a narrower study.

However, the diagnosis of our times may also be a problematic source of 'theory'. As Finnish sociologist Arto Noro (2000: 329) puts it: 'We cannot use [diagnoses of our times] in scientific discussion to interpret empirical evidence. The outcome would be that they would enchant us too much. We would find in our data what the diagnoses have already said' (my translation). Diagnoses of our times can inspire research questions and function as sources of ideas for formal theoretical formulations, but to conduct a case study on, say, social media use and then conclude that the results are explained by the 'age of surveillance capitalism' would mean being too enchanted by the concept to see anything else in the data. In an example from my own field, many scholars now use the term 'spiritual revolution' as a term that captures something about the spirit of the age (pun intended). Then every case study of a spiritual practice can be taken as proof of the diagnosis. This not only misrepresents the original research that coined the term 'spiritual revolution' (for an extended discussion see Chapter 8), but is an example of a problematic use of diagnoses of our times.

Many characterisations of 'our times' – whether originating from academic sources or not – become fashionable and there may be a temptation to use them as 'theoretical frameworks' or key concepts in research. While they may point to interesting questions, such diagnoses are problematic as research theory. Because diagnostic and more formal theorisations often overlap, it requires diligence from the researcher to recognise when an idea or concept is in danger of becoming a self-fulfilling prophecy in empirical research.

Fit-the-box theory versus creative theory use

In disciplines and fields where theorisation is an integral part of research practice, students often learn their disciplines' pet theories by heart. When they come to the dissertation stage, however, many are baffled by how to apply these same theories in their own research. This sometimes leads to what I call 'fit-the-box' theorising. More than a couple of times, I have read dissertations and theses, but also journal article submissions, where the point seems to be either to confirm or refute this or that theory. This is not a problem as such, but becomes one when the theory is used with an incompatible combination of question, data and method. The problem is studies that use the theory-testing approach as a 'theoretical framework', when in other aspects the research design suggests a theory-building approach, or an approach based on key concepts. Using 'theory' in the broad sense adopted here means that some theories are testable, while some are meant to provide looser frameworks for interpreting the empirical world.

A special case of this is using definitions as 'theoretical frameworks'. In my own field, I sometimes see dissertations that discuss a definition of religion at length, then present examples from the data – say, interviews with yoga practitioners – and finally conclude that based on the definition, this is indeed 'religion'. The problem here, of course, is that definitions help us categorise phenomena, but answering whether a practice can be counted as 'religion' (or 'deviant', or 'political') is not necessarily a very interesting scholarly question. If you work for a government agency or a law firm, the situation is different, because the answer has practical outcomes. For research, I have always thought that sociologist Peter Berger's (1967: 175) maxim summarises the issue perfectly: 'Definitions cannot, by their very nature, be either "true" or "false," only more useful or less so.' Definitions may be useful in narrowing down your research's subject matter, but they are not 'theory' in the sense used in this chapter.

What is 'creative theory use', then? There is a bit of a paradox here: if I was able to give you detailed instructions, the theorising would not be very creative, would it? Then again, you can take courses in creative writing, which do not tell you what to write, but give you tools to let your creativity flow. Creative theory use would be a topic for a book of its own (for some ideas, see Woodiwiss, 2005; Karlsson and Bergman, 2017), so here I am going to mention just two possibilities – cross-disciplinary borrowing and the combining of theories – and some problems in their implementation.

Although some scholars complain about 'incremental and imitative theorising' (Williams et al, 2018), this is very likely what you will be doing in a dissertation or thesis. And that is completely fine. To apply a tried and tested approach to using theory in research practice demonstrates that you understand the role of theory in research design. However, you may have a passion for theoretical thinking, or there simply are no sufficient concepts or theories in your field to help you understand a phenomenon.

Disciplinary borrowing is rather straightforward – on the surface at least. Whole disciplines have changed as the outcome of disciplinary borrowing. So, for example, in the 1960s sociologist Harold Garfinkel rebelled against his teacher Talcott Parsons, whose functional systems theory had become a sociological orthodoxy in the 1950s. In this, Garfinkel was inspired by phenomenology, a branch of continental philosophy that focuses on human experience. Garfinkel's (1967) ethnomethodology, as he called it, brought sociology down from abstract levels of structure and system to how people created informal rules of interaction in everyday life. What started as an alternative approach to doing sociological research became an alternative 'school' that in many ways outlived its predecessor.

On the level of individual studies, borrowing theories from other disciplines can provide new avenues for explanation and interpretation. Speaking of comparative politics, Ross (2009: 33) says that '[b]orrowing tends to occur when comparativists have reached a theoretical plateau, when they judge their political explanations to be inadequate or incomplete or when they seek to make claims to innovation by radicalising how their research problems are defined and answered'. She offers the example of political scientists borrowing from economics 'to understand their institutions through the lens of rational choice theory' (Ross, 2009: 33). Another function of theoretical borrowing is to avoid 'reinventing the wheel' (Fellows and Liu, 2020). If a working theory exists in another discipline, why not use it instead of claiming dubious theoretical novelty? Theories thus adapted rarely survive intact and may become unrecognisable to people in the other discipline, but disciplinary defensiveness and boundary guarding should not deter anyone from theoretical creativity if there is something substantive to be gained from the borrowing.

Borrowing needs to take into account and explicate the different contexts in which it is used. In practice this means that you will need to spend more time on the theory section, explaining not only the content of borrowed theories and concepts, but also how they are used in the original disciplinary context and what modifications are required to implant the theories and concepts in the new context. This includes awareness of the theoretical debates and critiques of the theories and concepts in the original discipline. Creative theorising is rewarding, but it is also hard work.

Combining theories means that instead of just borrowing from another discipline, theoretical and conceptual insights (from one or multiple disciplines) are blended (Oswick et al, 2011). Unlike borrowing, which implies a one-way relationship, this is closer to the current buzzwords multi- and interdisciplinarity, where insights across disciplines are combined or used to create something entirely new. For example, Robert Heiner (2002) in his approach to the study of social problems combines insights from constructionist social problems theory and critical, Marxism-inspired theory, which he calls 'conflict theory'. Thus, Heiner argues that social problems are phenomena 'regarded as bad or undesirable by a significant number of people' – in other words, regardless of their actual objectively calculable harm, people construct these phenomena as problematic. This is the standard constructionist theory of social problems. However, Heiner (2002: 10) goes further and adds that what he calls 'critical constructionism', 'emphasises the role of elite interests in the process of problem construction'. Because of these elite interests, youth gangs are considered a social problem, but not so much youth poverty (as discussed earlier) – even when poverty could be said to be at the root of gang problems, and solving the former would take care of the latter, but not the other way around. Combination of theories such as Heiner's enables new insights on all of the levels of theory use – as inspiration for questions, as analytical lenses, and for joining theoretical conversations – and as such serves the same functions that Ross (2009) gives for borrowing theories.

Combining concepts and theories comes with a warning, though. First, although Layder (1993: 198) says that 'only by attempting to draw together what would otherwise be regarded as antithetical or incompatible viewpoints or positions can social scientific knowledge advance', this requires special attention to the background assumptions (ontology and epistemology) of different theories. An addition of a minor concept into a broader theoretical framework may work well, but especially in cases where two or more theories are combined on equal footing, there is a danger of ignoring their real differences and thus doing violence to their original intent (Modell et al, 2017: 63). That two theories start from a very different perspective on how we can know about social life in the first place (epistemology) does not necessarily invalidate the empirical research done with their help, but it does call into question your theoretical reflexivity, the ability to recognise these epistemological differences.

There is also a more practical concern regarding theory combination. One of my most common comments in the research seminars I run is 'Do you really need all these concepts and theories to understand your topic?'. There is a temptation, perhaps especially if in the literature you find one study using one theory and another using a different theory, to use both, just in case. However, the principle of parsimony (or 'Occam's razor', as it is sometimes called) discussed in Chapter 2 applies to all of the elements of research design, but perhaps particularly to the theory section. More is not more when it comes to theorising. First, as mentioned many times in this book, everything you say about the different elements of research design in your written report is a promise. If you list five concepts and theories, then you really need to show in the analysis how they provide lenses for interpretation and discuss in your conclusion how these concepts and theories helped you get there. Second, even if you avoid this problem, you should always be wary of theory–data balance. If your purpose is to use empirical data to answer a research question, then it will look bad to use two-thirds of a dissertation, thesis or article on illustrating theory while your empirical analysis is reduced to a blip. Finally, multiple concepts and theories only make sense if you are able to explain and show how they relate to each other. Five unrelated theories, which do not overlap in any way with each other in your research, do not make the work theoretically stronger. That is why I talk about *combining* theories and concepts rather than just stacking them on top of each other.

Conclusion

Whenever you use concepts, typologies or models to distil and capture something essential about the complex jumble of empirical data, you are engaged in theorising. This is why the 'holy trinity' of question, data and method is depicted as embedded in the 'halo' of theory (and research literature) in Figure 1.1. Theory becomes part of research practice as a source of research questions, as a lens for interpreting empirical data, and as a way to join a broader conversation beyond the particular empirical case. Despite the cacophony of particular disciplinary theories, there are ways to discern between different uses of theory in research practice, which has been the focus of this chapter. It is especially important to spot the difference between theory-testing approaches and the other approaches discussed. The former tends to be taken as the model of how to use theory in research, yet it does not work with some combinations of data and method. My point overall is that theory should not be considered just a necessary evil, but rather as something that will – at any stage of the process – enrich your research and connect it better with the scholarly community. Whatever your disciplinary background, it is important to recognise the role of concepts and broader theories in empirical research.

7

Ethics

On 26 July 2022, *The Washington Post* noted the 50th anniversary of the uncovering of what is now known as the Tuskegee Experiment. In this study, which launched in 1932, the US Public Health Service recruited mostly poor Black men from the southern state of Alabama who were suffering from syphilis, in order to study the effect of medication on the disease. The problem was that there was no medication for syphilis at the time and when effective antibiotics were discovered, they were not given to the research participants. Why? Because the aim of the research was all along to study the effects of the untreated disease on the victims, not to cure them. Only an expose published in *The New York Times* in 1972 – 40 years later – ended the experiment and led to 'congressional hearings and a class-action lawsuit' (Brown and Wiener, 2022).

There are good reasons why this chapter could have been the first in this book. Scholars of society and culture may not have as direct an impact on people's health and well-being as medical researchers do, but that still leaves a swathe of situations where ethical issues arise. Years ago, when I was doing fieldwork (in the project we called it 'street ethnography') in London's East End, my aim was to observe and talk to young people about where they hung out, with whom, and why they preferred certain areas over others. Going to 'the field' open-minded and (in hindsight) naïve, I was surprised that some of the youth I chatted with were clearly uncomfortable with what I thought were completely harmless questions about their everyday life. When I raised the issue with a youth worker, he explained that in the area I was studying, where more than a third of young people were of British Asian background, these were exactly the kinds of questions a police officer would ask. Knowing that minority ethnic youth in London are stopped by police much more frequently than White youth, I started to understand their reluctance to talk. I also understood that I had put them in an uncomfortable situation, which was against all my intentions. The lesson from that experience was that although I have discussed other elements of research first, my guiding idea – depicted in Figure 1.1 – is that research ethics is not a step or phase in the research process, but rather that all the elements of research are immersed in it, every step of the way. The point is that you may have the perfect research design, elements aligned and all, but *none of it matters if your research is not ethically sound.*

Research ethics, or 'responsible conduct of research' as some prefer to call it, has taken giant steps in the last couple of decades – both as a scholarly practice and a field of research in itself. When I finished my MA in the 1990s, we had few courses dedicated to research ethics, and very little supervision regarding responsible research conduct. Now it seems research ethics is ubiquitous. This also means that it may be difficult to keep pace with what research ethics includes. Some scholars have come up with helpful typologies to help begin to understand all the issues involved. Kenneth D. Pimple (2002: 193–194), for example, outlines a framework with six 'domains' of research ethics:

1. scientific integrity (relationship between research and truth);
2. collegiality (relationships among researchers);
3. protection of human subjects (relationship between researchers and human subjects);
4. animal welfare (relationship between researchers and animal subjects);
5. institutional integrity (relationships between researchers, sponsoring institutions, funders, and government); and
6. social responsibility (relationship between research and the common good).

According to Pimple, these domains answer the three key questions of research ethics: Is it true (domain 1)? Is it fair (2, 3, 4, 5)? Is it wise (6)? My presentation in this chapter follows Pimple's scheme, but in a slightly different order. I discuss the domains broadly in the order in which they become acute in the research process. So, I will first discuss how research questions may be ethically problematic, followed by ethical issues with literature reviews (collegiality), and then data and method (protection of participants). The latter part of the chapter then deals with writing and your research contribution (scientific and institutional integrity, and social responsibility). Although writing and the research contribution will be covered in subsequent chapters, this chapter foreshadows the ethical issues that may arise when thinking about your research report as a finished product with potential impact on the world. As always, research ethics has different 'weight' in different fields and disciplines. Clearly, a drug trial has different ethical implications than an analysis of a 19th-century French novel. Also, much of the following uses qualitative field research as an example for discussing ethical issues, simply because fieldwork intrudes more on participants' lives than other types. If you are doing statistical, textual or archival research, the ethical emphases may be somewhat different. However, awareness and acknowledgement of potential ethical problems – and being able to articulate the circumstances in which ethics may *not* be an issue – is relevant for every scholar.

Beyond rules

The growing awareness and acknowledgement of the fact that research has to be not just scientifically sound but also ethically sustainable has led governments, professional associations, funding bodies and other institutions to formulate guidelines for ethical research. In other words, research ethics has become institutionalised.

One of the forms this institutionalisation takes is ethics committees or Institutional Review Boards as they are called mainly in the United States (Tinker and Coomber, 2005; van den Hoonaard, 2011: 5). I will use 'ethics committee' as the generic term here. If you are doing research that involves living humans, especially those in a vulnerable position (for example, young, old, disabled), or studying personal and potentially sensitive topics (for example, sexuality, religion), then you will probably have to submit your research plan for review to your university's or institution's ethics committee. There a panel of your peers – one hopes, since the composition and working practices of ethics committees are often shrouded in secrecy (Palmer, 2017: 249–250) – assesses whether the different aspects of your research design (data collection methods, especially) are ethical, and whether there are potential risks involved. Often a passed review by the ethics committee is a precondition for starting the data collection part of the research. The committee may pass or reject the proposal as it is, but most of the time they point to some potentially problematic issues and ask you to consider these before commencing the research, although these recommendations may not be binding.

Another, more minor detail about the institutionalisation of research ethics is the change in terminology. As Pimple (2002: 203) noted more than 20 years ago, 'responsible conduct of research (RCR)' was 'clearly becoming the term of favor' over 'research ethics'. Although he discerned no difference between how the two were used, he mused that 'perhaps RCR is preferred by some because using the word "ethics" seems too preachy, judgmental, moralistic, or abstract'. I cannot say whether Pimple's assessment applies to the United States only, or whether there has been a more recent shift back to 'research ethics'. But his thoughts about the shift in terminology raise an important issue.

Both the institutionalised ethical review process and the change in terminology mask the fact that research ethics is not about *rules* of responsible conduct of research. Too often – much too often – I see research proposals where the ethics component is ticked off with a variation on the phrase 'I will seek/I have been granted approval for the project from the ethics committee of university X', or 'The research will be conducted in accordance with the ethical guidelines of [insert professional association]'. This is not an ethics statement. This is an announcement that you will play or have played by the rules. As Pimple (2002: 195) puts it, rules and ethics 'are generally intended to overlap, but sometimes following rules serves no moral value other than that of following rules'.

Thinking about research ethics requires you to step out of the 'I passed the review board' mindset of ethics as rules and start considering ethics from the perspective of good research design. It requires flipping the view from thinking that you are there for the ethics committee to thinking that the ethics committee is there for you. It requires a switch from an instrumental view where the ethics review provides you, your project and your institution with legitimacy and liability cover to a view where ethical pre-evaluation makes your research design stronger. (Cynics – and I often count myself as one – may point that liability cover is the one thing that institutions like universities and research institutes are interested in. If you passed the ethical review, but then mess up, they can throw their hands up and swing the ethics form under your nose: 'We agreed to *this*, not to *that*!'.) In what follows, I will discuss cases where ethics committees have obstructed rather than facilitated research projects. Whatever the shortcomings of ethics committees, their existence should prompt you to think about ethical questions early on in the research process. Ethical issues arise already at the idea stage, especially in field research, where some ideas are born in everyday interaction with people who only later become 'participants' (Denscombe et al, 2008). Recognising potential ethical issues in your research highlights the importance of good research design.

As you have learned by now, few research designs survive intact until the end of a project. Access to data and shortages of time, money or both often intervene. This is the reality of research. However, if you have done your ethical pre-evaluation well, there should be few reasons to amend it and no reasons to abandon ethical assessment completely. Slipping from ethical standards should not be part of these otherwise perfectly normal changes in research design. Not because it is your duty to follow rules of research conduct, but because good research is not only well executed but also fair and just.

Ethical research questions

Perhaps the most cherished principle of science is that it should be free. The story of science is – at least in its popular versions – a story of thinking freed from the fetters of 'superstition', religion and political control. Science is, in other words, autonomous. Hence, from a scientific point of view, scientists should be free to ask any questions in order to make the world more comprehensible.

Can there be, then, such a thing as an unethical research question? Creswell (2003: 63) suggests that the way that research problems and questions are identified and formulated should benefit participants, or at least not marginalise or disempower them. It is well known that research results can be used in ways that cannot be always anticipated. Cherry-picking scientific research for political and sensational purposes is an unfortunately common practice. But if that is out of your hands, then what *is* in your hands is how you frame your research question. A mini excursion into the sociology of deviance will hopefully illustrate my point.

When early sociologists started studying social problems, especially as they appeared in a rapidly industrialising and urbanising society, they asked 'What makes a deviant?'. They examined how street gang members became street gang members, marijuana users became marijuana users, but also how 'homosexuals' became homosexuals, and so on. The problem with this all was that many of the people they studied did not consider themselves deviant at all. The sociologists were framing their questions so that whomever they studied were deviant by definition. Whom they studied was in turn often based on a common-sense definition of what constitutes a deviant. If many people thought that marijuana users were deviant, then sociologists asked 'how do people become deviant marijuana users' (see Hjelm, 2014: chapter 3).

Later sociologists (especially Becker 1991 [1963]) questioned this framing and turned it on its head. What sociologists should be asking, Becker and others argued, is how society comes to define people and practices as deviant. Asking 'how do people become deviant' meant, then, that the object of interest was not the people engaging in particular practices (same-sex relationships, smoking marijuana) but rather how society (government, law enforcement, media) came to define those practices as deviant.

This is a long-winded way of saying that if you frame your question in a way that commits your participants to a category such as 'deviant', your research will likely contribute to their marginalisation. You are not giving them a 'fair hearing' no matter what the actual data say. This is a risk especially with politically charged topics.

The second potential issue regarding ethical research questions concerns deception. Deception occurs when you tell your participants that you are studying X, when in reality you are studying Y. Participants in the Tuskegee Experiment agreed to participate on the premise that they were guinea pigs for testing the effectiveness of medication, when in reality the question the research was interested in was the effect of untreated syphilis on the participants. If and when informed consent (see pp 111–113) is the basic building block of ethical research, a deceptive question makes informed consent impossible by default. Although there are arguments in support of 'deceptive experiments/research' in some contexts (for example, Herrera, 2001), they need extra ethical assessment.

Ethical literature review

The title of this section may raise some eyebrows. Most accounts of research ethics focus on the treatment of participants and being truthful in your analyses. What does reading and writing about previous literature on your topic have to do with the responsible conduct of research? Turns out, quite a bit. I think it is important that writers such as Pimple include *collegiality* as part of ethical research practice. Collegiality is manifested most clearly in the avoidance of plagiarism, discussed later in this chapter in the section on writing. It is also manifested in the literature review, in the form of giving credit where credit is due. Here I want to raise two issues that may impede a fair literature review: competing schools of thought and unacknowledged biases.

I have earlier touched upon disciplines and research fields as organising frameworks that affect what questions are considered relevant, what data is viewed as valuable, and what the approved methods are. However, within disciplines and research fields there are smaller units, which could be referred to as 'schools of thought'. These are clusters of scholars who work with similar epistemological, theoretical or methodological assumptions, distinguishing them from competing schools. To give an example from my own field: all sociologists of religion are more or less interested in how the status of religion changes as societies change. However, there are quite stark differences between those who argue that religion is diminishing ('the secularisation paradigm') and those who say that it is merely changing form. In International Relations, the distinction between 'realists' and 'constructivists' seems to be a well-established way of organising the discipline into schools of thought – as are attempts to bridge the two. These are, in my sense of the term, 'schools of thought'.

Rivalries between schools of thought may lead you to think that research from the other 'school' is not worth citing – or that citing it somehow endangers your loyalty to your school. It may also lead to shoddy or wilful misrepresentation. In the first case, which we might term 'passive-aggressive', rival research is not cited because doing so gives legitimacy to the competing approach. In the second case, the simply 'aggressive' one, the rival school is represented as a straw man, lacking any nuance in order to boost your own argument. This might be wilful misrepresentation, but the logic of academia also leads to situations where such straw men become received truth after having been repeated enough times. In these cases the misrepresentation is a product of shoddy analysis of the literature. If I had a cent every time someone in my field brushed off the secularisation paradigm with a sentence or two and without any real engagement with the actual ideas, I would be able to buy a decent pair of socks at least. Whether avoidance or misrepresentation, you are not giving a fair hearing to research relevant to your topic. Academic politics is unavoidable, but it is a virtue to try to rise above it. It may of course be that research from a rival school is not relevant to your particular study. However, it is good to recognise and acknowledge that you might have less noble reasons for ignoring some scholars in your field.

The second issue regarding collegiality in the literature review concerns unacknowledged biases. Gender and ethnic biases in academic citation practices are by now rather well established (for example, Greenwald and Schuh, 1994; Conklin and Singh, 2022), that is, men cite more men, and people tend to cite more scholars in their own ethnic group. Greenwald and Schuh (1994) argue that unacknowledged bias explains these imbalances better than the kind of wilful selective citation discussed earlier. Now the question is: should this matter? Is science not 'blind'? Whoever does the research should not matter, only whether the science is sound. Science may be disinterested, but you can always ask yourself: are there women or ethnic minority scholars (or transgender, queer, and so on) out there who might have something important to say about my topic? Is there a scientific reason why I am not citing them? This is of course especially relevant to researchers studying these communities and their histories. Again, unlike some voices determined to undermine academic research claim, the issue here is not that the authors' background should dictate who to cite, but rather that you are aware of possible unacknowledged biases in your own citation practices.

Ethical data and methods: informed consent

After the Tuskegee fiasco and other cases where people have been treated unethically by researchers, it is no surprise that much of the discourse around research ethics revolves around study participants (sometimes also referred to as 'subjects' and 'informants'). When humans are our data, what we collect as evidence and how we do it is pivotal to ethical and responsible conduct of research. This and the next section discuss two topics: informed consent and potential harm during the research process. Confidentiality is also part of protecting the research participants, but I will discuss that in the ethical writing section.

The term 'informed consent' is well summarised by Fujii:

> The term 'consent' presumes that the person's participation in the study is voluntary – that the person has not been pressured, coerced, or tricked into participating. The term 'informed' indicates that the person understands all the dimensions of the study and particularly those that involve him or her directly, including possible risks and benefits he or she may incur as a result of participating. Only by being fully informed, the logic goes, can a person give proper consent. (Fujii, 2012: 718)

The standard way of dealing with informed consent is to provide the participants with a *consent form* that covers two main areas: the research procedure and the participant's role in it; and the participant's rights.

The first should include an explanation of the purpose of the research (for example, 'this study examines what people think about the role religion plays in political decision-making'), and how the research will be carried out in practice (for example, 'a researcher will interview you in a location that you prefer, the interview lasts from 30 minutes to one hour'). The second should explain that the participant is completely free to participate and to withdraw from the research at any point, that the participant has a 'right to ask questions, obtain a copy of the results, and have their privacy respected' (Creswell, 2003: 65). The consent form should also outline how participating in the research benefits the participant.

Informed consent is the bedrock of ethical research involving human participants. The consent form is its bureaucratic manifestation. 'Real world conditions, however', Fujii (2012: 718) suggests, 'often call into question the way in which institutional rules conceive of this most basic task'. Both being 'informed' and getting 'consent' become complicated in everyday research contexts, in ways that the consent form cannot cover. The purpose of the discussion here is to sensitise you to some potential issues, but every research needs to be assessed individually. There are (at least) three such potential issues: when participants do not have full capacity of being informed; when participants do not know they are being studied; and when the participants are informed, but power imbalances between participant and researcher make free consent difficult to give.

Examples of the first type include people with learning disabilities (Cook and Inglis, 2009), children, young adults and school pupils (for example, Sherwood and Parsons, 2021; Maduka-Okafor et al, 2022), and people in nursing homes and hospitals, for example. The issues here pertain to inability to process what the research is about and how the generated data will be used. That is why in most countries there are procedures in place for studying such groups. In the case of schoolchildren, for example, consent needs to be sought also from parents, teachers and possibly the educational bureaucracy. The age limit requirement for parental consent may vary. In some cases, it is the legal age of adulthood, whereas in others it may be lower. Again, depending on context, consent may be required from carers in the case of elderly people.

Second, participants also cannot give informed consent when they do not know they are being studied. Feminist sociologist Meera Seghal joined a Hindu Nationalist women's association in order to study 'why and how women became involved in India's violent right-wing nationalist movement' (Seghal, 2009: 325). Being open about her researcher role and background would have made research impossible in the fiercely anti-feminist movement, so she signed on as a potential recruit. This approach allowed for an 'inside view' that would not have been possible otherwise. In general, however, this type of 'covert' research is disapproved of in modern social science. The discussion is, however, ongoing and there may be cases where a covert approach is warranted (Calvey, 2008; Spicker, 2011). The Economic and Social Research Council of Britain, for example, outlines the following principles regarding covert research:

> Covert research may be undertaken when it may provide unique forms of evidence or where overt observation might alter the phenomenon being studied. The broad principle should be that covert research must not be undertaken lightly or routinely. It is only justified if important issues are being addressed and if matters of social significance which cannot be uncovered in other ways are likely to be discovered. (Cited in Calvey, 2008: 907)

There might be good academic reasons for doing covert research, but these may not woo your ethics committee. You will probably have more trouble with your covert research design passing the committee review than with an 'overt' approach. If you are doing research for a degree, always discuss with your supervisor first before planning a covert field research design.

Covert research is not, however, mainly an issue of traditional field research nowadays. Increased use of social media as research data prompts similar questions. Clearly, you should not quote a personal Facebook story shared with friends only. But is it ethical to use a publicly posted social media post for research purposes? For a handful of people, you could possibly write to them and ask for consent, but what about when your data comprises hundreds or thousands of social media posts? Research ethics is still catching up with developments in social media and best practices vary. That is why I am not providing references here – they might be dated by the time the ink dries. The important thing is to be aware that social media content is not unproblematic data in the same sense as newspaper articles are.

Finally, there are cases where the participants are properly informed, but cannot give fully free consent because of their circumstances. Prisoners are one such example (Robinson, 2020). Pressure from prison administrators or a perception of the researcher as a representative of law enforcement distorts the basic idea of 'consent'. Young children are doubly affected, having perhaps insufficient understanding of the purpose of the research and not being in a position to say no. Both are examples of a power imbalance, where the participants may feel pressured to comply with the researcher's requests. Recognising the potential pitfalls regarding both the 'informed' and 'consent' parts of 'informed consent' enables you to design research that does not only pass the ethics review, but makes participation a better experience for everyone involved.

Ethical data and methods: minimising harm and maximising benefits

The second issue regarding data and methods that I want to discuss here is risk of harm to participants and researchers. The bottom line, of course, is that you should carefully consider using any type of data that may subject participants to physical danger or psychological stress, or refrain from using methods that subject participants to such risks. Everyone working in academia would agree to this idea in principle.

The principle becomes 'messy' with practice, however. How do you measure harm in social science and humanities research? It is quite clear that the unwitting participants in the Tuskegee Experiment were singularly harmed by the research, in many cases with fatal consequences. Participants in Stanley Milgram's study on obedience (see Chapter 1) were subjected to stress and potential trauma – especially the children on whom Milgram's experiment was replicated by later researchers. Similarly, Philip Zimbardo's Stanford Prison Experiment, which put participants in roles of prisoner and prison guard, certainly caused stress, even physical harm, after the guards took their jobs rather seriously. Most egregiously, it later transpired that the abusive treatment of the 'prisoners' was not due to the participants assuming the role too wholeheartedly, but that the experimenters had instructed the 'guards' to behave in abusive ways (Le Texier, 2019).

These famous cases are outliers, however. In the field, the balance of harm and benefit may be more difficult to weigh. Studying vulnerable populations like refugees, rape victims, or survivors of war and disaster may trigger emotional distress in participants who relive the horrors of their ordeal. Yet, at the same time, they may be eager to have their story heard. Should you, as a responsible researcher, pull the plug in order to save the participants from stress, while at the same time robbing them of the opportunity to tell their story and by doing so perhaps help improve the situation of future people with similar experiences? The same problem applies to cases where the research interview, for example, may be completely uneventful, but its aftermath is not. Participants involved in crime may be subjected to physical and psychological threats simply by virtue of speaking to a researcher. Confidentiality does nothing to alleviate the stress if participation itself – regardless of the researcher's results and interpretations – is seen as threatening by the participant's reference group, whether a street gang or a family. These are some of the most challenging situations in field research and there are few blueprints to follow. Needless to say, the point of this chapter is not to even try to provide any such. 'Lived' ethics is hard, and perhaps the best piece of advice is to acquaint yourself with as many studies as possible where researchers have faced such circumstances in order to learn how others have navigated the ethical quicksand.

Protection of participants – the researched – is clearly a priority for any ethical evaluation of research. What about the researchers, then? I once sat in a committee evaluating research proposals for a big national funding body of country X. I recommended a high score for a project that proposed to study youth street gangs (I am deliberately leaving the project description vague). I thought that the plan was bold and would have generated interesting and important new knowledge that had potential to have beneficial social impacts as well. My fellow reviewers agreed, but one of them pointed out that the project proposed to use MA students as research assistants to do the fieldwork among the gang youth. This had somehow slipped my attention (and my other colleagues' attention as well), but this small detail required a re-evaluation of the whole project: sending inexperienced researchers – even if they were trained well – to a potentially hazardous field was a clear miscalculation by the project leaders. Remember that, as with the researched, the safety and well-being of researchers includes not only safety from physical harm but also minimising stress (see Kaplan et al, 2023). Witnessing distressing situations is an obvious case, but fieldwork may also come back to haunt you in the form of pressure from the authorities to share information on your participants – for example, when they are suspected of illegal actions. I won't divulge what happened to the project proposal in order to avoid possible recognition – the ethical thing to do – but I have ever since thought of this incident as a prime example of the maxim I started the chapter with: you may have the perfect research design, elements aligned and all, but none of it matters if your research is not ethically sound. In this case, the project overlooked or at least underestimated the safety concerns of the people without whom the data for the project would not be generated. This was clearly an ethical flaw, but it was also a problem with the research design: is a project feasible if it requires, first, risking researcher safety and well-being, and, second, by so doing compromises the quality of the data if the researchers are not able to collect it because of the risks to safety?

In terms of participant and researcher protection, research designs should operate on the principle of minimising harm and maximising benefits (for example, Cassell, 1980). The latter refers not only to the benefits the researcher will accrue from the research, but potential benefits to the community studied (see the next section). It is, of course, entirely different even to think about potential harm and benefits in social research than it is for medical research. A drug may have adverse effects on the participants of an experimental study, but these harms may be balanced by the larger benefit of an effective treatment. Calculating such a utilitarian balance is, however, impossible in social research (Cassell, 1980: 31). This applies especially to considerations of 'harm' to organisations and broader units, such as societies or cultures. What if your research shows, say, that building a dam has adverse effects on indigenous people living in the affected area? The results will inevitably harm the company that profits from building the dam. While financial loss to a big corporation may not weigh much against the well-being of humans, what about the probable mass layoffs of poor workers resulting from loss of revenue? When we move beyond the individual, 'harm' acquires many meanings, not solvable by formalised ethics statements (Schrag, 2011: 126). Again, awareness of the difficult balance between harm and benefits is more important here than attempting to provide hard and fast rules. Indeed, in a later section I will also discuss how ethical considerations may in some cases do more harm than good.

Ethical contribution

In the next chapter, I will discuss the purpose of your research from the perspective of the contribution it makes to science and to society more broadly. Here I will discuss the ethical aspects of that contribution. Following Pimple's scheme, this pertains particularly to research as a truthful account of the world (is it true?) and to the potential for research to contribute to the 'common good' (is it wise?).

Giving a truthful account of the world is, of course, at the heart of big philosophical questions about science. They are important questions, but this is not the place for that discussion. Truthfulness becomes an ethical concern when you tamper with the evidence you have about the world in order to make it fit a preconceived idea. I will not go into detail here, but this can mean either making up (fabrication) or 'fixing up' (falsification) data (Pimple, 2002: 192). Critics sometimes point to 'critical' (feminist, Marxist, critical race theory, queer, and so on) approaches as the main culprit. These, supposedly, sacrifice objectivity for activism. However, this makes sense only if the scientific process is considered to involve no interpretation of data. Besides, disciplines most wedded to the idea of 'hard science', including a focus on quantitative methods, suffer from problems of falsification, but for different reasons. In quantitative research, statistically significant findings have more weight – and thus a much better chance of being published in major journals – than null findings (for example, Franco et al, 2014). It is impossible to assess the extent of deliberate falsification, but certainly the 'replication crisis', where results from repeated analyses do not support earlier results (see Chapter 8), seems to suggest that data have been manipulated in order to either fit established ideas, or simply in order to get published. Fabrication and falsification are against the very mission of scientific research, but also an affront to collegiality, because they erode scientific standards and trust in science more broadly.

As I will discuss in the next chapter, despite much pressure from governments (via funding agencies), not all research needs to be 'applied' research, in the sense that it should have direct commercial or social applications. Nevertheless, it is never a bad idea to think about whether and how your research might 'improve the human condition' (Pimple, 2002: 193). For example, when I was doing my field research in London's East End, my guiding idea was to 'give back to the community' whatever insights I may have gained from the research. I did not have any template solutions for the racism, police harassment or gang violence the youth had experienced. However, I thought that if they were given a chance to see themselves through the eyes of someone else, it might enable and inspire them to pay attention to aspects of their community they had not noticed before. (As it happened, for various reasons, I failed to do this properly, even though the plan for the project included a short film about the research.) Obviously, 'giving back to the community' may not sound appealing if you are studying violent White supremacists, but you should at least factor in that they will likely be interested in your results. Your 'application' need not be a blueprint for social change. The ethics of social engagement can also refer to how through your research you can educate people to see the world in new ways. Pimple (2002) also suggests that in the face of multiple options for doing research (different topics, different approaches) with limited time and resources, it is an ethical question to ask which option is 'wisest' from the perspective of the common good.

Ethical writing

While some of the issues discussed in this chapter are specifically relevant to ethnographic field research, the ethics of academic writing is something that touches every scholar. While you are doing the research, the analysis and interpretations are in your head and in your private notebooks (unless you are doing collaborative research, of course). Writing them up and letting them go 'into the world' adds a further layer of ethical considerations to your work. I will discuss three such considerations in this section: confidentiality and fair use; plagiarism; and authorship and conflict of interest. The first has to do with protection of participants, the second with collegiality, and the third with scientific and institutional integrity.

First, assuming that you have treated your informants so that they know what they are getting into and made sure they do not experience any untoward stress, you still have more obligations towards them once you start writing up your research. Unless you are researching public personae or have made it clear from the beginning that you are asking people to participate because of who they are (thus appearing under their own names), then your information sheet should already talk about anonymity and how individual participants (or organisations) will be represented without identifying information. Confidentiality, in this sense, refers to the situation where participants have divulged information to you with an understanding that it will be dealt with anonymously. Of course, it also includes the usual sense that they may have told you something they do not want discussed in your research.

Although my focus so far has been on fieldwork, protecting participants through anonymity is not just a matter for contemporary research. Writing up research brings up ethical issues in historical analysis as well. The dead will not mind what you are saying about them, but some living people might. Say you are studying crime in history and the archival research uncovers a connection to a well-known family, for example. I would assume that few people would be bothered about a relative convicted of witchcraft 15 generations away. But what about a great-grandfather convicted of rape? How do you balance between letting the world know and not causing harm to the living relatives? Biographers, especially, wrestle with this question (see Oakley, 2010). In some cases, legal issues may also be involved. If you think this might be the case, seek qualified advice before publishing your findings (publishers also demand that no potentially libellous material is included).

In addition to confidentiality, when writing about your participants you have the responsibility to truthfully convey what they have answered in a survey questionnaire, what they have told you, or what you have observed them doing. This means your quotations have to be accurate and not taken out of context. It means that you cannot represent an extraordinary event or practice in a community as commonplace. When in doubt, it is acceptable, even preferable, to write yourself into the narrative: let the reader know the reasons why you prefer one interpretation to others. This is the classic meaning of 'reflexivity' as discussed by anthropologists and others (for example, Clifford and Marcus, 1986).

Second, moving from protection of participants to collegiality, plagiarism is an ethical offence in the sense that it is an offence against the whole scientific community (Pimple, 2002: 196). In passing someone else's findings and words as your own, you are claiming authorship where you in reality have none. Of all the topics discussed in this chapter, plagiarism is thankfully quite well covered already in undergraduate studies. It is not an exclusively undergraduate phenomenon, however. With increasing competition and measurement comes the temptation to cut corners in research as well. Plagiarism is an embarrassing infraction, since we really should know better. I will not say more about this, partly because the whole question in is flux after the emergence of commercial artificial intelligence. I will say that if in doubt, please refer to the many online guides provided by universities.

Third, writing brings up issues of authorship and conflict of interest. If you are writing a dissertation or thesis, the authorship question is clear. However, if your supervisor suggests writing an article based on your work, and then inserts himself as first author, you have an ethical issue at hand. The supervisor–supervisee relationship is especially tricky, because there is a power imbalance. Good academic practice suggests that papers based on essays, dissertations or theses should always list the student as first author – although there is disciplinary variation on this. Fair supervisors do not demand first authorship unless their contribution changes the original argument. So-called 'honorary authorship' (where a person is attributed authorship based on their status as senior researcher or head of department, without any involvement in the research) is an unethical practice and should be avoided. Authorship attribution is rarely easy, even in a co-authorship between equal authors. The best advice is to start the conversation about authorship early on in any collaboration.

Finally, conflict of interest (COI) refers to situations where an organisation or business where you have a stake may benefit from your research. In the narrow sense, this refers to financial stakes in corporations, which is how most universities understand COI in their designated policies. This narrow sense is most relevant in areas such as engineering, medicine and bioscience. In social science and humanities research, COI is understood much more broadly, also meaning that it becomes the purview of ethical research conduct, not just narrow financial regulation. Participatory action research, for example, starts with the premise that the research will promote change (McIntyre, 2008). The researcher has a 'stake' in the situation by definition. Employing research participants not as passive sources, but active constructors of knowledge, participatory action research tries to give voice to members of the studied communities and groups and thus affect change. Debates continue about whether research should be disinterested or 'activist'. This is a question about the nature of (social) science. In terms of ethics, the question is not so much about researchers wearing their interests on their sleeve, but rather about researchers who do not openly do so. Everyone has interests, but the unexamined ones are the most problematic. As you remember, data do not speak for themselves. Therefore, readers need to have all the relevant information about possible conflicts of interest in order to assess the validity of your arguments.

The dark side of institutionalised research ethics

The purpose of this chapter is not academic polemics. Yet, as I have intimated earlier, institutionalised ethics procedures are not an unambiguous good for social scientific and humanities research. Consider the letter Canadian sociologist Susan J. Palmer received from her university's ethics committee (Research Ethics Board, REB) after she had submitted an application to study a secretive right-wing Christian Militia movement (and had already made contact with them):

> Cease and desist all research activity. Surrender all your records pertaining to this study. You may not retain any copies of the records in this study. These shall be promptly surrendered to the office of the REB to the attention of the REB Chair. Provide the REB with a list of all the sites, institutions and individuals to which the research findings have been distributed. Include in this list contact information for these parties. (Palmer, 2017: 241)

Why would an ethics committee send a letter like this to a professional researcher with 30 years of experience studying these kinds of movements? Before going into the details of Palmer's case, I will suggest two answers: first, ethics committees model all research according to medical and 'hard science' human research, where the participants are not in a position to negotiate with the researchers. The idea that the research encounter is a human encounter involving negotiations of trust and 'common sense' does not fit the medical model, where trust is based on a formal agreement. Second, universities are increasingly concerned with risk assessment and fear of litigation, and the ethics committee becomes an instrument of reputation control, rather than a body that promotes the goals and best practices of scientific inquiry (van den Hoonaard, 2011: 4).

There are several consequences to the increased power of ethics committees, which some critics call the 'ethics police' or even 'new priests' (Palmer, 2017: 255). First, van den Hoonaard (2011: 248) argues that 'there is no question that participant observation as a method is dying and others that fall outside the circumscribed ethics regime are taking it over'. He backs this up with Canadian data: in 1995, 40 per cent of MA dissertations ('theses' in Canada) involved fieldwork. In 2004, the figure was 5 per cent. In 1996, 31 per cent of MA dissertations involved research participants. In 2004, the figure was 8 per cent. I do not have data to track trends in other countries, but the indication here is clear. Since fieldwork methods (observation, interviews) are the most 'intrusive' of social research methods, they bear the brunt of scrutiny by ethics committees.

Second, paradoxically, ethics considerations may in fact harm vulnerable people. As van den Hoonaard (2011: 7) notes, the broader cultural climate tends to favour a view of research participants as 'fragile and needing protection'. However, by avoiding research with vulnerable populations or on sensitive topics, researchers are robbing the participants of agency and voice (see Schrag, 2011: 127). As the scholars Palmer (2017) interviewed attest, many simply give up on projects that require massive effort to convince a by default reluctant ethics committee.

Finally, and dovetailing the previous, when researchers evacuate a field of study (specifically, ethnographic/qualitative fieldwork), others will fill the vacuum. Journalists and government agencies do not adhere to similar ethical guidelines (Palmer, 2017). While there are many good investigative journalists, media logic dictates that the framing of news is by default negative. News organisations in search of ever more clicks tend to go for the sensational rather than the balanced. Government agencies, in turn, have their own agendas, where principles of scientific method matter little.

This may all sound pessimistic, but as Palmer (2017) discusses, there are strategies that enable living with a rigid ethics regime. As mentioned, many abandon projects, but many resist the ethics committees' overreach. Palmer herself took it a step further with her 'cease and desist' order from the ethics committee. She was able to find a higher authority that regulates ethics standards across Canada and made a formal complaint. The higher authority found that 'several of my institution's procedures were "not in place"', with the consequence that 'an overhaul of the research ethics board and the research office ensued' (Palmer, 2017: 254–255). As Palmer says, this was possible because as a senior scholar she would not be intimidated by the ethics committee. It would be too much to ask from a degree student to rise up against a hierarchical and secretive ethics committee, so many understandably forgo their research designs, leading to the 'pauperisation' of social research, as van den Hoonaard (2011: 19) puts it. I think it is important that we, as scholars, do not abandon important research questions and unique research methods in fear of the ethics review. Ethical research is not the same as research approved by the ethics committee.

To sum up, the point of this discussion is that it is important to cultivate a healthy scepticism towards ethics committees while adhering to rigorous ethical standards. As the cases discussed attest, sometimes the function of ethics committees is not to promote ethical research but to act as a liability insurance for the university. We do not even know the full scope of the effects that this has had on social research, but few would claim that it has been entirely positive. In practice, there may be little you can do about the ethics committee process. I like to think that most ethics committees are doing sincere work, even when they are in general hampered by ignorance of social scientific and humanities research and a focus on liability. Knowing this should make you better prepared for the process.

Conclusion

Research ethics cuts through your whole research design – or, to follow the visual image of Figure 1.1, your research design is immersed in ethical considerations. The importance of ethics is revealed nowhere better than in the fact that if it turns out that you have mistreated your participants, fabricated evidence or plagiarised, the value of your work becomes zero. Why spend years on a project only to lose all respect among your peers? 'Lived' ethics, especially in field research that requires intrusion into the lives of people, is hard because you will not be able to anticipate all the situations where ethical issues may arise in your research project. Research committees are in place to assess whether you have done as much as you can in advance to think about key issues, such as informed consent and harm and benefits, but many ethics committees have turned out to have a limited understanding of social science and humanities research. Partly for that reason, it is important that your 'ethics statement' does not consist of a single sentence saying that you have, or will look for, research committee approval for your project. Conforming to rules and regulations is not the same as doing ethical research. Although institutionalisation has turned research ethics into a chore, a solid ethical foundation means a stronger research design. There are few rulebooks to follow, but the recognition and acknowledgement of responsible research conduct as a key part of research design makes for a good start.

8

Contribution

The research design is aligned and justified, the data has been collected and analysed in a methodologically robust and ethical manner, and the analysis is in conversation with theory. Now it is just a matter of putting it all down on paper or polishing earlier rough drafts.

Not quite.

Results might be interesting in themselves, but the problem of 'results' is that readers can take away all kinds of things from them. Results do not speak for themselves, so it is a crucial part of the scholarly endeavour to be able to show the reader what *you* think these results *mean*. The final step in any academic work is to recognise, and to do so explicitly, the contribution the research is making. This is where you re-join the conversation you started in the literature review and in the formulation of the research question. This is where you say why the research matters.

I said the 'final' step, but there are very good reasons why this chapter could have been in the beginning. Journal editors especially will tell you that one of the main reasons they reject submitted manuscripts is that the submissions lack an explicit recognition of the significance of the results. This is commonly referred to as a 'purpose statement' in academic parlance. A more colloquial term is the 'so what?' question. To repeat: why does your research matter? What is its contribution? In this chapter I will show examples of informative purpose statements.

This is not an easy question. With experience, answering it becomes easier as the research builds on previous research and your place within the broader disciplinary conversation becomes more apparent. With experience, the so-what-question can be anticipated already before the research is done. However, for those embarking on their first projects, or tackling a completely new topic, the purpose may only crystallise during the research process and after the results are in. That is why I take up the topic at this point.

One possible reason why the purpose statement is less well known and less well understood by inexperienced researchers is that few university systems expect Bachelor or Master level dissertations to make a scholarly impact. Hence, the stressful bit about the contribution can be left out. This is unfortunate, as thinking about the significance of research should be a key element of researcher training. Even if the significance of the study is limited to the author's increased understanding of the topic, it is important from early on to practice recognising how your research contributes to the academic discussion and to learn how to express it. This is a crucial part of the promise you make in the beginning of a study.

In this chapter, I will discuss how researchers make claims – or more precisely, *contribution claims* – about the meaning and significance of results. These claims can be categorised in several ways, namely, empirical, interpretative, theoretical, methodological, and practical claims. A single piece of research can make several types of claims, so these categories should be considered as complementary. Importantly, I will also talk about how claims can be overstretched. Every solid research design needs to take into account the so-what-question. But it is important to keep a close eye on whether the evidence provided warrants the claims you make.

Empirical claims

Most research proceeds from the observation that it fills a gap in current knowledge. Indeed, research funding is often contingent on researchers being able to express clearly how the proposed study will fill these gaps. With the exception of philosophy and disciplinary theory-building, most of these identified gaps are empirical. In this case, the main research elements in consideration are data and research questions. Therefore, to make empirical claims, researchers ask new questions and identify untapped sources of data, or ask old questions using new data. I will discuss each in turn.

To take an example: 'the other' is a now-standard social scientific term. It refers to the ways in which certain groups are labelled as problematic and threatening. These groups are often minorities, such as national, racial or ethnic minorities or LGBTQIA+ people. Jews in Nazi Germany are the prime example of how this kind of 'othering' dehumanises whole groups of people and consequently legitimates their violent destruction. Academic attention has been increasingly directed at the role the modern media plays in such othering, starting with Edward Said's (1981) classic *Covering Islam*, where the celebrated cultural critic analyses how Western media talk about Islam and Muslims.

This is also the starting point of Ozan Aşık's (2022) analysis of Turkish media images of Kurds, a minority 'other', who are seen as an internal threat to Turkey's national identity and security. There are plenty of analyses of media images and discourses, but far less attention has been paid to the question of why and how journalists come up with these othering images and discourses. In a succinct statement worthy of emulation, Aşık outlines how his study contributes to the field: 'To fill this gap in the literature, I focus in this article on newsroom dynamics, and I explore the world of content-makers – news practitioners – to understand how Turkish journalists imagine, categorize, and articulate Kurds – a significant national 'Other' of Turkey – in the production of news' (Aşık, 2021: np).

There are two things going on here. First, the author asks a new question, which is not about the news itself, as in much of the previous research on the broader topic, but the production of this news, or the practice of journalism. Granted, this is not the first time ever this question has been asked, but it is the first time in this national context and regarding this particular topic. One aspect of the gap is, then, the previously unasked question. Second, the author generates his own data in order to answer the question. He observes and interviews journalists at two television channels, thus creating data that would not have existed without this particular research. The combination of a novel question and data warrants the claim made at the end of the study: 'This ethnographic study primarily argues that the way in which politics influence news production is more complex, shifting, and non-linear than recognized by past studies' (Aşık, 2022: np). Note that the author is not simply summarising results of this particular fieldwork but indicates the broader impact of this one case to the study of political journalism as a whole. All case studies are specific and context-dependent but can – and should – point to larger issues in academic disciplines and fields of research.

Although having a fresh question and a new set of data is the gold standard of empirical social science and humanities research, claiming novelty can be a dangerous business. As discussed in previous chapters, the likelihood that you have covered *everything* in your literature review is tiny. Your supervisor(s) and/or peer reviewer(s) should help you avoid the most glaring omissions. There is one type of research, however, that does not even claim to ask new questions, but rather on purpose asks the same question again. The purpose of this kind of research is to check the validity of earlier research either by using the same data or by using new data to check whether generalisations made from earlier data hold up with comparable but different data. In narrower terms, this is sometimes referred to as replication research, which is especially pertinent to disciplines employing quantitative methods. In psychology, especially, there has been much talk about a 'replication crisis' when it has turned out that replication of quantitative studies has not unambiguously supported some long-cherished concepts or ideas in the discipline. More specifically, critical analyses have unearthed straightforward scientific fraud, falsification of data, inflation of results and inability to replicate 'statistically significant findings … in new data and in new laboratories' (Shrout and Rodgers, 2018) The relevant point here, though, is that if you are doing this kind of research, its purpose and contribution to the field are quite clear from the beginning and it is unnecessary to expand on that at this point.

Interpretative claims

Now, consider the field of biblical studies. Since the discovery of the Dead Sea Scrolls in a cave in Palestine in 1946, there have been few major discoveries of manuscripts of biblical texts. Biblical scholars working in the original languages work, then, with a rather limited number of primary sources, and yet they constantly produce new research. The same applies more or less to ancient history in general, for that matter. So, the empirical contribution in these cases is not about the novelty of the data, but the new questions posed, and the new angles taken on familiar material.

Many (inter)disciplinary perspectives – such as gender studies – have been born from an incentive to provide new angles to familiar issues. To stick to my example, much of biblical studies and ancient history has so far asked only questions pertaining to the lives of men. What would the ancient world look like if we read the same historical and archaeological sources with the lives of women in mind? Sure, many if not most documents remaining from that period were written by men for other men, and explicitly concern men, but there are plenty of clues if one knows where to look and, most importantly, cares to find out about a so far underrepresented perspective.

Indeed, while biblical studies somewhat obviously implies an interest in religion, the Bible (both Old and New Testaments) has been mined for clues about many other things as well. Biblical scholars have discussed, for example, women's roles in the household economy among the Hebrew tribes using innovative combinations of close reading of Old Testament/Hebrew Bible texts and comparative ethnographic and archaeological data from all the world's cultures. Women's roles in patriarchal societies such as that of the Hebrew tribes has been often limited to childbearing, but reconsidering some biblical passages suggests that they also played key roles in textile production, for example, thus putting women in more significant economic positions than previously thought (Ackerman, 2016: np).

Further, new interpretations arise from previously unexamined combinations of perspectives and positions. 'Intersectionality' became politicised after conservatives and the far right started using it as shorthand for everything that is wrong with the world, in their view. In its scholarly sense, however, the concept highlights the fact that although feminism challenged male dominance, early manifestations of feminism took White women's experiences as the norm. The intersection of sexism *and* racism makes the experiences of Black women different, however. And the experiences of Black lesbian women are further different from both of these. The point of intersectionality is to show how these different positionalities produce different experiences and that 'single-axis' analyses exclude these experiences (Cooper, 2015: np). This brief summary barely scratches the surface of the complex debates around the concept, but for my purposes, it again points to how a new angle enables new interpretations on issues thought as of familiar. Indeed, intersectionality disturbs 'familiarity' itself by challenging taken for granted views on different topics.

In terms of research contribution, then, interpretive claims do not offer new evidence as such, but rather urge readers to rethink how to understand the existing evidence from a novel perspective. This can of course be – and often is – combined with new data to strengthen an argument even more, but even familiar data can yield new insights when seen through new lenses. This is why the myriad critical approaches to the social sciences – gender, race, decolonial, queer and intersectional – are so important: they literally make visible issues that are as old as humans, but which have been marginalised by mainstream approaches, which privilege the Western White male experience.

Theoretical claims

As discussed in Chapter 6, there are different ways of approaching theory. If you start from a theory-testing perspective, then a theoretical contribution is built into the research design. Theory-building, which may be the main purpose of a study, or happen as a side-product of an empirical project, will obviously contribute to the theoretical understanding of the phenomenon under study. In both cases, theoretical claims broaden the empirical 'conversation' you are engaging in. In my view, this is an opportunity that should not be missed, even if you were not initially planning to engage in theoretical discussion. Any new concept or refinement of theory that enables a better understanding of the world, no matter how minutely, is a worthy thing to aspire to.

Sometimes making theoretical claims is important also in a more instrumental sense. For example, I work a lot with Finnish data, which, cruel as it is, simply is not very interesting for international readers. Should I want to publish in the top three American sociological journals, my chances would be extremely slim indeed, with 60 per cent of the published empirical articles using US data and only 9 per cent data from Western Europe (Gruijters, 2021). However, should the main purpose of my article be theory development, then the situation might be different (although not necessarily in the case of the top three American sociological journals). I could sneak in my peripheral data in order to demonstrate a theoretical point and offer it for testing and application in other social contexts.

This is a special case, of course, and for dissertation and thesis writers, the significance of theoretical contributions depends on multiple factors beyond the research design, including disciplinary traditions and your supervisor's preferences. The important point here is, however, that theoretical contributions should not be left to those specialising in theory. Indeed, theory development without empirical output becomes unlikely. You do not need to consider yourself a 'theorist' to make theoretical claims.

While broadening the conversation from empirical cases to theoretical and conceptual contributions is in principle commendable, there is another side to the issue. As Michael Billig (2013) argues, academia nowadays prioritises competition, which in turn incentivises a lot of conceptual development as a form of scholarly self-promotion. Theory-building – in the style of *A General Theory of Crime* (Gottfredson and Hirschi, 1990) – is in many disciplines considered the highest prestige endeavour. Making a name as the progenitor of 'deindividuation', 'mediatisation', 'McDonaldisation' or any concepts that catches the imagination of your fellow scholars is the next best thing. For Billig, the price of this development is the unnecessary complexity of academic language and the narrowing down of the potential audiences when each subdiscipline operates its own vocabulary. As he puts it: 'what I contest, however, is the assumption that, in order to have original thoughts, you must inevitably create new nouns – or correspondingly, if you create new words, you are being original' (Billig, 2013: 10). Conceptual development may enable new approaches and understandings of empirical issues, but it should not be considered an end in itself.

Methodological claims

One common contribution claim concerns methodology. Methodological claims usually take the form of arguing that a particular methodological approach yielded interesting new results. A discourse analytical close reading of historical documents, for example, may say something new about the actors or ideas of a particular time, compared to reading that is more cursory. You are making a methodological contribution when you make recommendations regarding the use of a method that apply in the discipline or field more broadly. Thus, concentrating on a particular linguistic form would be appropriate for *any kind* of discourse analysis, even if originally applied to a historical text.

Methodological claims like these are easier to demonstrate – and perhaps more common – in quantitative approaches. Indeed, many statistical innovations carry their inventors' names (Bartlett's test, Cronbach's alpha, Friedman test, and so on), but a methodological contribution can go unnamed and still have a big impact on a field. For example, there has been a long-established tug-of-war between sociologists who claim that religious pluralism undermines religious participation and sociologists who claim, to the contrary, that the more religious 'supply' there is, the more vibrant the participation in religious services. Both positions are well established and have their supporters in the field. The standard way of assessing this relationship has been to correlate some measure of religious participation and indices of pluralism, often in a national setting. Any result yielding a nonzero correlation either way has been interpreted as a substantive effect of pluralism on religious participation. However, after more than a decade of disagreement over mixed results, Voas et al (2002: 212) dropped a bomb by arguing that 'almost all of these findings (both positive and negative) should be abandoned'. They demonstrated that the correlation tests produce nonzero effects because of previously overlooked mathematical reasons. These taken into account, the causal power of pluralism on religious participation whittles away. As another scholar assessed the impact of Voas et al's discovery almost 20 years later: 'This article had an effect similar to when parents come home unexpectedly early to find their teenage children having a party in their house: everything ended in general embarrassment, and scholars had to go back to the drawing board' (Stolz, 2020: 295). This genuine methodological contribution had a massive impact on one small, but vibrant field of study.

On the qualitative side of methodological innovation, one that stands out is the development of 'virtual ethnography' (Hine, 2000) or 'netnography' (Kozinets, 2010). With the explosion of internet use since the late 1990s, there was a growing pressure to figure out how to study the new phenomenon. Asking people about their internet use is fine, but what they actually do online is often different, like the difference between interviewing and observation in face-to-face research. And so was virtual ethnography, the observation of people online, born. One early pioneer, Christine Hine (2000), describes how she observed online the unfolding of the case of Louise Woodward, where the 19-year-old British au pair stood accused of the murder of the infant child she was taking care of in Massachusetts. Pre-internet, Hine would have been standing in front of the courthouse, observing and talking to the people often congregating there during famous cases. The difference was that she was sitting on her screen and following changes on websites and (back then) newsrooms in real time. Her point was to show not only how people reacted to the case or to the media reports of the case, but how interacting virtually shaped people's identities, their sense of authenticity, and different criteria for knowledge (Hine, 2000). Developing internet research methodology has since become a major endeavour in the social sciences and humanities, with regular new methodological contributions.

Methodological claims are sometimes positive side effects of substantive research. If you think you have demonstrated that a particular methodological approach may potentially change the way a topic is treated in the discipline, then that is a methodological contribution. Of course, developing methodology is a worthy endeavour in itself. However, dissertation and thesis writers especially should find out early on from their supervisors if a methodological contribution is a legitimate enough purpose for work in their field.

Practical claims

Karl Marx wrote many things that live on as slogans 150 years after his death. For academics, none has been evoked as often as 'philosophers have hitherto only *interpreted* the world in various ways; the point is to *change* it' (Marx, 1845; emphases in the original). Many scholars have taken heed – although this does not make anyone a Marxist – of Marx's words and see social change and social justice as an integral part of academic research. In other words, the purpose of research is not only analysis, but also applying that analysis in practice.

For the 'hard' sciences, this is standard practice. Many developments in biochemistry, for example, are aimed at having a public impact in the form of improved medicine. Indeed, commercial companies fund this kind of research in order to manufacture these medicines. However, when the research is about society or culture, 'impact' becomes a political issue by default. Few people have qualms about research that results in developing drugs to cure diseases. But when scholarship points to racial inequality, many are up in arms about 'politicised research'.

Research which aims at changing society – public scholarship – has been criticised internally (by scholars) for polluting 'pure' science, and externally (by politicians) for sneaking political agendas into often publicly funded and thus supposedly politically neutral institutions. Recent years have witnessed a massive backlash against such 'activist' research not only in authoritarian countries, but also in countries designated as liberal democracies, such as the United States, France and Denmark. At the same time, and paradoxically, there is increasing political pressure to make all scholarly research 'applicable'. There is, then, disagreement on which kind of applicable research is politically acceptable, but increasingly *all* research is expected to have an impact beyond academia.

I find it useful to think of practical contribution claims in two senses (here I am following the terminology of Michael Burawoy, who coined the term 'public sociology'): the traditional and the organic (Burawoy, 2007: 28). First, the traditional way scholarship can make a practical contribution is in the form of press releases, op-eds, popular books, overall in the form of writing. You put the knowledge out there and hope someone notices. You can promote your writing but have little control over its actual impact. Often, these kinds of traditional contributions take the form of policy recommendations, either explicitly or implicitly. Some social science disciplines such as social policy research and much of economics are, like the 'hard' sciences, expected by default to make such recommendations. These can be directly in the form of reports commissioned by governments, local authorities, and so on.

Economist Christian Dustmann, for example, has studied how cutting refugees' welfare benefits impacts their labour market integration. Using data from Denmark, where the political will has been to cut welfare benefits to refugees in order to incentivise them to take up jobs, Dustmann shows that the actual effect is quite the contrary. While there was a short-term increase in employment, this was offset by refugee men and women increasingly resorting to crime just to survive and weakened educational attainment among refugee youth. Dustmann concludes: 'Our study does show that there are indeed employment effects, but that the policy has also had negative social and financial consequences that policymakers ought to consider' (UCL News, 2019). This is a classic case of a traditional practical contribution.

Second, organic practical contributions weave research and activism tightly together. Sociologist Edna Bonacich's study of the Los Angeles garment industry unearthed a sweatshop industry often exploiting racialised – especially Asian American – labour (Bonacich, 2007: 76–77). This led her to associating with the garment industry union in an attempt to improve the working conditions of the lowest end of the manufacturing chain. She further cooperated with union officials in order, in her own words, to help unions 'assess the big picture' and help them 'think strategically'. Equally importantly, the hands-on experience helped her to understand the garment-worker's life better from the inside (Bonacich, 2007: 78–79). Bonacich worked with unions, but similar examples of activist scholarship can be found in feminist, racial justice and environmental initiatives. Indeed, much of the public brouhaha over the 'ideologisation' of universities revolves around several disciplines (for example, gender studies, critical race theory, critical environmental studies) that are at the forefront of these struggles and thus seen as inherently ideological. This sort of activist 'public sociology', which introduces students to research that aims to benefit the communities it studies, is much more common in North America than elsewhere, but there are certainly opportunities for it everywhere. The question is – especially if you are doing research towards a degree – if organic practical contributions are considered appropriate in your field and academic community.

Not all areas of research are amenable to practical contribution claims. This would be an unnecessary thing to mention if governments all around the world had not been pushing academic 'impact' so hard for the last couple of decades. Every year, around the time when the deadline for project proposals for major research funders nears, I see comparative literature scholars, social theorists and church historians – just to name a few off the top of my head – conjure up wild justifications for why their study of a forgotten 19th-century novel, the development of Max Weber's thought, or the life of a saint is beneficial for contemporary society. We can do little if there is external pressure to think about practical contributions. It is important to remember, however, that an increased scholarly understanding of a question or problem remains a completely legitimate contribution in and of itself.

Overstretching claims

Kendal is a town of 28,000 inhabitants in North-Western England. Situated on the edge of the idyllic Lake District, Britons know Kendal best as a tourist destination. Internationally, the town is probably better known by sociologists of religion than tourists. This is thanks to the 'Kendal Project', which from 2000 to 2002 studied the changing contours of religion in modern Britain, and the results of which were reported in the highly influential book, *The Spiritual Revolution: Why Religion is Giving Way to Spirituality* (Heelas et al, 2005).

The Spiritual Revolution's Preface begins with a fitting line: 'This book explores the spiritual revolution *claim*: that traditional forms of religion, particularly Christianity, are giving way to holistic spirituality, sometimes still called "New Age"' (Heelas et al, 2005: x; emphasis in the original). At the end of the research, the authors tone down the book's title, saying that 'the claim that a spiritual revolution has taken place is exaggerated' (Heelas et al, 2005: 149). Yet, the direction they point to is clear: the form of (British) religion is changing and traditional church Christianity will be, in their estimate, superseded by alternative spirituality.

Now, in order to understand the impact of the Kendal Project, I need to recount briefly the key debates in the sociology of religion. Secularisation theory was for a long time the main theoretical framework in the sociology of religion, before coming under increased criticism from around the 1990s onwards. It argues – in heavily condensed form – that the unintended consequence of certain social conditions (for example, religious pluralism, a non-confessional state, strong existential security) is that religion loses its social significance both as an institution (for example, education becomes detached from the churches) and on the individual level (people become religiously indifferent). *The Spiritual Revolution* was widely taken as a refutation of this idea. Instead of declining, many claim, religion in the Western world is changing as traditional communal Christianity is giving way to individual spirituality. Many of the almost 3,000 citations of *The Spiritual Revolution* are this kind of knee-jerk refutations of secularisation theory.

In response, sociologist Steve Bruce has shown how the claim that alternative spirituality is reversing secularisation is misguided. Although the Kendal Project displays an interesting panoply of alternative spiritual practices, these do not challenge secularisation theory. If these new practices do not compensate for the decline of traditional churchgoing, if the 'innovations attract few of the unchurched people or if the most popular innovations are also the least religious, the secularisation thesis stands' (Bruce, 2017: 120). Religion might indeed be changing form, but it is also declining. To use the Kendal Project as an example to counter secularisation theory is to overstretch the claims of the project. The claims are simply not warranted by the evidence (see White, 2009: 117–121).

The Kendal Project did a lot of counting, but much of the other research citing *The Spiritual Revolution* against secularisation theory is qualitative, which points to one of the basic problems regarding claims, that is, the incommensurability of evidence. The research design of these qualitative studies can be perfectly solid, and the results convincingly argued from the data, but when it comes to claims, they overstretch. Interviews with 30 fervent evangelicals may tell us a lot about one form of religiosity, but it is not evidence against statistical analysis of declining membership and belief in whole populations. This is not to argue for the primacy of either type – the classic quantitative-qualitative 'method wars' – but simply to point out that researchers need to be mindful of the *coverage of claims*. Results always yield *some* claims, but not *all kinds* of claims.

This is a bit of a side track, but reading *The Spiritual Revolution* closely, the authors actually acknowledge Bruce's point about overall decline, almost word for word (Heelas et al, 2005: 47–48). We can debate whether the authors' way of expressing the significance of their results is too amenable for an overstretched interpretation, but the right address for the sharp end of criticism should really be the other scholars who took home the first sentence of the Preface without the emphasised word 'claim'. What matters is that *The Spiritual Revolution* engendered a whole genre of research, which claimed to be contributing to debates about secularisation, yet looking at the research design, were simply not responding to the actual theory. Any group of friends playing with a Ouija board on the weekend can be taken as evidence against secularisation theory, if the theory is presented in caricature form as claiming that all religion will eventually disappear (Bruce, 2017: 55). This is not the place to speculate on why some scholars would fall into this trap, but it is a good reminder that scholarship is not immune to interests and trends, and the fact that sometimes academic capital can be garnered by taking sides in a debate even when the evidence is inconclusive at best.

The moral of the story is that claims about the significance of research are affected by extrinsic factors as well as the results of research. It is more than understandable that after a year, four years or ten years of intensive research, it is tempting to claim the broadest possible significance for your project. The more you are embedded in the disciplinary debates and trends, the more pressure there might be to demonstrate that your research is making a key contribution, even if the actual coverage of claims is narrower. The danger of overstretching might be especially salient with applied contributions. Everyone who wants to change the world through research wants their study to have an impact. It is, however, also an ethical question not to inflate the significance of your research. If results evaluating the benefits of a particular training course are inconclusive, it would be problematic to claim that there are clear benefits. This would certainly not benefit the participants (although it might benefit the providers). The point is that it takes not only methodological skills, but also self-reflexivity to recognise when research claims are not warranted by evidence.

Conclusion

The arc of a research project does not start with questions and end with answers. Yes, questions need to be answered, but as has been said, results do not speak for themselves – even when they are, for rhetorical purposes, said to do so. What is highlighted as the main contribution of the research is dependent not only on the results, but on the broader conversation around the topic. Are you filling an empirical gap, providing a new angle on a familiar topic, challenging current theoretical wisdom, improving methods, or thinking about policy recommendations? In this chapter, I have called these empirical, interpretative, theoretical, methodological and practical contribution claims. The point of all these is to connect your research to broader conversations in a discipline, topic or academic field. If you are unsure whether you have presented clear contribution claims, ask yourself: have I explicitly told readers *why my research matters*? If not, think about the different types of contribution claims presented in this chapter and where your work fits. If *none* fit, you may need to go back to the drawing board with your research design. It may be that you are genuinely not contributing new knowledge or that you have not identified your contribution clearly enough.

Understanding the role of contribution claims takes practice. At the Bachelor and Master level, you may not be officially required to think about this issue at all – although even then, I would say, your dissertation will be stronger for it. From the PhD thesis onward, however, contribution claims become a key aspect of demonstrating your academic skill. Without an explicit purpose statement – where you outline how you are going to contribute to a broader conversation – you will have even less luck in the academic article submission game. Besides, research is so much more inspiring when you know why it matters.

9

Writing

As long as your research is in your head or in the form of notebook scribbles, it is not quite science yet. The point of science is that it is available for public evaluation. In practice, this often means behind commercial publishers' paywalls and, therefore, accessible only to a limited public. Nevertheless, your research really only becomes science once it is submitted for assessment by peers. So far, at least, the main vehicle for this has been writing. There are some exceptions, like higher education in the arts, where 'reports' can be performances or works of art. There are also alternative ways of presenting research findings, but whether those would be an animated film or a YouTube video broadcast from your home office, they also require planning and writing.

The world is full of excellent academic writing guides. The point of this chapter is not to compete with any of those. If you need advice on academic English, writing style or citation management, I advise you to get your hands on a general academic writing guide. There are also useful guides to academic writing habits (read: avoiding procrastination). In the conclusion of the chapter, I have listed some books that have helped me. Dissertation and thesis writers will probably benefit more from books and websites aimed higher than the undergraduate essay-writing guide, but those can be helpful too. This chapter caters more to the immediate concerns of people like those sitting in my MA and PhD seminars, but also to any academic wanting to re-examine their routines: getting started, writing habits, the structure of written research reports, and the writing process.

I will start by presenting two academic writing strategies, drafting and planning. Others may have more elaborate typologies but, at the end of the day, I think the different approaches to writing boil down to these two. Concisely, drafters write and edit later, planners structure and start writing only when they know exactly what they want to write. It is important to recognise these types, because choosing one or the other matters when thinking about when to start writing and what the process looks like. I will then explore how to learn to read academic research from a writing perspective, and the role of revision and peer support. Finally, I will briefly discuss the importance of titles, abstracts and introductions. I close with some words about procrastination and writing habits and offer some further reading recommendations.

The whole chapter – and here all writing guides, fiction, non-fiction and academic alike, agree – is premised on the idea that writing is not some mystical property one either has or has not. Writing is a craft or skill that can be perfected with practice. 'I am not a writer' is not an excuse to shy away from writing. You may not be a great writer yet, but you can be a good writer. The much-used adage is correct: writing is about perspiration, not inspiration. Writing is not a 'necessary evil' (even if some students might think so), but a key element in the research process. Good writing skills make you a better researcher.

Writing strategy I: drafting (or, the 30:70 model)

In his half memoir, half writing guide *On Writing*, bestselling novelist Stephen King describes his writing process in two stages, 'the one you do with the study door closed and the one you do with it open' (King, 2000: 249). Opening the door means letting go of the manuscript and giving it out to trusted readers for comment. How he describes the first phase, however, is what is interesting at this point: 'With the door shut', King says, '*downloading what's in my head* directly to the page, I write as fast as I can' (King, 2000: 249; emphasis added). King uses a computer metaphor to express a common fiction writing advice: write it out of your head before thinking about grammar, sentence structure or anything else. No matter if something does not make sense in the first draft; you have the second, third and further drafts to revise it. I call this the 30:70 model to describe the percentage of time and effort spent in getting the first draft done versus the time and effort spent on revision. The drafting approach is, then, back-end heavy, meaning that most of the work lies ahead by the time you have written the final full stop on your document for the first time.

Chances are that you have been told something similar about the writing process either on a course or in a book on writing. The difference between Stephen King and the academic writer is that novelists have everything they need in their head – hence 'downloadable' directly on the page – whereas scholarship requires reading secondary literature and doing primary research. This is not to suggest that novelists do not do research, they do, but they can write the first draft without knowing all the real-world details of a scene, whereas the real-world details are the reason why academics write in the first place. Does the received writing guide wisdom apply to academic writing, then?

The drafting method is helpful for two reasons: first, as the metaphor suggests, it frees space from your 'hard drive'. So does the planning approach, so perhaps the important take home point for both is that you should regurgitate ideas, instead of letting them mellow in your head. There they get lost and jumbled, whereas on the screen or paper they are safely deposited for further use. Even if the ideas end up discarded, every bit of space you free up makes you a more focused writer.

Second, drafting works when you are not sure how to connect all the information you have gathered in your research. The underlined passages in library books and the highlighted interview excerpts are in your head, but trying to pull them together into a coherent whole puts your brain into overdrive. The solution is to let it all go, to 'download' every fact, interpretation and question in your head to the page. What you might end up with could look something like this:

> People who leave a religious community and then join another one have often experienced difficult life situations that make them seek holistic change, including questioning their current faith. Secularisation means that religious groups lose social power and individuals become indifferent to religion.

This is an invented micro-example from my own field (because I didn't want to risk embarrassing myself dabbling into something I am not intimately familiar with). If you are not familiar with sociology of religion, the two sentences may seem perfectly fine. However, it is not at all clear how the two claims – fine on their own – are related. *If* there is a relation, that needs to be established in the revision round. Right now the important thing is to get both ideas out there on the screen. I even bought a digital age version of the typewriter for just this purpose: the gadget has a keyboard and a small screen, but moving the cursor has been made quite difficult so that you would not even try editing in the middle of the first draft spree. That is the point: type, type, type until you run out of things to say.

Using this approach, what you have in your hands after you have finished the first draft of your dissertation, thesis or article is very likely a mess. Whether an obvious mess or a deceptively clean document, this is when the hard work of editing starts. It may be that you have been able to keep the structure coherent (especially in shorter texts) and the sentences crisp, and the text only needs a little polishing. But I prefer to say that this phase takes up 70 per cent of the drafting approach, because that highlights the importance of doing different levels of revision. With the drafting approach you rarely get your structure right the first time (see pp 142). So it is important to be able to cut and paste whenever something feels off. Detective stories withhold information from the reader in order to surprise them at the end, but the good ones never make the reader confused when they reach the end of the story. The same should apply to your scholarly prose: if readers need to go continuously retrace their steps through your argument, there is probably something wrong with the structure. Revision is the cure. That is why calling this approach drafting is somewhat misleading. Master drafters are, in fact, master revisers.

Writing strategy II: planning (or, the 70:30 model)

If the purpose of drafting can be summarised as 'closing the door' and 'writing it out of your head', then the purpose of planning would be to close the door and plan it out of your head. Instead of sitting in front of a pristine white word processing document like drafters do, planners spread their poster-sized mind maps on the dining table, slap their Post-it notes all over the wall, or craft elaborate visuals on a graphic creation app before they write a single word in the research report document. In this approach, the bulk of the work happens *before* the actual writing, which is why I also call it the 70:30 model – planning and outlining are 70 per cent of the work, the actual writing 30 per cent.

Everybody is a planner, to a degree. We constantly make notes about what we read, what we hear at lectures, or when the proverbial lightbulb goes on in our heads while sipping a hot drink. These ideas are largely unorganised, but they are the building blocks for structured writing. To truly call this approach 'planning' requires the next step, however, which is to put the different ideas in order. This can be helpfully portrayed as a two-step process: first, the unorganised ideas are visualised in a mind map through *clustering*. Second, the relevant ideas in the mind map/cluster are organised in a particular order by *outlining* your dissertation, thesis, article or book (see Lima, 2008).

Most people who have survived modern primary and secondary education have done mind maps at some point. The term has been around for several decades now and has been sold as a tool for problem-solving, teaching, revising and 'creative dreaming', among other things (Buzan, 2006). For a planning-oriented academic writing strategy, mind mapping (or 'clustering') can be a good way to 'vomit' out all the information you have gathered in the literature review and empirical analysis phases of the research process. At this point you do not need to worry about connections or research report structure. The idea is rather to get the information out of your head. There are myriad online resources for mind mapping, including apps, but the following procedure captures the process well:

1. Jot the key word down in the middle of a blank page; underline and circle it.
2. Moving quickly, draw a dash from your key word and jot down the first word or phrase that comes to mind; circle the word or phrase.
3. Draw a dash from that word or phrase and jot down the next word or phrase that comes to mind.
4. Repeat until you come to the end of your word association string; you will know instinctively when this happens as you find yourself going blank.

5. Return to your key word.
6. Moving quickly, draw a new dash from your key word and jot down the next word or phrase that comes to mind; circle the word or phrase.
7. Draw a dash from that word or phrase and ... continue on as described above until your mind is blank.
8. Return to your key word and repeat the process. (Lima, 2008: 26)

As you will recall, the point of drafting was to empty your head of sentences that haunt there. Clustering is the same, but with key words or phrases. The outcome may be a neat sheet of office paper or a massive monster of Post-it notes filling the entire bedroom wall. There is no right number of words and associations, so you should keep going until you 'find yourself going blank'.

The planning approach has three main benefits: first, like drafting, planning enables you to free up headspace for writing by letting all the information that is stored there out in the world. You do not have to make the connections and the structuring in your head after you have jotted down everything on paper/screen and organised your key terms and ideas into an outline. Second, especially relevant for academic writers, once you have an outline, you should be free of the 'what next?' sensation that often accompanies finishing one section of a research report. Your text may be fine, but you have no idea how to follow it up in the following sections or chapters. Since you can outline down to the level of paragraphs, you can literally map your entire work from start to finish before writing a single sentence. This is a strong tool to have, especially when writing under pressure. It also means that you need to rethink the whole writing process. Planners spend more than half, maybe up to 70 per cent, of the writing process on clustering and outlining. You will have few pages to show your supervisor or colleagues in the beginning, but when the time comes to actually write those sentences, you will do it much faster than an unorganised writer. Finally, writing a long text may seem daunting, but your outline enables you to treat the whole as a combination of smaller, more manageable chunks. As I discuss further later in this chapter, this is a major benefit in the fight against procrastination.

Finally, an important reminder: although I have talked about 'drafters' and 'planners', they are not *personality types*. It is not as if you could discover with some practice that you are one or the other and then be stuck with that for the rest of your life. Instead, drafting and planning are, as said, *writing strategies*. One is suitable for one project, the other for a different project. I was probably a mix of the two earlier. I made only vague structural notes, yet wrote quite polished text from the start. It worked, but it was only when I started actively thinking about the process – inspired by King and academic writing guides – that I discovered that the middle road is not the best in the case of writing. Rather, I would focus on learning which projects benefited most from a drafting approach, which from a planning one. I still do not get it right every time, but the important thing is to be reflexive, that is, to recognise the different requirements of different writing tasks and reflect on what works for you.

Reading for writing

Shinichi Suzuki (1898–1998) was a Japanese violinist and pedagogue, who developed a music learning method that carries his name and became a worldwide phenomenon. Suzuki – a self-taught pedagogue – likened musical learning to language acquisition, which he saw as a process where 'children learn Japanese through repetition and imitation by modeling of their parents' (Akutsu, 2020: 19). Instead of learning complex musical theory and notation first, music learners should learn by listening and imitating the sounds made by the teacher. This is what is colloquially referred to as 'learning by ear'. Advanced students later learn notation and music theory as well, but the Suzuki method enables them to focus on mastering getting the right sounds out of the instrument at early stages of learning.

Why this excursion into music pedagogy?

In Chapter 5, I discussed strategies for reading for research, that is, how to digest all the material you need for the literature review and for contextualising your research. You can find similar ideas in many research handbooks. However, what most such guides forget to mention is that all the articles and books that you cite for their empirical facts or theoretical and methodological insights can be – and should be – used for a second purpose. This is what I call 'reading for writing'. When you read for research, you focus on the *content* of the text. When you read for writing, you focus on the *form* of the publication. The former helps you think about *what* to write, the latter about *how* to write.

Here is where the Suzuki method can serve as a model. Read the texts that you find most interesting, captivating (not a word often used for scholarly writing, but they exist!) and useful for your research. We often have our favourite academic books and articles, even if we cannot quite put our finger on what makes them so interesting. Read them again, but this time ignore the method, the analysis and the results, and focus on how the authors build their argument. It may be helpful to read aloud the text you are trying to imitate. This enables you to focus better on the form rather than the 'distracting' content. Reading aloud is especially helpful for figuring out sentence-level techniques: how authors build captivating sentences that also flow logically from each other. This is, like the Suzuki method, 'learning by ear', quite literally.

There is no one right way of reading for writing, but it may be helpful to pay attention to at least two levels, structure and sentences.

Writing

Structure

Quantitative studies have a quite formalised way of reporting the research. Dissertations, theses and articles using statistical data usually follow the IMRAD (Introduction, Methods, Results and Discussion) structure and there is little room for improvising. In most other types of studies, you will have to come up with the best possible structure yourself (indeed, the IMRAD structure makes qualitative research look stiff and disguises the active interpretive processes involved in such research).

After you have chosen your favourite text, you should jot down its structure in your own words, titling each section by what that section *does* (see Table 9.1). Then see whether that same structure could be applicable to your research. Dissertation and thesis writers are required to have

Table 9.1: Reading for writing: the structure of 'One *Volk*, One Church? A Critique of the "Folk Church" Ideology in Finland'

Section	Function
Introduction (untitled)	*Tension:* international research classifies the Finnish Lutheran Church as a state church, Finnish research as 'folk church' *Aim:* instead of assessing whether one term is truer than the other, this article looks at *what is being done* when 'folk church' is used *Tools:* ideology critique *Outline of article* *Glimpse at conclusion:* 'folk church' is used to downplay the state church aspect and, as such, is an ideological concept
Contemporary Ideology Critique and the Discursive Construction of Church and State	*Key concept:* ideology *Method:* Critical Discourse Analysis
Milestones in Finnish Church-State Relations	*Contextualisation:* a brief history of church–state relations in Finland
'Folk Church' in Finnish Scholarly Discourse	First *'case study'* (although not called that explicitly in the article)*:* a review of the uses of 'folk church' in Finnish research
The Church's Self-Presentation	Second *'case study':* analysis of Church home pages
'Folk Church' and the Status Quo in Parliament	Third *'case study':* analysis of a parliamentary debate
Conclusion: The Ideological Function of 'Folk Church'	*Conclusion:* whether or not 'folk church' is more accurate than 'state church', it is used (ideologically) to argue that it is. Why this matters

Source: Hjelm, 2019

some sections – varying across disciplines – outlining the elements of the research design, but are free to organise the analysis section. Here is a (non-exhaustive) list of principles for structuring texts that do not require a fixed outline:

- Chronological (you proceed from earliest to latest; the point is to show change).
- Thematical (you structure the work by, say, different themes revealed in interviews; the point is to show the variety of ways people think about things).
- By data source (the chapters/sections are based on different types of data or source used in each; the point is to show how different data/sources complement each other and as such deepen knowledge gained from just one source).
- Theoretical (the analysis of empirical material follows a theoretical outline or is structured around key concepts used in the study).

Whatever your choice, the point is to make your structure part of the analysis. A well-structured study lets the reader discern your reasoning from just looking at the table of contents or the article headings. I organised my MA thesis according to my sources, but they were the same type of data (three newspapers) and as such only broadened, but did not really deepen, the analysis. This made for boring reading, led to repetition, and required me to spend more time explaining my argument in the conclusion. The point is, keeping the research question always in mind helps you keep out of structural trouble.

Sentences

Again, there are many books about writing good English prose and my point is not to try to cover the same issues in a short chapter like this. I will not get into the mechanics of sentence construction as such. Instead, I want to talk about sentences in the broader context of your text, specifically passive voice, sentence variation and the place of key sentences. I find these particularly relevant topics for academic writing. First, passive voice refers to sentences where the subject of the sentence is either not known or is purposefully or inadvertently downplayed. However, writing in the passive is not always as bad in academic writing as it is said to be. You can see many instances of passive voice in this book as well. Sometimes the point is to emphasise the verb in the sentence, which passive voice does well. It needs to be used in moderation, though. See how the authors in your favourite articles vary between active and passive construction. There are plenty of exercises online, if you worry about using passive voice too much.

Second, sentence variation, in a nutshell, means alternating short and long sentences. If academic prose sounds dead and you feel like blanking out, the reason might be that the paragraphs look like a string of short sentences – especially if the authors write in passive voice. For example:

> The experiment was conducted in a controlled environment. Eight participants were selected from a sample. They were given three tasks. Task scores were calculated. Strong correlation between age and task score was suggested.

Now that is caricature writing (I made it up), but unfortunately not too far from some academic abstracts. Not only is there excessive passive voice, but there is no sentence variation. If the abstract is the part that draws the readers in, making them want to know more, then this fails miserably. Finally, analyse where the article that you want to imitate places key sentences – sentences with the most important information. Academic authors have different preferences, but usually you will find the key sentence either in the very beginning or at the end of a paragraph. In any case, try to avoid burying the key sentence in the middle of a paragraph.

Now that you have analysed the form of your favourite text, you can imitate it and apply the conventions that work to your own writing. Remember, 'imitating' the *content* of scholarly texts is plagiarism, but there is no copyright on *form*. As long as your research design is composed of your own combination of elements, you may imitate the ways in which authors structure their argument and build sentences.

If you are unsure which scholarly texts would be good examples, you can ask your supervisor or colleague for suggestions. As a rule, academic articles are better models for dissertation and thesis writers than academic books, because even research-based monographs are missing many of the elements required in university-level research reports. Dissertations and theses, in turn, can be good guides for structuring because of often-standardised outlines, but may not be great writing in terms of style. As I mentioned earlier, if you are interested in writing, you can learn much from popular non-fiction and even fiction writing guides – especially in terms of style, if not so much in terms of structure. And if you are aiming to publish your work in a journal, it is always a good idea to analyse the writing previously published in that journal.

My experience is that students, at all levels, struggle most with the structure of their dissertations and theses. Similarly, as journal editor – and author! – I have noticed that many problems in articles that just do not seem to work can be fixed by rethinking the organisation of the text and revising too complex sentences to clarify the argument. This can be hard, because you know your own text inside out and it is difficult to achieve a critical distance from it. But you do not have to wait for inspiration for structural edits to strike when you can read a previously published article, analyse its form, and imitate its structure and style. Academic peer-review does not guarantee good writing, but the best articles combine rigorous research with accessible and inspiring writing. Use these as models until you feel confident enough in your own structuring and style.

Show, don't tell

The adage 'show, don't tell' is often used in conjunction with fiction writing. The point is to say that instead of narrator voice telling how characters feel, it is much more interesting for the reader to be shown how the feeling of anger, for example, manifests in the character's actions. So, the usual advice would be to avoid writing 'Stella was excited about the end of term' and instead write 'As the clock struck four on the last day of term, Stella raced down the college steps, shouting "freedom"!' Showing the action instead of telling how things are makes for more interesting and better flowing writing in fiction.

However, the 'golden rule' should not be restricted to fiction alone. In fact, I think there is a special case to make for showing, not telling in academic writing. Academic writing is about backing everything you say with weighed reasons and evidence. Let's look at sentence, the likes of which I sometimes see in dissertations:

> The theoretical concept that best helps me in examining my research question is Bourdieu's *habitus*. Habitus means …

Now, there is nothing wrong with the content of this sentence as such. But what do readers learn from it? They learn that *you think* that habitus is the best concept for your study. They will need to trust your word on it. However, 'when you show people something, you are trusting them to make up their minds for themselves' (Provost, 1985: 68). This is the essence of academic writing. The reasons and evidence for your claims should be so obvious that the readers never have to take the claims on your authority. Scholarship is not determined by the status of the authors, but by their ability to convince that their claims are reasonable and supported by evidence. In this case, this would mean something like:

> In my research I study how social structures constrain the actions of individuals in particular contexts. Bourdieu's *habitus* is a concept which tries to capture that interplay and tension between structure and action. Habitus, for Bourdieu, means …

You will want to be more specific about your aims than this example, but it nevertheless shows why habitus is the best concept for that piece of research. To the readers the choice of concept now seems justified without you needing to cajole them or force it down their throats.

Check your text for any occasions where it sounds like you are telling the readers to take your word without showing them why they should do so. Sometimes it may turn out that you have not thought about the reasons enough yourself. Sometimes the readers may infer your justifications from other parts of the text. But why not make it easier for them with small changes that make your writing more convincing overall?

Revision, revision, revision

When former British Prime Minister Tony Blair campaigned to oust the Conservatives in 1997, he famously said that the three top priorities of the future Labour government would be 'education, education, education'. Whatever one thinks of Blair and his legacy, that was a powerful rhetorical tool. For the writer, the top three priorities should be, similarly, 'revision, revision, revision'.

Why I want to emphasise this so much is because inexperienced writers often do not even think about revision when they think of writing. Many find writing hard, because they think the first draft is the final version (except for typos perhaps). If the text does not turn out to be brilliant, it must mean that they are simply bad writers. Note that this not about the difference between drafters and planners, but rather the difference between unreflexive and reflexive writers. The former feel adrift in the process of writing, while the latter recognise that writing research reports (of any kind) is a process, which requires multiple revisions. There will be more revising if you are a drafter rather than a planner, but both strategies require going back to the text and editing it multiple times. There are many aspects to revision, but internalising the following four will get you off to a good start: readiness to revise; pruning for relevance; making the reader your ally; and knowing when to stop.

Readiness to revise. Knowing that revision is a key element in successful academic writing is one thing, coping with it in real life is another. It is never easy to submit something personal – and your writing is personal, even if it is on an impersonal topic – for scrutiny. 'Impostor syndrome' is an academic professional disease, if you will. This means that we often think we are not qualified to write the things we write and downplay our own capabilities (for a philosophical assessment of impostor syndrome, see Hawley, 2019; for an empirical meta-analysis of studies on impostor syndrome, see Bravata et al, 2020). A lot of my time as supervisor is spent telling my students that they are the experts in their field and while an examiner or reviewer may disagree with them on some points, as long as the students understand themselves where the criticism is justified and where not, disagreement is fine and a normal part of academic life. More advanced students or scholars may have horror stories about strict supervisors, examiners or reviewers, and there are indeed plenty of upsetting cases. But it will help a lot if you assume a basic attitude that all supervisors, examiners and reviewers do this work not in order to make your life more difficult, but to make your research better.

Pruning for relevance. 'RELEVANCE???' is the single most common thing I scribble in the margins of my students' dissertation and thesis manuscripts. If I am reading a study of contemporary Buddhist nuns in rural Finland, do I need to know about how Siddharta Gautama – later known as Buddha – became enlightened under the Bodhi tree 2,500 years earlier? Or is it necessary to discuss the structure-action problem in a sociology dissertation, which does not employ either concept in its analytical framework? There is sometimes a temptation to write everything you know about a topic (and this is not limited to students!), without stopping to think whether it is relevant for the question that the work is trying to address. 'Pruning for relevance', in my vocabulary, means exactly this: checking every sentence, paragraph and section against the research question. If the sentence, paragraph or section does not advance answering the question, then you need to consider if it is superfluous. If you are not 100 per cent sure, you can be sure a diligent reader will wonder why you are straying off course. Sometimes the issue is not so much that the content is not at all relevant, but that it is placed in the wrong context. In these cases pruning means rearranging rather than deleting. Letting go of cherished sentences is hard, but the point is always to keep your eye on the question. Every sentence, paragraph and section needs to be relevant for the aims set by your question.

Making the reader your ally. What I mean by this is that no matter how great your research, if your presentation is made up of half-page-long sentences and filled with typos, the reader will usually pay more attention to your deficient form than your brilliant content. With careful sentence construction and diligent editing, you make the reader your ally. They will focus on what you have to say, not how you say it. Further, you also make a reader your ally by paying attention to the previous point, relevance. Look at every sentence and ask yourself: Will this answer the reader's questions or raise more questions? If a reader needs to constantly wonder about the relevance of a sentence, paragraph or section in your writing – or needs to scribble in the margins, as I do with my supervisees – then you have failed to make the reader your ally. You can also think about this in terms of flow. Every time the reader needs to stop to think about where the text is going, you lose some of their sympathy. It is one thing to stop because an argument or idea is difficult – which is fine – and another to stop because it is not clear why you say what you say.

That said, it is also good to remember that yes, revision is important, but you need to stop at some point. I cannot remember now where I heard this line the first time, but I have for a long time used a variation of it in my teaching: *there are perfect dissertations/theses/articles that are never finished, and adequate dissertations/theses/articles that do get finished.* There is *always* room to tinker just a little bit more, but letting go is an important skill, especially if you are thinking about research as a career. There are two important things to remember if you feel uncertain about when your work is ready. First, as already discussed, academia is based on peer review. Your supervisor will read your dissertation or thesis and reviewers will comment on your article or book manuscript. You may get a lot of suggestions for revision, but you do not have to worry that you are publishing a complete disaster after a peer review. You should also volunteer to read the work of your friends and colleagues before they submit their texts and ask them to reciprocate. The best MA seminar I have had so far was one where the students read and commented on each other's work on their own initiative. It also produced the best dissertations so far. Sympathetic, 'safe' but constructively critical readers can catch a lot of problematic issues before submission, without you having to worry about their judgement.

Second, not only are adequate texts accepted or published more often than 'perfect' texts, they tend to be better than the latter. This is because of the simple fact that if you think you are submitting an already perfect piece of work, it will be much harder to accept the sometimes extensive suggestions for revision. 'Adequate' does not mean submitting a rough draft of disjointed text clips, of course. However, equally, it is no use in sitting on a text that might need polishing here and there, but which includes all the elements required of a scholarly work. Letting go is never easy, but you might surprise yourself reading the text after a couple of years. It is usually not bad at all!

Titles, abstracts and introductions

I have a somewhat odd habit of starting my article writing from the 'wrong' end. That is, whenever an article idea comes to my mind, I first try to come up with a title that best captures what I am trying to say. If academic writing guides are any measure, this should normally be the *last* thing you think about, when the argument and structure of the article are already down on paper. Needless to say, often my titles change by the time of publication, but the point is to capture the main claim, key concepts and context (not necessary in that order) of the article in one or two sentences. Doing this first is a good reminder of the task ahead, even if the research later requires revising the title.

Titles are important not only as distillations of your argument, however, but also for practical reasons. People will find your research largely based on the title. Institutional repositories for dissertations and theses, and academic journals will ask for separate keywords, but it is always a good idea to include the most important keywords in your title. That is the way to draw your potential reader in. With so much research published and posited in institutional repositories around the world every day, it is easy for your work to disappear in the flood. Article writers worry about this most, of course, but there is no reason why you shouldn't make your dissertation or thesis easily discoverable (if your university has a repository policy). There is always someone – another student perhaps – eager to read your work, no matter what the topic.

I tend to think of titles as the 'first base' of drawing potential readers to your writing. Abstracts are the 'second base'. Abstracts elaborate the title by discussing the context (often by showing a gap in the literature), the research question/problem, how the study was conducted (methods), and the results and their implications for the context – going back full circle. I admit that I often write my abstracts only at the point when I am required to and too often that means copy-pasting some key sentences from the text. On better days, my abstracts are more carefully written stand-alone texts in themselves. Good abstracts have the same double function as titles: they are concise reminders to not stray from the path. Even more importantly, the abstract may be the only thing a reader can access, so whether they take the step to write to you to ask for the text, or use interlibrary loans, depends largely on what is in the abstract.

Introductions are what I consider the 'third base' of making your writing inviting and accessible. Here you have even more space to show what it is exactly that you are studying and – most importantly – why it matters. A good introduction should include a purpose statement, where you explicate how the research contributes to the field. As discussed in Chapter 8, you may not be expected to leave a lasting mark on the discipline in your BA or MA dissertation, but if your research makes an identifiable contribution, no matter how small, the introduction is the place where you should announce it. Knowing why they should turn the page helps keep readers interested.

How you do this varies, inevitably. I remember a discussion from my PhD student days, where a colleague said that there is a 'German' style and an 'Anglo-American' style of writing academic introductions. In the German style, so the story went, you explain what the article is about and perhaps how you went about researching the topic, but the 'kicker' – the findings and their significance – you leave until the conclusion. This, apparently, builds tension and forces the reader to finish the article (or just skip to the end) for the juiciest parts. In the Anglo-American style, in contrast, you give a lot of information to the reader already in the beginning. You say what the topic is, why it matters, your methodology, what your main results are, and why they matter for the field of research. It is this up-front outlining that, supposedly, makes the text reader-friendly and as such encourages the reader to go on into more detail.

I could not say whether the national epithets have any basis in reality, but publishing in English-language journals made me switch from the 'German' to 'Anglo-American' in the beginning of my career. If you write in English, the latter is probably a safe bet. Supervisors will know what the particular expectations for dissertations and theses are. For academic journals, you need to do some studying yourself, because disciplines also have different traditions regarding writing formats.

Use the imitation method explained earlier to assess which kind of titles, abstracts and introductions best convey the main point of the dissertation, thesis or article. Investing some effort into this pays off – even when thinking about a title or abstract often become timely at the point when you are done with the main body of the text and can no longer be bothered. Not only do titles, abstracts and introductions all function as reminders for yourself about what your goal in the text is, they are also crucial in today's short attention economy, where uninformative titles, uninteresting abstracts and confusing introductions make the reader prone to move on to another study instead of finding out what wisdom lies within yours.

Against procrastination

Knowing everything that I have said in this chapter should put you on the right path to becoming a good academic writer – at least in an ideal world. In reality, you might do everything I have recommended and read a ton of other guides on top, yet be stuck with a blank first page. Whether you are a drafter or a planner, nothing comes out. Your home is cleaner than ever, you have discovered your inner chef, and you may have read a ton of other books unrelated to your research. In other words, you are procrastinating.

I speak from some experience here: I signed a book contract in 2002, promising to deliver the manuscript in two years. The book was published in 2014. I did publish a lot of other books and articles in the meantime, but it is hard to live for 12 years with a sense of not having delivered something I promised to do. I have since read a lot of books about procrastination and reflected on that time. The less useful ones give detailed time management advice and exercises to strengthen your willpower. But for me it was important to understand that, according to research, procrastination is largely a way to avoid negative feelings. If you are under pressure to finish your dissertation, thesis, article or book, even thinking about the writing may trigger negative feelings. So you procrastinate. As most students and academics are under constant pressure, it is no wonder that most of them find themselves procrastinating at one time or another.

If and when procrastination is a reaction to negative emotions, it may help to do some CBT (cognitive behavioural therapy) exercises, meditation, or whatever. The two things that have worked for me have been creating a routine around writing (see Silvia, 2007) and breaking the writing task into smaller chunks. Regarding routine, I try to schedule my week so that before noon every day, my time is dedicated to writing. I say 'try', because of course some weeks there are meetings or classes in the morning hours. In that case I either reschedule for later that day (although writing in the afternoon is much harder for me) or skip the day. Right now, I know my duties as journal editor will take me a whole day a week, so I do not even try to schedule more than four writing days a week. Whatever your routine, as long as you have a clear plan when to write, the writing progresses. If you wait for an ideal opportunity for writing (the right 'air and light and time and space', as writer Charles Bukowski put it; cited in Sword, 2017: ix) you will find that there are always other demands on your time. Routinisation is important, because it decreases the amount of conscious thinking you need to spend on your writing habits. Once you have settled into a routine, you do it without a second thought, as the saying goes.

Coming from a Nordic country with long winters, one student's characterisation of the empty page as 'the long white tundra' has stayed with me ever since. The white emptiness is especially daunting if you are writing the opening words of your dissertation, thesis or article, and counting forward towards the amount required by your degree or the journal you are submitting to. When a task seems too big to handle, it is easy to postpone it until the famous 'right' moment, when you have enough time, a quiet office, or whatever. Having learned the hard way, I can confirm that the right moment strikes perhaps twice a year, which means that if was dependent on that, I would still be doing my 30th year of undergraduate studies. Breaking down writing tasks into smaller chunks has been extremely liberating psychologically for me, and I believe is for everyone. When my immediate concern is not 'finish article!', but 'finish the method section', I have a much more manageable task ahead. A 10,000-word dissertation will likely take many weeks to finish, sometimes even months. A 1,000-word theory section can be managed in a week or two. The former can be a soul-crushing thought, the latter a much more concrete matter of time management and organisation. Having a clear sense of your outline early in the project (even if you are a drafter) will help also work habit-wise, because the outline can be used as a map of the smaller, more manageable pieces.

As with any 'trick of the trade' of writing, you need to find what works best for you. You may be someone who flourishes in chaos and is able to snatch the needed minutes for writing amid the turbulence of life. In that case, routinisation may not be for you (even in that case, breaking down writing tasks into smaller chunks is probably helpful!). The point with procrastination is the same as with writing strategies: the important thing is to be reflexive – to recognise and acknowledge what works best for you in different situations. It may also be a comforting thought that you are most definitely not alone.

Conclusion

More than any other chapter in this book, this one could have been twice as long and, even then, would not have covered half of the important things there are to know about writing. Although you can successfully plan a research project without much writing, in order to finish the project, you need to learn to know yourself as a writer. That is why I think a chapter on writing belongs in a book on research design. However, since there is much more to discover, I will, as promised, mention a couple of books that have been inspirational for me. Johnson and Mullen's (2007) *Write to the Top: How to Become a Prolific Academic* focuses on writing habits and time management, as does Silvia's (2007) *How to Write a Lot*. Helen Sword's (2017) *Air & Light & Time & Space: How Successful Academics Write* also discusses writing habits but reads more like a study than a how-to book – which works as encouragement by showing that you are not alone in your struggles with academic writing. Joe Moran's (2018) *First You Write a Sentence* is not only useful for any writer, but a pleasure to read. Finally, Michael Billig's (2013) *Learn to Write Badly: How to Succeed in the Social Sciences* is not a writing guide at all, but an indictment of the competitive culture of modern academia. According to Billig, this competition creates a linguistic style where coming up with new obscure words for social processes and phenomena has become a mark of distinction, all the while making our writing poorer. I may not have followed Billig in everything he says, but I think everyone should know his argument. In addition to academic writing guides, I have benefited from having a keen interest in all kinds of writing advice. Popular non-fiction writing guides include useful insights on chapter organisation, for example, and even books on fiction writing can be helpful. Knowing how to build tension, think about viewpoint and so on can make your academic writing much better, without compromising the focus on researched knowledge.

Science is not just knowledge based on evidence and rigorous reasoning. It is also, by definition, public knowledge. So far, at least, the way we make our research public is by writing dissertations, theses, articles and scholarly books. Writing is a large part of your research process in terms of time and effort, so it pays off to learn to know yourself as a writer. But writing can also influence your research design. For certain, good writing can highlight why your research design is the best for the study at hand – just as bad writing can obscure it. It may be true that few academic writers create exciting prose as such, but everyone can become a clear communicator of complex ideas and realities. You too.

10

Proposal

Congratulations!

If you have read the previous chapters and applied them to your research idea, you should have a fairly good sense of the research design puzzle – what the different elements are and how they relate to each other. However, these ideas might be disorganised in your head or as a jumble of electronic notes. Although you have done by far most of the work, what remains to be done is a structured written report of your research design. In academic parlance, this is referred to as a research proposal.

There are solid instrumental reasons for knowing how to write a good research proposal. Applying to higher degree programmes almost always requires some account of what you plan to do for your research project. In MA (and equivalent) programmes this might be a shorter box on a form, but PhD (and equivalent) programmes require a full proposal, even if the format may vary. Importantly, in the race for research funding (whether PhD or postdoc), a proposal is your ticket. Put more cynically, the proposal is your lottery ticket. Although I like to think that good research ideas and well written proposals have a better chance of 'winning' than a random list of numbers, there is one similarity: you will have no chance of success at all unless you have a ticket/proposal to submit.

Applicants for degree programmes and research funding are obvious beneficiaries for research proposal writing skills. There are also, however, good non-instrumental reasons for writing proposals. Seeing your research design on paper or screen makes it much more concrete than a pile of notes. Seeing the connections between the different elements unfold in text forces you to look for weak spots and missing ingredients. If you are planning, say, an article or essay, which does not require extra funding, it may be helpful to write a 'proposal' for the article or essay, even if it is for your eyes only. In order to publish your research as a book, you will need to provide publishers with a book proposal, which in many ways follows the research proposal framework. The proposal is the logical final step in research design, whether you write it for someone else, or just for yourself.

This final chapter is, then, dedicated to the research proposal. It is somewhat different from the others in the sense that instead of discussing broad outlines and helpful ways of thinking about the different elements, in this chapter I focus on an example of a research proposal. It is one that I put together with colleagues for research project funding. In that sense, it is somewhat different from individual research proposals submitted for degree programmes or funding bodies. The proposal does, however, demonstrate common features that are applicable to proposals of different types. It is also relatively short, unlike some proposals required by large funders, such as the European Union (which I also refer to in this chapter). You should not take it as a template to follow and students especially should always consult their supervisors, who know well what formats work best in your discipline. I will begin by discussing some general features of research proposals and then proceed to analyse the model proposal section by section, pointing out instances where other types of projects might express things differently.

What's in a proposal?

The purpose of a research proposal is to answer three questions: *what* does the research want to find out? *How* does it propose to find it out? *Why* is it important to find it out? The first question is about *content*, the second about *procedure*, and the third about *purpose*. These relate to the chapters in this book (see Table 10.1).

Ideally, then, a research proposal covers all the elements of research design we have discussed (writing is included only implicitly). Remember that application forms and proposal templates may have different titles for these three questions, or may put them in a different order. The main point remains that good proposals need to cover all of the questions.

Table 10.2 is a sample outline of a European Research Council template proposal. These are heavy, two-phase project funding proposals that extend to over 20 pages altogether. The format requires the proposal to include the section headings (a, b, c), but individual proposals may vary as to content and structure within the three required sections. The subheadings are from a project proposal of mine. Section (a) covers content and purpose, the 'state of the art' referring to what you know about the phenomenon you propose to study at the moment (literature review and theory) and how you propose to add to that knowledge (research question). Although not spelled out in the headings, this section also includes the purpose statement of the study (contribution). The second section answers the 'how' question (data, method, ethics). Note the somewhat misleading heading about 'project design' because the whole document is about project design! The final

Table 10.1: Research proposal questions and themes

Question (theme)	Relevant chapters
What? (Content)	Question, Literature, Theory
How? (Procedure)	Data, Method, Theory, Ethics
Why? (Purpose)	Contribution, Question

Table 10.2: European Research Council template proposal structure

---
Section a. State-of-the-art and objectives
A1 Overview
A2 State of the Art
A3 Research Questions, Themes and Objectives
Section b. Methodology
B1 Data, Method, and Project Design
B2 Research Practice: Data Collection, Analysis and Comparison
B3 Work Packages
B4 Team Structure and Project Management
B5 Risks and Feasibility
B6 Timetable
B7 Outputs, Dissemination, and Impact Plan
Section c. Resources (including project costs)
C1 Personnel
C2 Fieldwork and travel costs
C3 Event organisation
C4 Publication and dissemination costs
C5 Equipment costs
C6 Other
References

---

section (c) is the most practical one. I will not cover the intricacies of budgeting in this book, as the practices vary wildly, but be aware that unless applying for a personal grant or salary, you need to factor in time (and assistance!) to figure out budgeting.

Before going to a more detailed analysis of a somewhat simpler proposal, I want to highlight two additional issues to consider when writing a proposal: feasibility and audience.

Even the best articulated purpose statement, which promises to change the field of the discipline, will fail if the project is not practically feasible. I have mentioned this earlier when discussing the feasibility of a particular element of your design, but the proposal is the one place where you need to demonstrate that the research is feasible and doable as a whole. Your access to data, research method skills, proposed timeline and ethics need to be in sync.

Second, when writing research proposals, you need to write for a non-specialist audience. This may sound counterintuitive: are you not supposed to demonstrate your deep knowledge of the specialised discipline, field and topic? Yes, but at the same time degree programme, scholarship and project funding committees are almost always composed of scholars from various disciplines and specialisations. This means that you need to be able to convince someone who might not be very familiar with your particular field. What unites these committees is an understanding of the basics of research design. Speaking from experience, no amount of fancy terminology will convince a committee more than a straightforward, easy to follow proposal.

The model proposal

In the next pages you will find a model proposal for a research project on religious literacy, which was submitted to a Finnish research foundation (in English). The foundation had a template for what the proposal should include as a minimum, which the proposal follows. I have redacted some details from the text but left everything relevant for the purposes of this chapter untouched. Neither the topic nor the methodology may be anywhere close to your interests but consider this as an exercise in 'alternative reading'. As with the imitation method in Chapter 9, the point is not so much about the substance, but the structure and logic of the proposal. I have cut the proposal into sections, each of which I discuss in detail.

Please note that this is an example of a highly structured project. Writing a proposal for a quasi-experimental research design is 'easy' in the sense that the practical procedures are defined by type of data and method. It is also possible to envision the different phases of the project in a relatively detailed way. This is of course different with a more open-ended project, where, for example, research questions become clear only after an initial immersion into fieldwork. I will try to cover different types in the analysis, but do not be discouraged if putting together a structured proposal like the one shown here feels difficult. Some proposals cannot include all the detail, and this is fine as long as you are aware of that and are able to justify it.

Introduction

Religious Literacy in Action (RELIACT): An Experimental Inquiry into the Impact of Religious Education Courses in Finnish Upper Secondary Schools

Introduction

Interest in religious literacy has grown exponentially in recent years. Increasing cultural and religious diversity has prompted claims that people in secularised societies are incapable of encountering religious difference. This religious illiteracy, it is claimed, manifests in the misrecognition of the role of religion in politics, as well as in misunderstanding religious identities (Asani 2011; Dinham & Francis 2016). Religious illiteracy is most visible when minorities are "othered" through religious stereotypes, which further their stigmatization and marginalization. As Dinham and Shaw (2017, 1) put it: 'As religion and belief come under renewed scrutiny now, under pressure from extremism, migration and globalisation, we find that the ability to talk well about religion and belief has largely been lost'. Offered as a solution, religious literacy is defined as the ability to understand the history, central beliefs, and practices of different religions and their embedment in social, cultural and political contexts (Davie and Dinham 2019; Dinham & Shaw 2017; Moore 2016; Sakaranaho, Aarrevaara & Konttori 2020). Importantly, in addition to cognitive internalisation of information, religious literacy aims at attitudinal and emotional effects to enable respectful relationships in a religiously plural context (Dinham and Jones 2010).

The problem with the literature on religious literacy so far, however, is that it assumes rather than demonstrates these cognitive and attitudinal effects. We are told that religious literacy is needed for harmonious social life and, indeed, considering the frequent misinformation and disinformation about religion and religions circulating in public discourse, this seems like common sense. What we do not know, however, is the key question: *Does religious literacy work?* Much ink has been spilt on the justification for religious literacy training in all levels of society, but very little has been said about the effectiveness of such training. The Religious Literacy in Action (RELIACT) project seeks to fill this gap in knowledge.

Somewhat surprisingly, the literature on religious literacy nowhere refers to the vast research on different types of 'literacy', e.g. health literacy, information literacy, even 'financial literacy'. For our purposes, perhaps the most relevant point of comparison is media literacy, which has been widely studied in different contexts, including Finland (e.g. Ferguson, 2011; Hobbs 2007; Kupiainen & Ruokamo 2013; Rantala 2011). While some of the work focuses on building and analysing curricula for media literacy education (e.g. Fedorov, Levitskaya & Camarero 2016), there are, importantly for our purposes, experimental studies which investigate the effectiveness of media literacy interventions and their impact on students' critical thinking (e.g. Bergstrom, Flynn & Craig 2018; Byrne 2009). Comparable studies on the impact of religious literacy interventions are almost non-existent (but see Conroy 2015 for a limited example). RELIACT will draw on the research on media literacy impacts and apply that to religious literacy.

Finland is a good case study for testing the effects of religious literacy learning. In the Finnish context, one of the main goals of the educational system is to promote cultural diversity in a way that enables students to develop their intercultural competence (Mäkelä et al. 2017; Opetushallitus 2014). This includes religious diversity, so the premise of religious literacy is embedded in the broader curriculum.

Finnish Religious Education (RE) is organised according to 'the student's own religion'. In practice, this means that the vast majority of students at primary and secondary school level attend Evangelical Lutheran RE. The second largest group – those unaffiliated with a religious institution, or minority religion students whose own religion is not taught (because of minimum group size requirements) in a particular school – take an Ethics (*elämänkatsomustieto*) class. Finally, some minority religions with an approved curriculum (e.g. Orthodox Christianity, Islam, Buddhism) have their own courses. RE and Ethics are compulsory in the Finnish system, which means we can avoid selection bias (i.e. training tends to be more effective when participants seek it).

The Evangelical Lutheran RE curriculum explicitly mentions that the goal of RE is to familiarise students with their own and other religions, and to encourage students to be responsible, active, and independent members of a plural society (see Sakaranaho, 2013). Opinions differ, however, on whether the RE curriculum offers a balanced context for learning religious literacy (Poulter 2019; Sakaranaho 2013; 2019; Zilliacus, Holm & Sahlström 2017; Ubani 2013; Åhs, Kallioniemi & Poulter 2019; Kimanen & Poulter, 2018). Significantly, this debate is conducted over the principles of RE delivery, not over expected or (even less) demonstrated effects of this delivery. For our purposes, the important point is that the goals mentioned in the religious literacy literature and the those of the Finnish Evangelical Lutheran RE curriculum – better understanding and acceptance of religious diversity – are similar enough that it is appropriate to treat them as mutually co-inhabiting (despite some critical voices against equating the two; Hannam et al. 2020). The context is unique, as always, but the pioneering approach of RELIACT will be of international interest in a situation where religious literacy is offered as a partial cure, at least, to problems of religiously and culturally diverse societies.

The 'introduction' here does two main things: it places the study within a conversation (religious literacy) and shows what is missing from that conversation (an assessment of the actual efficacy of religious literacy). The latter provides the study with a purpose statement: this study is important because it tests some of the key claims on the topic and thus adds much-needed new knowledge to several cognate fields. Note that although this is the place to show the gaps in the literature, it is *not* the place to engage in a fully-fledged literature review. An assessment of the main arguments regarding your topic will suffice for the reader to understand both where you come from and the conversation you are contributing to.

In addition to the two main functions, the introduction justifies the research design in two ways: first, the text shows that 'literacy' has been used beyond its literal meaning in 'media literacy', for example. This increases the feasibility of the study because there are models to follow, even if they are in another field. Second, the last two paragraphs justify the case study (Finland). Studying public religious education avoids selection bias (which would likely happen if the research asked volunteers to participate in a religious literacy course), and although a small country at the periphery of Europe, the curricular objectives of Finnish religious education come close to definitions of religious literacy, thus making them a suitable proxy for studying the latter.

Aims and objectives

Aims and objectives

Religious literacy literature proceeds from several assumptions that the RELIACT project aims to test. First, the basic assumption is that knowing more about religion and religions (the cognitive side of religious literacy) is beneficial or even essential for active citizenship in a plural world (Dinham & Francis, 2016; Poulter 2019). Second, a corollary assumption is that religious literacy increases acceptance of religious diversity (the attitudinal side of religious literacy) (Dinham & Francis, 2016). Finally, it is argued that secularisation leads to religious illiteracy and, consequently, lesser understanding and acceptance of religious diversity (Dinham & Francis, 2016; Davie and Dinham 2019; Dinham & Shaw 2017).

The aim of the RELIACT project is to measure the cognitive and attitudinal impact of religious literacy as practiced in Evangelical Lutheran RE in Finland. We use the first year upper secondary school RE course that discusses religion as a phenomenon, with a reference to Christianity, Judaism, and Islam (*UE1 Uskonto ilmiönä – juutalaisuuden, kristinuskon ja islamin jäljillä*) as the test course ('the intervention'). One of its learning objectives is to 'develop skills (*valmiuksia*) to function in a religiously and culturally plural environment and working life, and skills to discuss topical questions related to religion' (Opetushallitus 2019, 299). Our control group will consist of students taking the first year Ethics course on 'the good life' (*ET1 Minä ja hyvä elämä*). Only a small element of the course discusses religious and secular views. Because of this, and since Ethics students come from a non-religious or minority religion background (members of the Evangelical Lutheran Church are not allowed to take Ethics classes), we assume differences in outcomes between the control group and the test group. Finally, we study two different populations to test the secularisation claim. Although church membership is not a comprehensive measure of religiosity, regional differences in membership give an indication of differences in the level of secularisation, which we will control with further measures in the questionnaire. The contrast between the Helsinki metropolitan area (53 percent membership rate) with the western region of central Ostrobothnia (peaking at 94 percent membership rate, target municipalities to be confirmed) is significant enough to indicate possible differences.

Presented in hypothesis form, the RELIACT project will test five claims:

H1: Students exposed to RE have significantly higher cognitive religious literacy scores after the intervention, as well as having a higher score in comparison to the control group (students in Ethics).

H2: Students exposed to RE score higher on positive attitudes towards religious diversity after the intervention, as well as having a higher score in comparison to the control group (students in Ethics).

H3: The cognitive aspect of religious literacy co-occurs with the attitudinal aspect.

H4: Religious literacy is lower in more secularised contexts, higher in more religious contexts.

H5: The impact of RE on cognitive and attitudinal religious literacy is higher in more secularised contexts.

Collecting information about students' background, such as ethnicity, class and gender enables us to control them as extraneous variables. Besides, we can further investigate their effect on religious literacy. Successful testing of these hypotheses will contribute entirely new knowledge to the field of religious literacy research, religious education research, and more broadly, to the sociology of religion, in that it will shed light on some of the key concerns of the discipline, such as the centrifugal forces of secularisation and religious diversity. The project will also generate new data for future research on religious literacy and education.

Course descriptions in British universities often include a section on 'aims and objectives' and, despite working in the system for over a decade, I never quite understood the difference between the two (and I was not the only one). Had I had power over the proposal section titles, I would not have called this section 'aims and objectives', but here we are.

If the opening section introduced the conversation and its deficiencies in broad outlines, this section narrows down the discussion (always remember the funnel!) to workable hypotheses. It outlines some of the assumptions in the literature regarding the effects of religious literacy and presents the comparative design, which enables the testing of these assumptions. The 'aim' of study in the second paragraph could also be expressed in question form: what is the cognitive and attitudinal impact of religious literacy as practiced in Evangelical Lutheran RE in Finland? Put in question form, the study seems mainly descriptive (answering a 'what' question). This is true, because the research examines some key beliefs in the literature, which have so far however gone untested. The more detailed aims, expressed in this research as hypotheses, complicate the picture somewhat.

Analysing the impact of secularisation (as stated in H4 and H5) and controlling for ethnicity, class and gender enables discussion of correlations and possible causations as well, thus adding the 'how' and 'why' questions into the mix.

Research materials and methods

Research materials and methods

In order to test for pre- and post-intervention conditions, we have chosen *survey experiment* (Mutz 2011) as the key method. Unlike experiments in artificial settings, exposure to the intervention in this study will be in a natural setting (upper secondary schools), without interference of the researchers (who do not have any input into the curricular makeup of the courses), and thus has a high level of external validity (see Jackson and Cox 2013; Mutz 2011).

Another privilege of our experimental design (compared with experimental studies on media literacy, e.g. Bergstrom, Flynn & Craig 2018; Byrne 2009) is that we provide a comprehensive picture of religious literacy in Finland by assessing representative samples from the Helsinki Metropolitan area and Ostrobothnia. We use a *stratified sampling* technique to reach a representative number of participants. The sampling will be based on the number of schools and their students as well as ethnic and social class composition of neighbourhoods. Then, we recruit a representative number of pupils in selected schools. Informed consent will be taken before data collection. We ask the participants to fill in a questionnaire twice: once before the intervention (approximately one week before RE course at the beginning of semester) and once after they have finished the course (after the intervention at the end of semester). The time gap between pre-intervention and post-intervention allows to avoid the immediate effect of the intervention. The questionnaire for students taking the RE course and the Ethics course will be identical. Data collection will be administered by the project researchers during the second year of the project and supplemented, if required, by research assistants.

The content validity of the measurement will be guaranteed through our collaborative team of experts who assess the operationalisation of religious literacy. We use Likert scaling to assess the score of each question given by our expert panel and the level of their agreement (S-CVI) on each question. To keep a question in our questionnaire S-CVI should be ≥0.78 (Sangoseni, Hellman & Hill 2013). In addition, we will arrange a pilot test with 20 to 30 students to check if our questionnaire successfully captures the different dimensions of religious literacy (cognitive, attitudinal). For this purpose, factorial validity analysis will be administered to finalize our questionnaire. Following the reliability principle of a measurement (the replicability of the questionnaires) we use the pilot data to test coefficient Cronbach alpha. A reliability coefficient (Cronbach alpha) of ≥0.70 will be considered acceptable.

We use different statistical techniques to test the results against null situations, such as *comparative multivariate analysis of variance and covariance (ANOVA and MANOVA), regression*, and *factor analysis*. We first use ANOVA to test and retest the effect of each religious teaching period on students' level of cognitive and attitudinal religious literacy. Then we use MANOVA for testing hypotheses with more than one dependent variable. We also test the differences between students in rural and urban regions. Hierarchical ordinary least squares regression model (OLS) and Factor analysis are employed to see if we can offer a theoretical model for religious literacy learning.

Finnish Advisory Board on Research Integrity (TENK) guidelines and the European Code of Conduct for Research Integrity will be followed throughout the research project and after, when data is stored. We will also obtain research permission from the municipal education boards. Full confidentiality is guaranteed to all participants, as personal identifier such as names will not be stored or reported. It will be clearly explained to the students that they can drop the experiment at any stage. When the project ends, the data will be safely stored at University of Helsinki server according to the data management guidelines.

This is a straightforward heading and section. Here you present your data and your collection and analysis methods. Remember that you are writing to non-specialists here. This proposal could have stopped at stating that 'we have chosen *survey experiment* as the key method'. A specialist would have understood from the term and the reference what we understand by the survey experiment and that may have been enough. However, the proposal goes into detail about the practicalities of data collection and analysis, so that readers unfamiliar with this kind of quasi-experimental research can follow the logic of the study. You should always be explicit about your terms – that is, not expecting that 'discourse analysis' or another 'named' method has an immutable meaning – and you should try to outline, as much as you can, how the research proceeds in practice. As said earlier, the RELIACT study is 'front-heavy' in the sense that, ideally, the research will unfold more or less as depicted in the proposal. Proposals for ethnographic research with much more open-ended aims cannot be similarly detailed – but even then, it is a good idea to try to anticipate potential detours as much as you can.

Many proposal forms have a separate section for ethics. Here, the paragraph on ethics starts with a sentence dangerously close to what I explicitly told you *not* to say in a proposal. Remember: 'sometimes following rules serves no moral value other than that of following rules' (Pimple, 2002: 195). Thankfully, the proposal goes to some detail at least as to what following the guidelines entails.

Work outline

Work outline

2023 March–August: Desk work on theoretical and methodological literature and designing questionnaire; Ethics certificate preparation and submission; assessing the questionnaire by experts; introducing project through public presentation at Helsinki University and social media and project's website
August–December: Pilot data collection and evaluation of the measurement; finalizing the questionnaire; sampling; preparation and arrangement with selected schools.
2024 January–June: Writing first article (conceptual)
July–December: Data collection; data management; submitting book proposal; conference participation
2025 January–June: Preparing data for analysis; data wrangling and analysis; submitting second article; conference participation
July–December: Public presentation; submitting third and fourth article
2026 January–March: Submitting fifth article; finalising book manuscript; Academic conference and public seminar for stakeholders (ministry of education, municipal education administration, etc.); storing data for open access at Helsinki University archive

This is a section where the people reviewing your proposal look to when assessing the feasibility of the project. They will ask: will you be able to accomplish everything needed to bring the project to a happy end within the timeline you present here? In the model proposal, this is simply a timeline. This section could be also used to elaborate on potential issues that could delay the plan. In this case, the proposal says very little about access to schools and the timing of the RE courses studied. Although quasi-experimental research like this can be planned to a large degree in advance, everything hangs on the access to data.

Project team and outputs

Project Team and Outputs

The RELIACT project team consists of Professor Titus Hjelm (PI, University of Helsinki), a sociologist of religion who specialises in secularisation and religion-state relationships; Dr Zeinab Karimi (University of Helsinki), a sociologist with a background in demography and statistics; Dr Tuomas Äystö (University of Helsinki), a religion scholar who works on computer-assisted text data analysis and statistics. In addition, we will use research assistants for data gathering, when applicable.

The RELIACT project will be supported by an interdisciplinary international advisory board, who will also evaluate the questionnaire. Members of the board include: [Names redacted]

The RELIACT project is the first systematic empirical inquiry into the much-used concept of religious literacy, and as such, will contribute to academic conversations in sociology of religion, education, law, religious studies, and theology. The planned *five academic articles* will be published in peer-reviewed open access journals, such as: [Titles redacted]. A collaborative and transdisciplinary book will be submitted to [Name redacted]. The findings will be presented in interdisciplinary conferences, seminars, and workshops.

In addition to scholarly outcomes, the project will contribute to broader public debate by organising a public discussion seminar with stakeholders (ministry of education, municipal education administration) and submitting op-eds to newspapers [names redacted], professional magazines [names redacted], and popular academic blogs [names redacted]. We will also write a blog and establish social media accounts to disseminate the results.

References [List redacted]

This is the other section where the study's feasibility is assessed. This time, however, it is not about time but your skills (and in this case, the skills of the team) and suitability for carrying out the research. Self-promotion is always difficult for me, but it has been a skill worth learning – as long as you do not take yourself *too* seriously! Here you also present a realistic estimate of the 'outputs' (publications, conference talks, public engagement) of your project. Obviously, a project has a team, whereas for an individual grant you will talk about yourself. In both cases, it is good to mention the 'supporting cast' of the project. For dissertations and theses, this is your supervisory team or committee. For postdocs and projects, this is an advisory board, comprised of researchers who are able to support you with the research. Many funders, especially for postdocs and projects, also require an account of how the institution where you undertake your research will support you and why that institution is the best place to do it.

Note that your proposal should always have a list of references after the main document. Make sure to check whether the references are counted towards your maximum word limit, so that you do not go over it.

Abstracts

The proposal presented here does not have an abstract (sometimes referred to as a 'synopsis'), but in addition to proposals you will need abstract-writing skills for many other academic endeavours. Conference paper submissions and scholarly articles are the two most common ones. Even if you are not (yet) contemplating either, learning how to write abstracts helps you condense your research, which also forces you to think about what really is the key information you want to convey in about 200 words.

The best abstracts answer the same questions as the full proposal. Opening with the research aim or question draws the reader's attention immediately (the 'what' question). You will need to show the relevance of your question by pointing out the gaps in the literature. The middle part of an abstract should explain briefly but comprehensively your data and method (the 'how' question). You will then need to justify why your research is important (and, indirectly, why you should be admitted to a programme and/or supported financially) (the 'why' question).

An abstract for a conference talk or a scholarly article – which you would present after the research is done – would add a line or two about the results of the empirical or theoretical investigation. For a long time, I thought that it was a good practice to keep the reader in suspense about actual results (the 'German style', see Chapter 9), so that they would need to read the actual paper to get the full picture. This was a mistaken view, however, since often people skim abstracts for interesting things to cite, and only read further if they think the results and discussion sound interesting and relevant. Suspense may work in other writing genres, but for abstracts you need to spill the beans, as the saying goes.

Conclusion

Research proposals are a key component of academic work. If you have spent some time thinking about the role of the different elements discussed in this book, putting together a proposal should not be a major effort. Even if not required, it is a good exercise to write down your research design. Writing is a way to clarify your thoughts and seeing the structured document may enable you to comprehend something about your design that you were not able to see previously. Proposals are a great way to wrap up the 'thinking about' part of your research before engaging in data collection, analysis and writing. Although not all research can be planned in detail in advance, a proposal is useful as a blueprint whenever you feel like you are lost in the middle of the research process.

This is the end of this book. For dramatic effect, I originally planned to follow this by saying, 'but it is the beginning of your research journey'. That would not be quite right, however. You have already started the journey. Whether your ideas are in your head, as notes on random slips of paper, or in proposal form, you have already gained an appreciation of what goes into a research project. Research design is the first half of the journey, where you make sense of the different elements and, importantly, their interconnections. With a good research design, you will (almost) always know what you are doing and why you are doing it. In my experience, 'what am I doing?' is a common question students, early-career scholars and even more experienced researchers grapple with when engaging in new research. Just as no map will take you to your destination by itself, no research design can anticipate all the contingencies you may face. Your creativity in the face of challenges makes the work your own. That is part of the beauty of research.

References

Ackerman, S. (2016) 'Women in Ancient Israel and the Hebrew Bible', in J. Barton (ed) *Oxford Research Encyclopedia of Religion*. DOI: 10.1093/acrefore/9780199340378.013.45 [Accessed 27 May 2021].

Adamczyk, A., Freilich, J.D. and Kim, C. (2017) 'Religion and Crime: A Systematic Review and Assessment of Next Steps', *Sociology of Religion* 78(2): 192–232.

Akutsu, T. (2020) 'Changes after Suzuki: A Retrospective Analysis and Review of Contemporary Issues Regarding the Suzuki Method in Japan', *International Journal of Music Education* 38(1): 18–35.

Alexander, M. (2010) *The New Jim Crow: Mass Incarceration in the Age of Colorblindness*. Harlow: Penguin Books.

Allan, S. (2010) *News Culture*. 3rd Edition. Maidenhead: Open University Press.

Alvesson, M. and Sandberg, J. (2020) 'The Problematizing Review: A Counterpoint to Elsbach and Van Knippenberg's Argument for Integrative Reviews', *Journal of Management Studies* 57(6): 1290–1304.

Aşık, O. (2022) 'How Does the Political Enter the Newsroom? The Representation of the Kurdish "Other" in Turkish Journalism', *Journalism* 23(11): 2434–2451. DOI: 10.1177/14648849211015604 [Accessed 27 May 2021].

Atkinson, P. and Coffey, A. (2003) 'Revisiting the Relationship between Participant Observation and Interviews', in Holstein, J.A. and Gubrium, J.F. (eds) *Inside Interviewing: New Lenses, New Concerns*. Thousand Oaks: SAGE, pp 415–428.

Baker, S.E. and Edwards, R. (2012) *How Many Qualitative Interviews Is Enough? Expert Voices and Early Career Reflections on Sampling and Cases in Qualitative Research*. np: National Centre for Research Methods.

Barbour, R. (2007) *Doing Focus Groups*. London: SAGE.

Bartlett, R. and Milligan, C. (2021) *Diary Method*. London: Bloomsbury Academic.

Bauman, Z. (2000) *Liquid Modernity*. Cambridge: Polity.

Baumrind, D. (1985) 'Research Using Intentional Deception: Ethical Issues Revisited', *American Psychologist* 40(2): 165–174.

Beck, U. (1992) *Risk Society: Towards a New Modernity*. London: SAGE.

Becker, H.S. (1991 [1963]) *Outsiders: Studies in the Sociology of Deviance*. New York: Free Press.

Becker, H.S. (2017) *Evidence*. Chicago: University of Chicago Press.

Becker, H.S. and Geer, B. (1957) 'Participant Observation and Interviewing: A Comparison', *Human Organization* 16(3): 28–32.

Berger, P.L. (1967) *The Sacred Canopy: Elements of a Sociological Theory of Religion*. Garden City: Anchor Books.

Biggs, J. (1996) 'Enhancing Teaching through Constructive Alignment', *Higher Education* 32: 347–364.

Billig, M. (2013) *Learn to Write Badly: How to Succeed in the Social Sciences*. Cambridge: Cambridge University Press.

Bitektine, A. (2008) 'Prospective Case Study Design: Qualitative Method for Deductive Theory Testing', *Organizational Research Methods* 11(1): 160–180.

Blaikie, N. (2010) *Designing Social Research*. 2nd Edition. Cambridge: Polity Press.

Blair, P. (2016) 'Liberalism', in Ray, S. and Schwarz, H. (eds) *The Encyclopedia of Postcolonial Studies*. https://doi.org/10.1002/9781119076506.wbeps208 [Accessed 18 October 2022].

Blake, A. (2017) 'Kellyanne Conway Says Donald Trump's Team Has "Alternative Facts." Which Pretty Much Says It All', *Washington Post*, [online] 22 January. https://www.washingtonpost.com/news/the-fix/wp/2017/01/22/kellyanne-conway-says-donald-trumps-team-has-alternate-facts-which-pretty-much-says-it-all/ [Accessed 14 November 2022].

Blumer, H. (1971) 'Social Problems as Collective Behavior', *Social Problems* 18(3): 298–306.

Boland, R. and Katzive, L. (2008) 'Developments in Laws on Induced Abortion: 1998–2007', *International Family Planning Perspectives* 34(3): 110–120.

Bonacich, E. (2007) 'Working with the Labor Movement: A Personal Journey in Organic Public Sociology', in Nichols, L.T. (ed) *Public Sociology: The Contemporary Debate*. New Brunswick: Transaction Publishers, pp 73–94.

Bouko, C., Naderer, B., Rieger, D., Van Ostaeyen, P. and Voué, P. (2022) 'Discourse Patterns Used by Extremist Salafists on Facebook: Identifying Potential Triggers to Cognitive Biases in Radicalized Content', *Critical Discourse Studies* 19(3): 252–273.

Bravata, D.M., Watts, S.A., Keefer, A.L., Madhusudhan, D.K., Taylor, K.T., Clark, D.M., et al (2020) 'Prevalence, Predictors, and Treatment of Impostor Syndrome: A Systematic Review', *Journal of General Internal Medicine* 35(4): 1252–1275.

Briggs, R. (1998 [1996]) *Witches and Neighbors: The Social and Cultural Context of European Witchcraft*. New York: Penguin Books.

Brown, D.L. and Wiener, A. (2022) 'The Racist Tuskegee Syphilis Experiment was Exposed 50 Years Ago', *The Washington Post*, 26 July. https://www.washingtonpost.com/history/2022/07/26/tuskegee-syphilis-experiment-50-years/ [Accessed 13 December 2022].

Bruce, S. (2017) *Secular Beats Spiritual: The Westernization of the Easternization of the West*. Oxford: Oxford University Press.

References

Burawoy, M. (2007) 'For Public Sociology', in Clawson, D., Zussman, R., Misra, J., Gerstel, N., Stokes, R., Anderstone, D.L. and Burawoy, M. (eds) *Public Sociology: Fifteen Eminent Sociologists Debate Politics & the Profession in the Twenty-First Century*. Berkeley: University of California Press, pp 23–64.

Burchardt, M. (2020) *Regulating Difference: Religious Diversity and Nationhood in the Secular West*. New Brunswick: Rutgers University Press.

Burke, P. (2005) *History and Social Theory*. 2nd Edition. Cambridge: Polity Press.

Buzan, T. (2006) *Mind Mapping: Kick-Start Your Creativity and Transform Your Life*. Harlow: BBC Active.

Calvey, D. (2008) 'The Art and Politics of Covert Research: Doing "Situated Ethics" in the Field', *Sociology* 42(5): 905–918.

Carlsson, M. and Eriksson, S. (2017) 'Do Attitudes Expressed in Surveys Predict Ethnic Discrimination?', *Ethnic and Racial Studies* 40(10): 1739–1757.

Cassell, J. (1980) 'Ethical Principles for Conducting Fieldwork', *American Anthropologist* 82(1): 28–41.

Chandler, D. (2000) *Bosnia: Faking Democracy after Dayton*. 2nd Edition. London: Pluto Press.

Chaves, M. (2013) 'Serendipity in the Study of Religion and Society', in Hjelm, T. and Zuckerman, P. (eds) *Studying Religion and Society: Sociological Self-Portraits*. London: Routledge, pp 105–115.

Clifford, J. and Marcus, G. (eds) (1986) *Writing Culture: The Poetics and Politics of Ethnography*. Berkeley: University of California Press.

Conklin, M. and Singh, S. (2022) 'Triple-Blind Review as a Solution to Gender Bias in Academic Publishing: A Theoretical Approach', *Studies in Higher Education* 47(12): 2487–2496.

Cook, T. and Inglis, P. (2009) 'Making our Own Decisions: Researching the Process of "Being Informed" with People with Learning Difficulties', *Research Ethics* 5(2): 55–64.

Cooper, B. (2015) 'Intersectionality', in Disch, L. and Hawkesworth, M. (eds) *The Oxford Handbook of Feminist Theory*. DOI: 10.1093/oxfordhb/9780199328581.013.20 [Accessed 7 June 2021].

Cooper, H. (2017) *Research Synthesis and Meta-Analysis*. Thousand Oaks: SAGE.

Creswell, J.W. (2003) *Research Design: Qualitative, Quantitative, and Mixed Methods Approaches*. 2nd Edition. Thousand Oaks: SAGE.

Crotty, M. (2003) *The Foundations of Social Research: Meaning and Perspective in the Research Process*. London: SAGE.

D'Ancona, M. (2017) *Post-Truth: The New War on Truth and How to Fight Back*. London: Ebury Press.

Daniels, J. (1946) *The Wilson Era: Years of War and After 1917–1923*. Chapel Hill: University of North Carolina Press.

Denscombe, M., Dingwall, G. and Hillier, T. (2008) 'At the Genesis of a Research Idea: Defending and Defining a Duty Prior to Ethics Review', *Research Ethics* 4(2): 73–75.

de Wit, H. (2020) 'Internationalization of Higher Education: The Need for a More Ethical and Qualitative Approach', *Journal of International Students* 10(1): i–iv.

Do, T.T. and Van Nguyen, A.T. (2020) '"They Know Better than We Doctors Do": Providers' Preparedness for Transgender Healthcare in Vietnam', *Health Sociology Review* 29(1): 92–107.

Doerschler, P. (2004) 'Education and the Development of Turkish and Yugoslav Immigrants' Political Attitudes in Germany', *German Politics* 13(3): 449–480.

Doesburg, C. (2022) *The Adaptation of the Kalevala and Folk Poetry in Finnish Metal Music*. Doctoral thesis (PhD), University College London. https://discovery.ucl.ac.uk/id/eprint/10153465 [Accessed 3 January 2023].

Drisko, J.W. and Maschi, T. (2016) *Content Analysis*. Oxford: Oxford University Press.

Durkheim, É. (1979 [1897]) *Suicide*. New York: The Free Press.

Elsbach, K.D. and van Knippenberg, D. (2020) 'Creating High-Impact Literature Reviews: An Argument for "Integrative Reviews"', *Journal of Management Studies* 57(6): 1277–1289.

Evans, A.R., Parutis, V. and Hart, G. (2009) 'The Sexual Attitudes and Lifestyles of London's Eastern Europeans (SALLEE Project): Design and Methods', *BMC Public Health* 9: 399. DOI: 10.1186/1471-2458-9-399.

Evans, R.J. (1997) *In Defence of History*. London: Granta Books.

Fakunle, O. (2021) 'International Students' Perspective on Developing Employability during Study Abroad', *Higher Education Quarterly* 75(4): 575–590.

Fellows, R. and Liu, A.M.M. (2020) 'Borrowing Theories: Contextual and Empirical Considerations', *Construction Management and Economics* 38(7): 581–588.

Franco, A., Malhotra, N. and Simonovits, G. (2014) 'Publication Bias in the Social Sciences: Unlocking the File Drawer', *Science* 345(6203): 1502–1505.

Franklin, B. (2005) 'McJournalism: The Local Press and the McDonaldization Thesis', in Allan, S. (ed) *Journalism: Critical Issues*. Maidenhead: Open University Press, pp 137–150.

Fujii, L.A. (2012) 'Research Ethics 101: Dilemmas and Responsibilities', *PS: Political Science & Politics* 45(4): 717–723.

Fuller, S. (2018) *Post-Truth: Knowledge as a Power Game*. London: Anthem Press.

Fuller, S. (2020) *A Player's Guide to the Post-Truth Condition: Name of the Game*. London: Anthem Press.

Furnham, A. (2013) *Lay Theories: Everyday Understanding of Problems in the Social Sciences*. Oxford: Pergamon Press.

Garfinkel, H. (1967) *Studies in Ethnomethodology*. Oxford: Blackwell.

References

Glaser, B.G. and Strauss, A.L. (2017 [1967]) *The Discovery of Grounded Theory: Strategies for Qualitative Research*. New York: Routledge.

Gobo, G. (2008) *Doing Ethnography*. Translated by Adrian Belton. London: SAGE.

Gopal, P. (2013) 'Renegade Prophets and Native Acolytes: Liberalism and Imperialism Today', in Huggan, G. (ed.) *The Oxford Handbook of Postcolonial Studies*. https://doi.org/10.1093/oxfordhb/9780199588251.013.0028 [Accessed 18 October 2022].

Gottfredson, M.R. and Hirschi, T. (1990) *A General Theory of Crime*. Stanford: Stanford University Press.

Gover, A.R., Jennings, W.G. and Tewksbury, R. (2009) 'Adolescent Male and Female Gang Members' Experiences with Violent Victimization, Dating Violence, and Sexual Assault', *American Journal of Criminal Justice* 34: 103–115.

Grant, M.J. and Booth, A. (2009) 'A Typology of Reviews: An Analysis of 14 Review Types and Associated Methodologies', *Health Information & Libraries Journal* 26(2): 91–108.

Green, D. (2022) *Social Science Experiments: A Hands-on Introduction*. Cambridge: Cambridge University Press.

Greenwald, A.G. and Schuh, E.S. (1994) 'An Ethnic Bias in Scientific Citations', *European Journal of Social Psychology* 24(6): 623–639.

Greetham, B. (2009) *How to Write Your Undergraduate Dissertation*. Basingstoke: Palgrave Macmillan.

Gregory, A. (2008) *The Last Great War: British Society and the First World War*. Cambridge: Cambridge University Press.

Gribble, C., Blackmore, J. and Rahimi, M. (2015) 'Challenges to Providing Work Integrated Learning to International Business Students at Australian Universities', *Higher Education, Skills and Work-Based Learning* 5(4): 401–416.

Gruijters, R. [@RobGruijters1] (2021) 'Western-centrism in sociology? Following @brankomilaniv tweet I decided to check the geographic focus of top sociology publications since 2019. Here are the results'. [Tweet]. https://twitter.com/RobGruijters1/status/1394955343608811520 [Accessed 22 September 2023].

Günther, E. and Quandt, T. (2016) 'Word Counts and Topic Models', *Digital Journalism* 4(1): 75–88.

Guzzini, S. (2013) *Power, Realism and Constructivism*. London: Routledge.

Harvey, D. (2003) *The New Imperialism*. New York: Oxford University Press.

Hawley, K. (2019) 'I—What Is Impostor Syndrome?', *Aristotelian Society Supplementary Volume* 93(1): 203–226.

Heelas, P. and Woodhead, L. with Seel, B., Szerszynski, B. and Tusting, K. (2005) *The Spiritual Revolution: Why Religion is Giving Away to Spirituality*. Oxford: Blackwell.

Heiner, R. (2002) *Social Problems: An Introduction to Critical Constructionism*. New York: Oxford University Press.

Herbert, D.E.J. (2011) 'Theorizing Religion and Media in Contemporary Societies: An Account of Religious "Publicization"', *European Journal of Cultural Studies* 14(6): 626–648.

Herrera, C.D. (2001) 'Ethics, Deception, and "Those Milgram Experiments"', *Journal of Applied Philosophy* 18(3): 245–256.

Hilgartner, S. and Bosk, C.L. (1988) 'The Rise and Fall of Social Problems: A Public Arenas Model', *American Journal of Sociology* 94(1): 53–78.

Hilton, S., Patterson, C. and Teyhan, A. (2012) 'Escalating Coverage of Obesity in UK Newspapers: The Evolution and Framing of the "Obesity Epidemic" From 1996 to 2010', *Obesity* 20(8): 1688–1695.

Hine, C. (2000) *Virtual Ethnography*. London: SAGE.

Hjelm, T. (ed) (2011) *Religion and Social Problems*. New York: Routledge.

Hjelm, T. (2014) *Social Constructionisms: Approaches to the Study of the Human World*. Basingstoke: Palgrave Macmillan.

Hjelm, T. (2015) 'Is God Back? Reconsidering the New Visibility of Religion', in Hjelm, T. (ed) *Is God Back? Reconsidering the New Visibility of Religion*. London: Bloomsbury Academic, pp 1–16.

Hjelm, T. (2019) 'One *Volk*, One Church? A Critique of the "Folk Church" Ideology in Finland', *Journal of Church and State* 62(2): 294–315.

Hjelm, T. and Maude, G. (2021) *Historical Dictionary of Finland*. Lanham: Rowman & Littlefield.

Hraundal, T.J. (2014) 'New Perspectives on Eastern Vikings/Rus in Arabic Sources', *Viking and Medieval Scandinavia* 10: 65–97.

Hobsbawm, E. (1962) *The Age of Revolution: Europe 1789–1848*. London: Abacus.

Hobsbawm, E. (1975) *The Age of Capital: 1848–1875*. London: Weidenfeld & Nicholson.

Hobsbawm, E. (1987) *The Age of Empire: 1875–1914*. London: Weidenfeld & Nicholson.

Hobsbawm, E. (1994) *The Age of Extremes: The Short Twentieth Century, 1914–1991*. London: Michael Joseph.

Howse, E., Watts, C., McGill, B., Kite, J., Rowbotham, S., Hawe, P., et al (2022) 'Sydney's "Last Drinks" Laws: A Content Analysis of News Media Coverage of Views and Arguments about a Preventive Health Policy', *Drug and Alcohol Review* 41(3): 561–574.

Huff, A.S. (1999) *Writing for Scholarly Publication*. Thousand Oaks: SAGE.

Humfrey, C. (2011) 'The Long and Winding Road: A Review of the Policy, Practice and Development of the Internationalisation of Higher Education in the UK', *Teachers and Teaching* 17(6): 649–661.

Hutchinson, S.A. (1986) 'Education and Grounded Theory', *Journal of Thought* 21(3): 50–68.

Jenkins, R. (2008) *Social identity*. 3rd Edition. Abingdon: Routledge.

References

Johnson, W.B. and Mullen, C.A. (2007) *Write to the Top: How to Become a Prolific Academic*. New York: Palgrave Macmillan.

Kaas, L. and Manger, C. (2012) 'Ethnic Discrimination in Germany's Labour Market: A Field Experiment', *German Economic Review* 13(1): 1–20.

Kalberg, S. (1994) *Max Weber's Comparative-Historical Sociology*. Cambridge: Polity.

Kalmijn, M. (1998) 'Intermarriage and Homogamy: Causes, Patterns, Trends', *Annual Review of Sociology* 24: 395–421.

Kapferer, B. (1979) 'Entertaining Demons: Comedy, Interaction and Meaning in a Sinhalese Healing Ritual', *Social Analysis: The International Journal of Social and Cultural Practice* 1: 108–152.

Kaplan, L., Kuhnt, J., Picot, L.E. and Grasham, C.F. (2023) 'Safeguarding Research Staff "In the Field": A Blind Spot in Ethics Guidelines', *Research Ethics* 19(1): 18–41.

Kaptchuk, T.J. (2013) 'The Placebo Effect in Alternative Medicine: Can the Performance of a Healing Ritual Have Clinical Significance?', in Miller, F.G., Colloca, L., Crouch, R.A. and Kaptchuk, T.J. (eds) *The Placebo: A Reader*. Baltimore: Johns Hopkins University Press, pp 64–70.

Karlsson, J.C. and Bergman, A. (2017) *Methods for Social Theory: Analytical Tools for Theorizing and Writing*. Abingdon: Routledge.

Kazansky, B. (2021) '"It depends on your threat model": The Anticipatory Dimensions of Resistance to Data-Driven Surveillance', *Big Data & Society*, 8(1). doi: 10.1177/2053951720985557.

Kim, J.S., Samson, J.F., Fitzgerald, R. and Hartry, A. (2010) 'A Randomized Experiment of a Mixed-Methods Literacy Intervention for Struggling Readers in Grades 4–6: Effects on Word Reading Efficiency, Reading Comprehension and Vocabulary, and Oral Reading Fluency', *Reading and Writing* 23(9): 1109–1129.

King, S. (2000) *On Writing: A Memoir of the Craft*. London: Hodder & Stoughton.

Knopf, J. (2006) 'Doing a Literature Review', *PS: Political Science & Politics* 39(1): 127–132.

Kozinets, R. (2010) *Netnography: Doing Ethnographic Research Online*. Thousand Oaks: SAGE.

Kuhn, T.S. (1996 [1962]) *The Structure of Scientific Revolutions*. 3rd Edition. Chicago: University of Chicago Press.

Kundnani, A. (2012) 'Radicalisation: The Journey of a Concept', *Race & Class* 54(2): 3–25.

Larja, L., Warius, J., Sundbäck, L., Liebkind, K., Kandolin, I. and Jasinskaja-Lahti, I. (2012) *Discrimination in the Finnish Labor Market: An Overview and a Field Experiment on Recruitment*. Työ ja yrittäjyys (Employment and Entrepreneurship), Työ- ja elinkeinoministeriö, Helsinki. http://www.tem.fi/files/32827/TEMjul_16_2012_web.pdf [Accessed 11 October 2021].

Layder, D. (1993) *New Strategies in Social Research*. Cambridge: Polity Press.

Lester, J. (2009) 'Not Your Child's Playground: Workplace Bullying Among Community College Faculty', *Community College Journal of Research and Practice* 33(5): 444–462.

Le Texier, T. (2019) 'Debunking the Stanford Prison Experiment', *American Psychologist* 74(7): 823–839.

Lichtblau, K. (1995) 'Sociology and the Diagnosis of the Times or: The Reflexivity of Modernity', *Theory, Culture & Society* 12(1): 25–52.

Lima, P. (2008) *How to Write a Non-Fiction Book in 60 Days*. np: Five Rivers Chapmanry.

Lin, L. and Miller, S.L. (2020) 'Protective Factors against Juvenile Delinquency: Exploring Gender with a Nationally Representative Sample of Youth', *Social Science Research* 86. https://doi.org/10.1016/j.ssresearch.2019.102376.

Maduka-Okafor, F.C., Okoye, O.I., Oguego, N., Udeh, N., Aghaji, A., Okoye, O., et al (2022) 'Recruiting Pupils for a School-Based Eye Study in Nigeria: Trust and Informed Consent Concerns', *Research Ethics* 18(1): 13–23.

Marginson, S. (2012) 'Including the Other: Regulation of the Human Rights of Mobile Students in a Nation-Bound World', *Higher Education* 63(4): 497–512.

Martin, N. (2015) '"And all because it is war!": First World War Diaries, Authenticity and Combatant Identity', *Textual Practice* 29(7): 1245–1263.

Marx, K. (1845) 'Theses on Feuerbach', *Marx Engels Archive*. https://www.marxists.org/archive/marx/works/1845/theses/ [Accessed 7 June 2021].

Maynard, D.W. and Heritage, J. (2005) 'Conversation Analysis, Doctor–Patient Interaction and Medical Communication', *Medical Education* 39(4): 428–435.

McIntyre, A. (2008) *Participatory Action Research*. Thousand Oaks: SAGE.

McIntyre, L. (2018) *Post-Truth*. Cambridge, MA: MIT Press.

Meldrum, R.C. (2016) 'Low Self-Control Takes Flight: The Association Between Indicators of Low Self-Control and Imprudent Airline Passenger Behavior', *The Social Science Journal* 53(4): 444–454.

Merriam-Webster (nda) 'Method', *Merriam-Webster.com Dictionary*. https://www.merriam-webster.com/dictionary/method [Accessed 23 September 2023].

Merriam-Webster (ndb) 'Parsimony', *Merriam-Webster.com Dictionary*. https://www.merriam-webster.com/dictionary/parsimony [Accessed 31 August 2021].

Messamore, A. (2023) 'The Effect of Community Organizing on Landlords' Use of Eviction Filing: Evidence from U.S. Cities', *Social Problems*. https://doi.org/10.1093/socpro/spac061.

Mindess, H. (1967) 'Freud on Dostoevsky', *The American Scholar* 36(3): 446–452.

References

Miner, J.B. (2000) 'Testing a Psychological Typology of Entrepreneurship Using Business Founders', *The Journal of Applied Behavioral Science* 36(1): 43–69.

Minkler, M. (2005) 'Community-Based Research Partnerships: Challenges and Opportunities', *Journal of Urban Health* 82(2): ii3–ii12.

Modell, S., Vinnari, E. and Lukka, K. (2017) 'On the Virtues and Vices of Combining Theories: The Case of Institutional and Actor-Network Theories in Accounting Research', *Accounting, Organizations and Society* 60: 62–78.

Moran, J. (2018) *First You Write a Sentence: The Elements of Reading, Writing … and Life*. London: Penguin.

Morroni, C., Myer, L. and Tibazarwa, K. (2006) 'Knowledge of the Abortion Legislation Among South African Women: A Cross-Sectional Study', *Reproductive Health* 3(7): np. https://doi.org/10.1186/1742-4755-3-7.

Mortensen, M. and Baarts, C.A. (2018) 'Killing Ourselves with Laughter … Mapping the Interplay of Organizational Teasing and Workplace Bullying in Hospital Work Life', *Qualitative Research in Organizations and Management* 13(1): 10–31.

Mouritzen, H. (1988) *Finlandization: Towards a General Theory of Adaptive Politics*. Avebury: Ashgate.

Nisbett, G.S. and DeWalt, C.C. (2016) 'Exploring the Influence of Celebrities in Politics: A Focus Group Study of Young Voters', *Atlantic Journal of Communication* 24(3): 144–156.

Nissilä, P. (2018) 'Young People at a Revivalist Summer Gathering: Rituals, Liminality, and Emotions', *Social Compass* 65(2): 278–294.

Noro, A. (2000) 'Aikalaisdiagnoosi sosiologisen teorian kolmantena lajityyppinä', *Sosiologia* 37(4): 321–329.

Oakley, A. (2010) 'The Social Science of Biographical Life-Writing: Some Methodological and Ethical Issues', *International Journal of Social Research Methodology* 13(5): 425–439.

Oktay, J.S. (2012) *Grounded Theory*. Oxford: Oxford University Press.

O'Mahony, K. and Garavan, T.N. (2012) 'Implementing a Quality Management Framework in a Higher Education Organisation: A Case Study', *Quality Assurance in Education* 20(2): 184–200.

Ost, J., Wright, D.B., Easton, S., Hope, L. and French C.C. (2013) 'Recovered Memories, Satanic Abuse, Dissociative Identity Disorder and False Memories in the UK: A Survey of Clinical Psychologists and Hypnotherapists', *Psychology, Crime & Law* 19(1): 1–19.

Østebø, M.T., Haukanes, H. and Blystad, A. (2013) 'Strong State Policies on Gender and Aid: Threats and Opportunities for Norwegian Faith-Based Organisations', *Forum for Development Studies* 40(2): 193–216.

Oswick, C., Fleming, P. and Hanlon, G. (2011) 'From Borrowing to Blending: Rethinking the Processes of Organizational Theory Building', *Academy of Management Review* 36(2): 318–337.

Pakkasvirta, J. (2018) 'Latin American Stereotypes in Finnish Social Media', *Iberoamericana – Nordic Journal of Latin American and Caribbean Studies* 47(1): 94–107.

Palamar, J.J., Rutherford, C. and Keyes, K.M. (2019) '"Flakka" Use among High School Seniors in the United States', *Drug and Alcohol Dependence* 196: 86–90.

Palmer, S.J. (2017) 'Renegade Researchers, Radical Religions, Recalcitrant Ethics Boards: Towards the "McDonaldization" of Social Research in North America', *Fieldwork in Religion* 12(2): 239–258.

Parker, J. and Stanworth, H., with Mars, L. and Ransome, P. (2015) *Explaining Social Life: A Guide to Using Social Theory*. London: Palgrave.

Patrick, H., Mantzicopoulos, P. and Samarapungavan, A. (2009) 'Motivation for Learning Science in Kindergarten: Is There a Gender Gap and Does Integrated Inquiry and Literacy Instruction Make a Difference', *Journal of Research in Science Teaching* 46(2): 166–191.

Pimple, K.D. (2002) 'Six Domains of Research Ethics', *Science and Engineering Ethics* 8(2): 191–205.

Provost, G. (1985) *100 Ways to Improve Your Writing*. New York: Mentor.

Purcell, K. and Elias, P. (2004) *Seven Years On: Graduate Careers in a Changing Labour Market*. Report. HECSU.

Randolph, J. (2009) 'A Guide to Writing the Dissertation Literature Review', *Practical Assessment, Research, and Evaluation* 14(1): Article 13. https://scholarworks.umass.edu/pare/vol14/iss1/13 [Accessed 17 October 2022].

Resignato, A.J. (2000) 'Violent Crime: A Function of Drug Use or Drug Enforcement?', *Applied Economics* 32(6): 681–688.

Richardson, J.E. (2007) *Analysing Newspapers: An Approach from Critical Discourse Analysis*. Basingstoke: Palgrave.

Ritzer, G. (1983) 'The "McDonaldization" of Society', *Journal of American Culture* 6(1): 100–107.

Ritzer, G. (1992) *The McDonaldization of Society*. Newbury Park: Pine Forge Press.

Robinson, C. (2020) 'Ethically Important Moments as Data: Reflections from Ethnographic Fieldwork in Prisons', *Research Ethics* 16(1–2): 1–15.

Robinson, J.P. (2002) 'The Time-Diary Method', in Pentland, W.E., Harvey, A.S., Lawton, M.P. and McColl, M.A. (eds) *Time Use Research in the Social Sciences*. Boston: Springer (pp 47–89). https://doi.org/10.1007/0-306-47155-8_3.

Rocha, Z.L. and Yeoh, B.S.A. (2023) 'Orang Cina Bukan Cina: Being Peranakan, (Not) Being Chinese and the Social Construction of Race in Singapore', *Identities*, 30(4): 568–587. Published online 14 November 2022. DOI: 10.1080/1070289X.2022.2145775.

References

Römgens, I., Scoupe, R. and Beausaert, S. (2020) 'Unraveling the Concept of Employability, Bringing Together Research on Employability in Higher Education and the Workplace', *Studies in Higher Education* 45(12): 2588–2603.

Ross, E. (2021) '"What we see and what we hear": Combining Children's Drawings with Child and Educator Interviews to Assess Child Well-being in Child Support Grant (CSG) Beneficiaries in South Africa', *Journal of Human Behavior in the Social Environment* 31(7): 848–866.

Ross, F. (2009) 'Degrees of Disciplinarity in Comparative Politics: Interdisciplinarity, Multidisciplinarity and Borrowing', *European Political Science* 8(1): 26–36.

Said, E. (1981) *Covering Islam: How the Media and the Experts Determine How we See the Rest of the World*. London: Routledge & Kegan Paul.

Sartori, G. (2005) 'Party Types, Organisation and Functions', *West European Politics* 28(1): 5–32.

Schedler, A. (1998) 'What is Democratic Consolidation?', *Journal of Democracy* 9(2): 91–107.

Schrag, Z.M. (2011) 'The Case against Ethics Review in the Social Sciences', *Research Ethics* 7(4): 120–131.

Schwartz-Shea, P. and Yanow, D. (2012) *Interpretive Research Design: Concepts and Processes*. New York and London: Routledge.

Sedgh, G., Finer L.B., Bankole, A., Eilers, M.A. and Singh, S. (2015) 'Adolescent Pregnancy, Birth, and Abortion Rates across Countries: Levels and Recent Trends', *Journal of Adolescent Health* 56(2): 223–230.

Seghal, M. (2009) 'The Veiled Feminist Ethnographer: Fieldwork Among Women of India's Hindu Right', in Huggins, M.K. and Glebbeek, M.-L. (eds) *Women Fielding Danger: Negotiating Ethnographic Identities in Field Research*. Lanham: Rowman & Littlefield, pp 325–352.

Shah, A., Pell, K. and Brooke, P. (2004) 'Beyond First Destinations: Graduate Employability Survey', *Active Learning in Higher Education* 5(9): 9–26.

Sherwood, G. and Parsons, S. (2021) 'Negotiating the Practicalities of Informed Consent in the Field with Children and Young People: Learning from Social Science Researchers', *Research Ethics* 17(4): 448–463.

Shrout, P.E. and Rodgers, J.L. (2018) 'Psychology, Science, and Knowledge Construction: Broadening Perspectives from the Replication Crisis', *Annual Review of Psychology* 69(1): 487–510.

Shuell, T.J. (1986) 'Cognitive Conceptions of Learning', *Review of Educational Research* 56(4): 411–436.

Silverman, D. (2007) *A Very Short, Fairly Interesting and Reasonably Cheap Book about Qualitative Research*. London: SAGE.

Silvia, P.J. (2007) *How to Write a Lot: A Practical Guide to Productive Academic Writing*. Washington, DC: American Psychological Association.

Soares, M.E. and Mosquera, P. (2020) 'Linking Development of Skills and Perceptions of Employability: The Case of Erasmus Students', *Economic Research* 33(1): 2769–2786.

Somekh, B. (2006) *Action Research: A Methodology for Change and Development*. Maidenhead: Open University Press.

Spickard, J.V. (2017) *Research Basics: Design to Data Analysis in Six Steps*. Los Angeles: SAGE.

Spicker, P. (2011) 'Ethical Covert Research', *Sociology* 45(1): 118–133.

Stark, R. and Bainbridge, W.S. (1996) *Religion, Deviance, and Social Control*. New York: Routledge.

Starr, M.A. (2014) 'Qualitative and Mixed-Methods Research in Economics: Surprising Growth, Promising Future', *Journal of Economic Surveys* 28(2): 238–264.

Stearns, P.N. (2008) 'History of Emotions: Issues of Change and Impact', in Lewis, M., Haviland-Jones, J.M. and Barrett, L.F. (eds) *Handbook of Emotions*. 3rd Edition. New York and London: Guilford Press, pp 17–31.

Stolz, J. (2020) 'Secularization Theories in the Twenty-First Century: Ideas, Evidence, and Problems. Presidential Address', *Social Compass* 67(2): 282–308.

Strand, K.J., Cutforth, N., Stoecker, R., Marullo, S. and Donohue, P. (2003) *Community-Based Research and Higher Education: Principles and Practices*. San Francisco: Jossey-Bass.

Suddaby, R. (2006) 'From the Editors: What Grounded Theory is Not', *Academy of Management Journal* 49(4): 633–642.

Swedberg, R. (2020) 'Exploratory Research', in Elman, C., Gerring, J. and Mahoney, J. (eds) *The Production of Knowledge: Enhancing Progress in Social Science*. Cambridge: Cambridge University Press, pp 17–41.

Sword, H. (2017) *Air & Light & Time & Space: How Successful Academics Write*. Cambridge, MA: Harvard University Press.

Teichler, U. (1999) 'Research on the Relationship between Higher Education and the World of Work: Past Achievements, Problems and New Challenges', *Higher Education* 38(2): 169–190.

Tinker, A. and Coomber, V. (2005) 'University Research Ethics Committees: A Summary of Research into Their Role, Remit and Conduct', *Research Ethics* 1(1): 5–11.

Tsegaye, K.K. (2020) 'The Role of Regional Parliaments in Conflict Resolution: The Case of the Pan-African Parliament (2004–2011)', *African Journal of Political Science and International Relations* 14(4): 168–179.

UCL News (2019) 'Cutting Refugees' Benefits Results in More Crime and Less Education', *UCL News*, [online] 22 March. https://www.ucl.ac.uk/news/2019/mar/cutting-refugees-benefits-results-more-crime-and-less-education [Accessed 8 June 2021].

References

van den Hoonaard, W.C. (2011) *The Seduction of Ethics: Transforming the Social Sciences*. Toronto: University of Toronto Press.

Ventresca, M.J. and Mohr, J.W. (2017) 'Archival Research Methods', in Baum, J.A.C. (ed) *The Blackwell Companion to Organizations*. Oxford: Wiley-Blackwell, pp 805–828. https://doi.org/10.1002/9781405164061.ch35.

Voas, D., Olson, D.V.A. and Crockett, A. (2002) 'Religious Pluralism and Participation: Why Previous Research is Wrong', *American Sociological Review* 67(2): 212–230.

Wagner, H.R. (1968) Book review of *The Discovery of Grounded Theory*, *Social Forces* 46(4): 555.

Walseth, K., Engebretsen, B. and Elvebakk, L. (2018) 'Meaningful Experiences in PE for All Students: An Activist Research Approach', *Physical Education and Sport Pedagogy* 23(3): 235–249.

Weber, M. (2001 [1904–1905]) *The Protestant Ethic and the Spirit of Capitalism*. Translated by Talcott Parsons. London: Routledge.

White, P. (2009) *Developing Research Questions: A Guide for Social Scientists*. Basingstoke: Palgrave Macmillan.

Wienke, B. and Jekauc, D. (2016) 'A Qualitative Analysis of Emotional Facilitators in Exercise', *Frontiers in Psychology* 7: np. https://www.frontiersin.org/articles/10.3389/fpsyg.2016.01296/full [Accessed 3 September 2021].

Wilde, M. (2020) *Birth Control Battles: How Race and Class Divided American Religion*. Oakland: University of California Press.

Williams, C.K., Wynn D.E. Jr., Hassan, N.R., Mingers, J. and Stahl, B. (2018) 'A Critical Realist Script for Creative Theorising in Information Systems', *European Journal of Information Systems* 27(3): 315–325.

Woodiwiss, A. (2005) *Scoping the Social: An Introduction to the Practice of Social Theory*. Maidenhead: Open University Press.

Woodside, A.G. (2017) *Case Study Research: Core Skills in Using 15 Genres*. Bingley: Emerald.

Yan, M.C. (2008) 'Exploring Cultural Tensions in Cross-Cultural Social Work Practice', *Social Work* 53(4): 317–328.

Yin, R.K. (1994) *Case Study Research: Design and Methods*. 2nd Edition. Thousand Oaks: SAGE.

Yin, R.K. (2018) *Case Study Research: Design and Methods*. 6th Edition. Thousand Oaks: SAGE.

Yorke, M. (2004) 'Employability in the Undergraduate Curriculum: Some Student Perspectives', *European Journal of Education* 39(4): 409–427.

Zuboff, S. (2019) *The Age of Surveillance Capitalism: The Fight for a Human Future at the New Frontier of Power*. London: Profile Books.

Index

References to figures appear in *italic* type; those in **bold** type refer to tables.

A

abstracts 143, 148, 149, 165
action research 58
activist research 119, 130, 131
Adamczyk, Amy 83
Alexander, Michelle 100
alignment of research elements 9–12
alternative facts 33
archival research 58–59
articulated positions 43–46
Aşık, Ozan 124–125
audio methods 60
authorship attribution 118–119

B

Bauman, Zygmunt 99
Beck, Ulrich 99
Becker, Howard S. 35, 37, 40, 59, 109
Berger, Peter L. 101
bias 46, 111
bibliographies 74
Billig, Michael, *Learn to Write Badly* 127–128, 151
Blaikie, Norman 55
Blair, Peter 74
Blair, Tony 145
Blumer, Herbert 96
Boland, Reed 35–36
Bonacich, Edna 131
Booth, Andrew 84
Bosk, Charles L. 96
Bouko, Catherine 81
Briggs, Robin 3
broad topics 22
Bruce, Steve 132, 133
Bukowski, Charles 150
Burawoy, Michael 130
Burchardt, Marian 20–21

C

case study research 47–48
Chandler, David 90, 91
change-driven questions 27–28
Chaves, Mark 45–46, 67

children, as research participants 112, 113
coding 63, 94
collegiality 106, 110–111, 116, 118
combining theories 102–104
community-based research 18
confidentiality 114, 117–118
conflicts of interest 119
consent 109, 111–113
constructionist approaches 27–28, 41, 57–58
constructive alignment 9
content analysis 62–63
contribution claims *see* research contribution
convenience samples 62
conversation analysis 57, 64
Conway, Kellyanne 33
covert research 112–113
COVID-19 pandemic 31, 37–38
Creswell, John W. 108
critical approaches 116
cross-disciplinary borrowing 19, 101–102
Crotty, Michael, *Foundations of Social Research* 12

D

data analysis
    articulated/hidden positions 43–46
    importance of method 51–52, 52–54
    practical importance of 4–5
    theory and 90–91
    types of methods 57–58, 62–65
data collection
    covert research 112–113
    importance of method 51–52, 52–54, 58
    inaccessible/unachievable data 3–4, 30–31, 37–38, 48
    informed consent 109, 111–113
    resource issues 31, 38, 48
    risk of harm 114–116
    sample sizes 46–49
    skills and competencies 38
    types of methods 58–62
data triangulation 40, 43, 45–46, 54, 67–68
data-driven research interests 13–14
dead end questions 28–31

deceptive experiments 105, 109
deductive model of research 91–93
definitions, use of 51, 101
descriptive questions 25–26
descriptive statistics 63–64
DeWalt, Christina Childs 60
diaries 42, 57, 61–62
disciplinary borrowing 19, 101–102
disciplinary traditions 19–20, 34–35, 53, 54
discourse analysis 9–10, 57, 62, 64
discursive methods 62–63
Doerschler, Peter 66
Doesburg, Charlotte 79
Dostoyevsky, Fyodor 30
Drisko, James W. 62–63
Durkheim, Émile 75, 84–85, 99
Dustmann, Christian 130–131

E
Economic and Social Research Council (UK) 113
Elsbach, Kimberly 84, 86
empirical contribution claims 124–125
epistemology 12–13, 56–57
ethics *see* research ethics
ethics committees 107, 108, 119–120, 121
ethnic bias 111
ethnographic research 14, 31, 38–45, 54–55, 59, 65, 105, 114–116, 120, 129
European Research Council template proposal 154–155, **155**
experiments 59
expert knowledge 43, 74
explanation-driven questions 26–27, 35
explanatory research 66–67
exploratory research 66, 67

F
fabrication of research 116, 125
fair use 118
Fakunle, Omolake 76–77, 80
falsification of research 116, 125
fieldwork methods *see* ethnographic research; interviews
Finnish Literature Society 61
first-order data 38–39
focus groups 59–60
Franklin, Bob 95
Freud, Sigmund 30
Fujii, Lee Ann 111, 112

funnel approach (literature review) 79
funnel method (research question) 22–25

G
Game of Thrones 43–44
gaps in literature 18–19, 72, 79–81, 124–125
Garavan, Thomas N. 48
Garfinkel, Harold 102
Geer, Blanche 40
gender bias 111
Glaser, Barney G. 65, 94
Gopal, Priyamvada 74
Gover, Angela R. 42
government agencies, research by 120–121
  see also official data
Grant, Maria J. 84
Greenwald, Anthony G. 111
Gregory, Adrian 57
Grounded Theory 65, 91, 93–95

H
Harvey, David 74
Heiner, Robert 102–103
Herbert, David E.J. 95–96
hidden positions 43–46
Hilgartner, Stephen 96
Hine, Christine 129
Hobsbawm, Eric 93, 100
'holy trinity' figure 6
honorary authorship 119
how-questions 27–28
Howse, Eloise 63
hypotheses 24–25, 66

I
identity (articulated positions) 44–45
identity (construction of) 57
impostor syndrome 145
informed consent 109, 111–113
interdisciplinarity 19
  see also disciplinary borrowing
interpretative contribution claims 125–127
intersectionality 126
interviews 37, 39–43, 47, 48–49, 59–60, 60–61, 114–116
introductions 148–149

J
Jekauc, Darko 30
Jenkins, Richard 44
Johnson, W. Brad, *Write to the Top* 151

Index

journal article submissions 10, 101, 116, 123, 149
journalism 43, 46, 120–121
justification of research design 10–11

K
Kaplan, Jeffrey 21
Katzive, Laura 35–36
Kazansky, Becky 24
Kendal Project 131–133
keyword searches 73, 82, 85
keywords in title 148
King, Stephen 136
Kuhn, Thomas S. 71

L
Lavoisier, Antoine 71
lay theory, as research question 18
Layder, Derek 94, 98, 103
Lester, Jaime 39
letting go 147
Lichtblau, Klaus 99
Lin, Liu 92
Lincoln, Abraham 21–22
literature, gaps in 18–19, 72, 79–81, 124–125
literature review 71–88
    broad reviews of emerging topics 85
    checklist **87**
    competing schools of thought 110
    critical analysis and creative synthesis 76–79
    functions of review 71–72, 73
    narrative reviews 73, 82–83
    narrow reviews of mature topics 84–85, 86–87
    positioning 79–81
    relevance to topic 72, 73–76, 85
    sources 73–76
    systematic reviews 83–84
    theory section distinguished 86–87
    unacknowledged biases 111
    writing 87

M
Martin, Nancy 57
Marx, Karl 89, 129–130
Maschi, Tina 62–63
material methods 60
memory-writing method 61–62
Messamore, Andrew 64–65
meta-analysis 83

method *see* research methods
method-driven research interests 52–53
methodological contribution claims 128–129
Milgram, Stanley 8, 114
Miller, Susan L. 92
Miner, John B. 19
mixed methods 65–68
Moran, Joe, *First You Write a Sentence* 151
Morroni, Chelsea 36
Mortensen, Mille 39
Mullen, Carol A., *Write to the Top* 151

N
narrative analysis 57, 64
narrative reviews 73, 82–83
naturally occurring data 35–38
netnography 129
Nisbett, Gwendelyn S. 60
non-probability sampling 62
Noro, Arto 100

O
objectivist approach 57–58
'Occam's razor' *see* parsimony principle
official data 36–37
O'Mahony, Kim 48
one question rule 21
online questionnaires 48
ontology 12–13, 56–57
originality in research 19

P
paintings 42–43
Palmer, Susan J. 119–120, 121
parsimony principle 20–22, 103–104
Parsons, Talcott 102
participant observation *see* ethnographic research
participatory action research 58, 119
peer review 71, 144, 147
Pimple, Kenneth D. 106, 107, 117
plagiarism 118
positioning 79–81
    see also gaps in literature
positivism 13
positivistic paradigm 91–93
practical contribution claims 129–131
practical research questions 18
prisoners, as research participants 113
probability sampling 62
problem-driven research interests 15

process-driven questions 27–28
procrastination 149–151
proposals *see* research proposals
purpose statements *see* research contribution

Q
quantitative versus qualitative methods 34–35, 55–56, 57–58
question-driven research interests 15

R
reading for research 73–79
reading for writing 140–144, **141**
reflexive ethnography 40–41
reflexivity 118
RELIACT project 156–164
replication crisis 116, 125
replication research 125
research contribution 123–134
    empirical claims 124–125
    ethical aspects 116–117
    interpretative claims 125–127
    methodological claims 128–129
    overstretching claims 131–133
    practical claims 129–131
    theoretical contributions 91, 127–128
    writing 148–149
    see also gaps in literature
research data *see* data analysis; data collection
research design, defined 1–2
research elements
    alignment of 9–12
    core elements 5–8, *6*
    justification of 10–11
    see also individual elements
research ethics 105–122
    the common good 116
    confidentiality 114, 117–118
    ethical writing 117–119
    ethics committees 107, 108, 119–120, 121
    fundamental importance of 105
    informed consent 109, 111–113
    research questions 108–109
    risk of harm 114–116
    rules distinguished 107–108
    six 'domain' framework 106
    terminology 107
    truthfulness 116
research interests 13–15
research literature *see* literature, gaps in; literature review

research methods
    background assumptions 56–58
    balanced attitude toward 51–54
    choice of method 54–55
    contribution claims 128–129
    data analysis methods 62–65
    data collection methods 58–62
    disciplinary differences 53
    'method' defined 7, 51
    methodology distinguished 7, 51
    mixed methods 65–68
    as research interest 14–15
    risk of harm 114–116
research paradigms 13–14
research proposals 153–165
    feasibility 155, 163–164
    model proposal 156–164
    introduction 156–159
    aims and objectives 159–161
    research materials and methods 161–162
    work outline 163
    project team and outputs 163–164
    non-specialist audience 155–156
    sample outline 154–155, **155**
    uses for 153
research questions 17–31
    dead end questions 28–31
    ethical issues 108–109
    funnel method 22–25
    importance of 2–3, 17
    parsimony principle 20–22
    question types 25–28
    sources of 17–20, 90
research theory 89–104
    application and development of concepts and models 95–97
    creative theory use 101–104
    diagnoses of our time 98–100
    'fit-the-box' theorising 101
    functions of theory 90–91
    general theorising 89, 97–98
    Grounded Theory 65, 91, 93–95
    literature review distinguished 86–87
    as research interest 14
    as research practice 89
    as research question 19–20
    theory-building approach 93–95, 127–128
    theory-testing approach 91–93, 101, 127
Resignato, Andrew J. 29
resource issues 31, 38, 48, 54–55

Index

rhetoric 57, 64
Ritzer, George 95
Rocha, Zarine L. 44–45
Ross, Eleanor 22–23
Ross, Fiona 102

S
Said, Edward 124
SALLEE project 66–67
sample sizes 46–49
Schuh, Eric S. 111
Schwartz-Shea, Peregrine 1–2
scientific rigour 10
second-order data 39–43
secularisation theory 92, 95–96, 132–133
Seghal, Meera 112–113
Silverman, David 60
Silvia, Paul, J., *How to Write a Lot* 151
Skłodowska-Curie, Marie 71
social engagement 117
social media posts 113
solicited writing 61–62
    see also diaries
so-what-questions *see* research contribution
Spicer, Sean 33
Spickard, James V., *Research Basics* x, 11, 23, 49
statistical analysis 63–64, 64–65
Stearns, Peter N. 42–43
step models of research 11–12
Strauss, Anselm L. 65, 94
surveys 27, 42, 62
Suzuki, Shinichi 140
Sword, Helen, *Air & Light & Time & Space* 151
systematic reviews 83–84

T
theoretical sampling 65
theory *see* lay theory; research theory
Thompson, E.P. 93
time limitations 31, 38, 48, 54–55
time-diary method 61–62
titles 147–148, 149
triangulation 40, 43, 45–46, 54, 67–68
truthfulness 116
Tsegaye, Kebede Kassa 20, 23, 24
Tuskegee Experiment 105, 109

U
unacknowledged bias 46, 111
unverifiable questions 30

V
van den Hoonaard, Will C. 120, 121
van Knippenberg, Daan 84, 86
virtual ethnography 129
visual methods 60
Voas, David 128–129

W
Walseth, Kristin 28
Weber, Max 27, 89, 95, 97, 99
what-questions 25–26
White, Patrick 22, 23
why-questions 26–27
Wienke, Benjamin 30
Wilde, Melissa 56
Wilson, Woodrow 21–22
writing 135–151
    authorship attribution 118–119
    confidentiality 117–118
    conflicts of interest 119
    drafting approach 136–137, 139–140
    fair use 118
    learning through reading 140–144, **141**
    literature review 87
    plagiarism 118
    planning approach 138–140
    procrastination 149–151
    revision 145–147
    sentences 142–144
    showing not telling 144–145
    structure 141–142, **141**
    see also research proposals

Y
Yan, Miu Chung 65
Yanow, Dvora 1–2
Yeoh, Brenda S.A. 44–45
yes/no questions 28–30
Yin, Robert K. 47–48

Z
Zimbardo, Philip 114
Zuboff, Shoshana 100